Edexcel Spanish Grammar for A Level

Edexcel Spanish Grammar for A Level

Phil Turk and Mike Zollo

HODDER EDUCATION
PART OF HACHETTE LIVRE UK

Acknowledgements

The authors would like to thank the following for their help in the preparation of this book.

- teachers in Devon and the Bath area whose reactions were sought on the basic principles of the book and who provided helpful comments on the material
- students at Britannia Royal Naval College in Dartmouth with whom some of the material was tried out
- José-Luis García Daza, Geneviève García Vandaele, Matilde Gutiérrez-Manjón and Gloria Schumperli Soria for their meticulous checking of the Spanish typescript and for many invaluable comments on the content
- our wives for help proofreading and printouts
- finally, our wives, families and friends for their patience, cooperation and encouragement throughout.

The Publishers would like to thank the following for permission to reproduce copyright material: El País pp. 15, 277, 279; Cambio 16 p. 260.

Every effort has been made to trace all copyright holders, but if any have been inadvertently overlooked the Publishers will be pleased to make the necessary arrangements at the first opportunity.

Although every effort has been made to ensure that website addresses are correct at time of going to press, Hodder Education cannot be held responsible for the content of any website mentioned in this book. It is sometimes possible to find a relocated web page by typing in the address of the home page for a website in the URL window of your browser.

Hachette's policy is to use papers that are natural, renewable and recyclable products and made from wood grown in sustainable forests. The logging and manufacturing processes are expected to conform to the environmental regulations of the country of origin.

Orders: please contact Bookpoint Ltd, 130 Milton Park, Abingdon, Oxon OX14 4SB. Telephone: (44) 01235 827720. Fax: (44) 01235 400454. Lines are open 9.00–5.00, Monday to Saturday, with a 24-hour message answering service. Visit our website at www.hoddereducation.co.uk

© Phil Turk and Mike Zollo 2008
First published in 1993 by Hodder Murray
Second edition 2000
Third edition 2006
This edition first published 2008 by Hodder Education,
part of Hachette Livre UK,
338 Euston Road,
London NW1 3BH

Impression number   5 4 3 2 1
Year   2010 2009 2008

Cover photo © David Jackson/Alamy
Typeset in 45 Helvetica Neue Light 9/10pt by Pantek Arts Ltd, Maidstone, Kent
Printed in Spain

A catalogue record for this title is available from the British Library

ISBN: 978 0340 968 543

Contents

Our contents list has been mapped against the latest Edexcel GCE A Level specification, highlighting the language and grammatical structures which you will be required to demonstrate in the AS and A2 examinations. Grammar and structures are divided into AS and A2 level. For the A2 level, all grammar and structures listed under AS, along with those marked A2, will need to be actively demonstrated. For structures marked (R), receptive knowledge only is required.

Introduction

Edexcel Spanish Grammar for A Level is the comprehensive grammar reference textbook of choice for students studying for A level. Taking a contemporary approach to language, it pairs detailed explanations with graded reinforcement exercises. A range of open-ended communicative activities is also included to encourage and develop the creative use of language using the grammar points covered.

 Our contents list has been mapped against the latest Edexcel GCE A Level specification, highlighting the language and grammatical structures which you will be required to demonstrate in the AS and A2 examinations.

Edexcel Spanish Grammar for A Level aims to provide a systematic presentation of grammar points together with sufficient back-up practice to ensure that the points are adequately reinforced.

The book is divided into 50 chapters, most of which have three sections:

 Mecanismos – the 'mechanics' of the language
The first section of each chapter sets out grammatical rules and/or verb tables, with clear explanations in English. This section is also useful for reference purposes.

 ¡Ponte a punto! – 'tune yourself up'
This provides practice and reinforcement exercises on a particular grammatical point. Where possible, these exercises are set within a realistic context and are designed to be suitable for individual study. There is a key at the end of the book for self-correction. Apart from a few translation exercises, this section is in Spanish.

 ¡. . . Y en marcha! – 'off you go to exploit the freedom of the road!'
This section offers a range of more open-ended communicative activities in Spanish, ranging from the fairly elementary to the more sophisticated. The activities are set in a variety of contexts in which the grammar point is likely to occur.

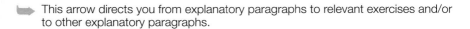 This arrow directs you from explanatory paragraphs to relevant exercises and/or to other explanatory paragraphs.

1 Grammar – what is it?

Any language is a mechanism, and grammar is the system – or the rules and patterns – by which the language works.

Although at first you might sigh heavily at 'all the grammar' that has to be absorbed, once you have done so, you will find it does in fact help you enormously. It can often provide useful short cuts. For example, once you have learned one 'regular' verb, you know the pattern for hundreds of others. And, most importantly, once you have mastered each point of grammar, you are on the way to speaking and writing the language correctly!

But why do we need technical terms, such as verb, adjective, or noun? Well, like any system or area of knowledge, such as engineering, information technology or horticulture, grammar has its technical terms, which enable us to talk about, explain and describe that subject. What follows is a brief explanation of some of the more common and useful grammatical terms which you will encounter in this book. If you really do know them all, just skip this chapter. If not, read it thoroughly and refer back to it when you need help in understanding these terms.

We have arranged this chapter so that you can use it in two ways. 1) You can read it through to revise your knowledge of grammatical terms, and perhaps learn some new ones, or 2) you can use it as a quick reminder if you come across a term that you have forgotten in the body of the book. To this end, we have provided below a quick alphabetical reference table, giving you the number of the paragraph in which you will find the term in question.

accents	1.1.3	indirect object	1.2.3	register	1.5
adjectives	1.2.4	infinitives	1.4.1	regular verbs	1.4.5
adverbs	1.2.5	interrogatives	1.2.10	relative pronouns	1.2.9
clauses	1.3	irregular verbs	1.4.5	sentence	1.3
comparatives	1.2.6	main clause	1.3	sentence structure	1.3
conjugations	1.4.5	negatives	1.4.6	singular	1.2.1
conjunctions	1.2.8	nouns	1.2.1	spelling	1.1
consonants	1.1.1	number	1.2.4	style	1.5
definite article	1.2.1	objects	1.2.3	subject	1.2.3
diphthongs	1.1.1	parts of speech	1.2	subjunctive mood	1.4.4
direct object	1.2.3	person	1.4.2	subordinate clause	1.3
finite verbs	1.4.2	phrase	1.3	superlatives	1.2.6
gender	1.2.1	plural	1.2.1	syllables	1.1.2
indefinite article	1.2.1	prepositions	1.2.7	tenses	1.4.2
indicative mood	1.4.3	pronouns	1.2.2	verbs	1.4
				vowels	1.1.1

1.1 Spelling

1.1.1 Letters

There are two categories of letters. The **vowels** are *a, e, i, o, u*.

A **diphthong** is a combination of two or more vowels pronounced as a single syllable (but with each vowel keeping its normal sound), such as the following:

*farmac**ia**, b**ie**n, c**ua**ndo, b**ue**no, f**ui***   chemist, well, when, good, I went

Note that Spanish never has more than two vowels pronounced together.

All the other letters are called **consonants**, but note that the letter *y* in a sense acts and sounds like the vowel *i* in the word *y* – and.

1.1.2 Syllables

These are the consonant + vowel units that make up a word:

cri-sis, ce-le-ste, per-sua-si-vo   cri-sis, heav-en-ly, per-sua-sive

1.1.3 Accents

These are the marks written above letters, usually to alter the way they are pronounced or to alter the sound of the letter itself. (See also Chapter 48.)

The most frequently used accent ´ (the acute accent) is used above vowels to indicate that the stress falls on that syllable:

*caf**é**, c**é**sped*   coffee/café, lawn

You will also come across the tilde ~ above *-n-* : *-ñ-* as in *Espa**ña*** – Spain, and the diaeresis ¨ used above *-u-* to indicate that it should be pronounced separately from the following *-e-* in words like *verg**ü**enza* – shame (*u* and *e* pronounced separately).

1.2 Parts of speech

1.2.1 Noun

A person, name, animal, thing or concept:

señora, Juan, gato, tenedor, identidad   lady, Juan, cat, fork, identity

In Spanish, all nouns are either masculine or feminine. This is called **gender**.

The gender of the noun determines the form of the **definite article** (the ... *el/la, los/las*) and the **indefinite article** (a/an ... *un, una*).

A noun can be **singular** (*un texto* – a text) or **plural** (*dos texto**s*** – two texts).

1.2.2 Pronoun

A pronoun is used in place of a noun, so that we don't have to keep repeating it:

*Tiene un nuevo móvil; **lo** compró ayer.*
He has a new mobile phone; he bought **it** yesterday.

1.2.3 Subjects and objects

The noun or pronoun that *does an action* is called the **subject**; a noun or pronoun that *has the action done to it* is called the **direct object**. The noun or pronoun that is the *recipient* (i.e. the person or thing something is given, sent etc. **to**) is called the **indirect object**.

Subject:

Mi novia *vive en Huelva.* **Ella** *trabaja allí.*
My girlfriend lives in Huelva. **She** works there.

Direct object:

*Me mandó **un e-mail**; **lo** leí esta mañana.*
She sent me **an email;** I read **it** this morning.

Indirect object:

*Mi amigo dio su tarjeta de crédito **a la camarera**.*
My friend gave his credit card **to the waitress**.

Le *dio también cinco euros de propina.*
He also gave (to) **her** a five euro tip.

1.2.4 Adjectives

These are words that describe or 'qualify' nouns. They change their form to 'agree' with the gender and number of the noun. **Number** in this sense means singular or plural.

un DVD <u>*interesante*</u>, **una película** <u>*larga*</u>, **las torres** <u>*altas*</u>, **los campos** <u>*verdes*</u>
an **interesting** DVD, a **long** film, the **tall** towers, the **green** fields

1.2.5 Adverbs

These words describe or qualify verbs, adjectives and other adverbs:

*El chico sale **lentamente**.*
The boy goes out **slowly**.

*Es un estudiante **bastante** bueno.*
He's **quite** a good student.

*Aquella actriz cantó **muy** bien.*
That actress sang **very** well.

3

1.2.6 Comparatives and superlatives

The **comparative** of adjectives is used to compare nouns and pronouns, and the comparative of adverbs to compare other parts of speech (i.e. 'more', 'less' or 'as…as'):

una casa más grande, *menos cómodamente*, *tan pequeño como*
a **bigger** house, **less comfortably**, **as small as**

The **superlative** of adjectives and adverbs is used to indicate 'the most' or 'the least'.

la persona más importante, Este atleta salta mejor.
the **most important** person, This athlete jumps **best**.

1.2.7 Prepositions

They tell you where something/someone is in relation to another in time or place, or they can indicate direction:

con mi amigo, *cerca del colegio*, *antes de la reunión*, *hacia la plaza*
with my friend, **near** school, **before** the meeting, **towards** the square

They are also used to link verbs together:

> *Habíamos comido **antes de** salir.*
> We had eaten **before** going out.

> *Escucha **sin** hablar.*
> Listen **without** speaking.

1.2.8 Conjunctions

They join words, phrases or clauses to each other:

té y café, *rápido pero silencioso*, *volveremos a casa si llueve*
tea **and** coffee, quickly **but** silently, we'll go back home **if** it rains

1.2.9 Relative pronouns and adjectives

These words join two clauses in order to give more information about a noun or pronoun. Compare the following:

> *Mi amigo compró una casa **que** era muy moderna.*
> My friend bought a house **which** was very modern.

> *El profesor **cuyas** clases os gustan…*
> The teacher **whose** lessons you like…

As you can see, the relative **which/que** links the two parts of the sentence, but relates to a noun in the first part of the sentence, or relates the noun to the extra information given about it.

1.2.10 Interrogatives

These are words used to form questions – the word may remind you of interrogation.
Here are some examples:

¿quién? ¿cuándo? ¿qué?   who? when? what?

1.3 Sentence structure

A **phrase** is a meaningful group of words:

con mi hermano, en la habitación, a velocidad máxima, antes de las ocho de la tarde
with my brother, in the room, at top speed, before eight o'clock in the evening

A **clause** is a meaningful group of words containing a verb, usually in a tense.

A **main clause** is a clause that can stand by itself:

Éste es el hombre...
This is the man...

A **subordinate clause** is a clause that cannot stand alone, but depends on a main clause:

...que habla catalán.
...who speaks Catalan.

A **sentence** consists of a main clause, and any number of subordinate clauses.

1.4 Verbs

A **verb** is a word describing an action or state of being:

Maite juega, pensamos, existen   Maite plays, we think, they exist

1.4.1 Infinitives

The infinitive is the basic form of the verb which you will find in dictionaries and vocabulary lists.
It is indeed *in-finite*, i.e. it is not in a tense or person. You could call it the verb 'in neutral'.

viajar, pensar, existir   to travel, to think, to exist

1.4.2 Tenses

A **finite verb** is a verb which is in a **tense**. A tense relates the verb (i.e. the action) to time –
past, present or future – telling you for example when the action took/takes/will take place.
There are a number of different tenses in Spanish, which you will find explained in the body
of the book.

Verb tenses vary their endings according to the **person**. There are 3 persons singular – *yo*,
tú, *usted*/*él*/*ella*/*sujeto nominal* – I, you, he/she/noun subject, and 3 persons plural –
nosotros/as, *vosotros/as*, *ustedes*/*ellos*/*ellas*/*sujeto nominal* – we, you, they/noun
subject.

1.4.3 Indicative

Most verb tenses belong to the **indicative mood**. For want of a better word, these are the 'ordinary' tenses.

1.4.4 Subjunctive

The **subjunctive mood** is used to express something which is 'less than fact', such as where there is doubt about the action expressed, or expressing an action as yet unfulfilled, for example future possibility.

1.4.5 Conjugations

A **conjugation** is a group of verbs which all have the same pattern of tense and person changes according to the infinitive ending. A **regular verb** is a verb which follows one of these conjugation patterns. An **irregular verb** is one which does not conform in this way, and whose 'irregular' parts have to be learnt separately.

1.4.6 Negatives

The **negative** is when you say something does **not**/did **not** happen. It includes other negative words such as 'never', 'nothing', etc.

> **No** fuimos al club anoche.
> We did**n't** go to the club last night.

> **Nunca** van al cine.
> They **never** go to the cinema.

> **No** tiene **nada** en la mano.
> She's got **nothing** in her hand.

1.5 Style and register

This refers to the level of formality or informality of the language you are using. The Spanish are nowadays less conscious of the style or level of language to be used in a particular situation than in the past. The *tú/usted* distinction is less important than it used to be: you can use the informal form not just to address a friend or relative, but also to address strangers of your own age group (*¡Hola! ¿Cómo estás?*). It is still safer to use the formal forms with a stranger, particularly if senior to you (*¡Buenos días! ¿Cómo está usted?*). Style and register vary from one Spanish-speaking country to another. It is also worth noting that *tú* is used less in Hispano-America, and *vosotros* is used hardly at all there.

This book indicates when a certain style of language would not be suitable, with exercises using a variety of registers or types of language. Our general advice about familiar language is: if in doubt, don't use it to strangers unless and until they invite you to!

1.6 Spanish grammar terms

While working through the exercises in the sections *¡Ponte a punto!* and *¡…Y en marcha!*
you may find it helpful to refer to the following list of grammatical terms:

el 'a' personal	personal 'a'
el acento	accent
el acento tónico	stress
el adjetivo	adjective
el adverbio	adverb
el antecedente	antecedent
el artículo	article
el auxiliar modal	modal auxiliary
la cláusula	clause
el comparativo	comparative
compuesto	compound
el condicional	conditional tense
la conjugación	conjugation
la conjunción	conjunction
el consonante	consonant
continuo	continuous
definido	definite
demostrativo	demonstrative
la dimensión	dimension
el diptongo	diphthong
el discurso directo	direct speech
el discurso indirecto	indirect speech
el estilo	style
la exclamación	exclamation
la forma pasiva	passive voice
la frase	phrase, sentence
el futuro	future tense
el género	gender
el gerundio	gerund
el imperativo	imperative
el imperfecto	imperfect tense
indefinido	indefinite
el indicativo	indicative mood
el infinitivo	infinitive
el interrogativo	interrogative
la medida	measure
(el) negativo	negative
el número	number
el objeto	object
la ortografía	spelling
el participio	participle
el perfecto	perfect tense
plural	plural

el pluscuamperfecto	pluperfect tense
posesivo	possessive
la preposición	preposition
el presente	present tense
el pretérito	preterite tense
el pronombre	pronoun
radical	radical-changing
reflexivo	reflexive
regular	regular
relativo	relative
la sílaba	syllable
singular	singular
el sujeto	subject
el subjuntivo	subjunctive mood
el sufijo	suffix
el superlativo	superlative
el sustantivo	noun
el tiempo	tense
el verbo	verb
la vocal	vowel

We hope these explanations of grammatical terms will help you to use this book. *¡Ánimo, y suerte!*

2 Nouns and articles

MECANISMOS

A noun is a person, animal, object, or concept, for example: Sandra, man, horse, table, hope, inefficiency.

2.1 Gender

a) All nouns in Spanish are either masculine or feminine. There is no neuter gender in Spanish, so inanimate nouns – those denoting non-living objects or concepts – are also either masculine or feminine.

Generally speaking, nouns ending in **-o** are masculine (*el caso*, *el puerto*, *el chico*) and those ending in **-a** are feminine (*la casa*, *la puerta*, *la chica*). There are, however, a number of common exceptions to this rule.

- The following nouns ending in **-o** are feminine:

la foto, *la moto*, *la mano*, *la radio*.

- The following nouns ending in **-a** are masculine:

el día, *el mapa*, *el planeta*, *el tranvía*, *el yoga*.

- An appreciable number of nouns ending in **-ma** are also masculine:

el anagrama, *el clima*, *el crucigrama* (crossword), *el drama*, *el esquema* (scheme), *el fantasma* (ghost), *el panorama*, *el pijama*, *el problema*, *el programa*, *el sistema*, *el síntoma* (symptom), *el telegrama*, *el tema*.

- Nouns ending in **-ista** are invariable whether referring to a male or female person:

el/la socialista, *el/la ciclista*.

b) Some noun endings are helpful in determining gender:

- Nouns with the following endings or any stressed vowel are masculine: **-aje**, **-or**, **-án**, **-ambre**:

el paisaje, *el rigor* (but *la labor*, *la flor*), *el desván* (attic), *el enjambre* (swarm), *el sofá*, *el café*.

- Nouns with the following endings are feminine: **-ión**, **-dad***, **-tad**, **-tud**, **-umbre**, **-ie**, **-isis**, **-itis**:

la estación (but *el avión*, *el camión*, *el gorrión* [sparrow]), *la ciudad*, *la virtud*, *la muchedumbre* (crowd), *la superficie* (surface), *la crisis* (but *el chasis*), *la apendicitis*.

*Words ending in **-dad** and **-tad** correspond to English words ending in '-ty', for example: **la caridad** (charity), **la ciudad** (city), **la libertad** (liberty).

It could be said that in Spanish all **dad**s are feminine and most **ma**s are masculine!

c) Countries, regions, provinces, towns and places ending in **-a** are feminine, though some countries are masculine: **el Canadá, el Perú, el Uruguay**.

d) Compound nouns (those made by joining two or more words together) are masculine: **el rascacielos** (skyscraper), **el limpiaparabrisas** (windscreen wiper).

e) Some fruits which are feminine have a corresponding tree which is masculine:

la manzana (apple)	**el manzano** (apple tree)
la cereza (cherry)	**el cerezo** (cherry tree)
la naranja (orange)	**el naranjo** (orange tree)

f) Words imported from other languages, especially from English, tend to be masculine (though not always), for example: **el best-seller, el márketing**, while some from an obviously feminine noun in another Latin language are feminine, for example: **la roulotte** (caravan), **la élite**.

➡ **Exercise 1**

2.2 Plural of nouns

To form the plural of nouns, the general rule is to add **-s** to a vowel and **-es** to a consonant:

el niño/los niño<u>s</u>	**la niña/las niña<u>s</u>**
el reloj/los reloj<u>es</u>	**la red/las red<u>es</u>**

Foreign imported words, such as **el club**, should behave according to the rules as stated above, but you will hear and see both **los clubes** and **los clubs**.

Take care, however, with the following spelling changes in the plural.

Words ending in -z change this to -ces:	una vez/muchas veces
Words ending in stressed -án, -én, -ín, -ón, -ión, -és lose the accent. This category includes the many words ending in -ción / -ciones.	el catalán/los catalanes el andén/los andenes el maletín/los maletines el cajón/los cajones la ración/las raciones el francés/los franceses
Words ending in unstressed -en add an accent to the preceding syllable:	la imagen/las imágenes

Words ending in stressed -í, -ú should add -es but in spoken Spanish the -e- is sometimes omitted:	el iraquí/los iraquíes el champú/los champúes
Most words ending in unstressed -es or -is do not change:	el martes/los martes la crisis/las crisis
Note the change of stress in:	el carácter/los caracteres el régimen/los regímenes
Surnames do not usually change in the plural:	la familia Gómez/los Gómez

➡ **Exercise 2**

2.3 Articles

There are two articles, the 'definite' (= the) and the 'indefinite' (= a/an). The definite article has four forms in Spanish, for masculine and feminine singular, and masculine and feminine plural:

masculine: **_el_ coche** (the car)   **_los_ coches** (the cars)
feminine: **_la_ casa** (the house)   **_las_ casas** (the houses)

The indefinite article has a masculine and feminine singular and a form which can be used in the plural to mean 'some':

masculine: **_un_ coche** (a car)   **_unos_ coches** (some cars)
feminine: **_una_ casa** (a house)   **_unas_ casas** (some houses)

✏ Note: **el** and **un** are used before a feminine noun beginning with a stressed **a-** or **ha-**: **el agua**, **un águila** (eagle). This is just for the sake of the sound, but any adjective describing it still has a feminine agreement: **el agua está fría**. When article and noun are separated by an adjective, the normal rule applies: **una hermosa águila**.

Remember:

• **de** + **el** = **del** (of the, from the)

la puerta del comedor   the door of the dining room/the dining-room door

• **a** + **el** = **al** (to the)

Voy al comedor.   I'm going to the dining room.

These are the only two cases of two words contracting to form one in Spanish.

2.3.1 Use and omission of the definite article

You can use the definite article in Spanish much as in English, but there are exceptions.

a) The definite article is omitted in Spanish but not in English with numbers of monarchs, Popes, etc:

*el rey Juan Carlos **primero***
King Juan Carlos **the First**

b) It is also usually omitted in Spanish with a noun in apposition to another:

*Juan Carlos, **rey** de España*
Juan Carlos, **the King** of Spain

*Tokio, **capital** del Japón*
Tokyo, **the capital** of Japan

'Apposition' is when the second noun is an alternative title or provides further information about the first.

c) It is used in Spanish but not in English when you talk about nouns in a general sense:

*En esta región se produce **el vino**.*
Wine is produced in this region.

***El café** me desvela.*
Coffee keeps me awake.

*Lo más importante es **la esperanza**.*
Hope is the most important thing.

In these cases the nouns denote the whole of what they represent – all coffee, all hope, etc. When the noun only refers to part or some of it, the article is omitted:

*Ese hombre tiene **valor**.*
That man has **courage**. (i.e. some courage)

*Yo tomo **carne**.*
I'm having **meat**. (i.e. some meat)

If you know French, resist the temptation to put in a 'partitive' article (***du** vin, **de la** viande, **des** croissants*), as this does not exist in Spanish:

*Nous allons prendre **du café**. = Vamos a tomar **café**.*
We're going to have **(some) coffee**.

d) It is used with a language when the language is the subject of a verb:

***El alemán** es difícil para los españoles.*
German is difficult for the Spanish.

It should also be used when a language is the direct object, except after *hablar*, but its use seems to be becoming increasingly optional:

> *No entendemos (el) inglés pero aprendemos (el) francés.*
> We don't understand **English** but we're learning **French**.

e) Use the definite article to express 'on' a day of the week:

el martes   **on** Tuesday   *los martes*   **on** Tuesdays

f) It is used before titles, such as *el señor, la señora, la señorita, el doctor, el padre,* when people are being talked about, but not addressed:

> **El doctor** *Jiménez es muy bueno.*
> **Dr Jiménez** is very good.

> **El rey** *Juan Carlos*
> **King** Juan Carlos

> *– Buenos días, **Señora** Carrascal.*
> 'Good morning, **Mrs** Carrascal.'

2.3.2 Use and omission of the indefinite article

You can use the indefinite article in Spanish much as in English, but there are exceptions.

a) It is omitted when used after *ser* or *hacerse* + profession, occupation, status:

> **Soy estudiante** *de español.*
> **I'm a student** of Spanish.

> *Quiero **hacerme traductora**.*
> I want to **become a translator**.

b) It is not usually used after *sin*, or with *¡qué... !, tal, semejante, medio, cierto, otro*:

> *sin camisa*
> **without a** shirt

> *¡Qué risa!*
> **What a** laugh!

> *En mi vida he visto **tal/semejante cosa**.*
> Never in my life have I seen **such a thing**.

> *Déme **medio litro** de otro vino.*
> Give me **half a litre** of another wine.

c) It is used with an abstract noun qualified by an adjective:

> *La pintó con **un esmero excepcional**.*
> He painted her with **exceptional care**.

➡ **Exercise 3**

¡PONTE A PUNTO!

1 ¿Macho o hembra?

Has perdido tu diccionario y tienes que adivinar el género (*m* o *f*) de las siguientes palabras.
¡A ver cuántas adivinas correctamente!

bronquitis	diploma	parabrisas
cuidado	igualdad	civilización
dilema	ama de casa	tesis
goma	Ecuador	equipaje
amor	tragaperras	cumbre
programa	Paraguay	Argentina
paraguas	footing	software
coma	rugby	guitarrista

2 Arca de Noé

En la lista de animales y otras cosas que Noé tuvo en su arca, su mujer sólo escribió uno de
cada especie. Claro que había dos; entonces cambia las palabras de la lista al plural. Si hay
palabras que no conozcas, ¡búscalas en un diccionario! ¡Cuidado con los acentos!

Ejemplo:

una jirafa ⟶ *dos jirafas*

un rinoceronte	un hipopótamo	un cocodrilo
un gato	un ratón	una rata
un gorrión	una serpiente	un pitón
un jabalí	una res	un chimpancé

... además de:

una crisis	una tos	una inundación
un régimen	una serie de problemas	un club de vela
un inglés	una portuguesa	un israelí

3 Un concierto de José Carreras

En este extracto de un reportaje de *El País* faltan los artículos definidos e indefinidos. Rellena los espacios en blanco con el artículo necesario. ¡Cuidado! a) porque un par de espacios no requieren artículo y b) ¡no te olvides de que *a + el = al,* y *de + el = del*!

Diez años después de **(1)** multitudinario concierto que reunió en Barcelona a 150.000 personas y con **(2)** que José Carreras volvió a cantar tras superar **(3)** leucemia que padeció, **(4)** tenor ofreció anteanoche, ante más de 50.000 personas, **(5)** concierto gratuito de dos horas ante **(6)** fuentes de Montjuic de Barcelona, conmemorativo de **(7)** aniversario de **(8)** creación de **(9)** fundación de lucha contra **(10)** leucemia que lleva su nombre.

Fue **(11)** concierto popular y solidario. **(12)** programa elegido por Carreras mezcló **(13)** canción catalana y napolitana, que se convirtió en **(14)** verdadera protagonista de **(15)** noche, y **(16)** ópera. **(17)** tenor alternó sus intervenciones con **(18)** que en solitario ofreció **(19)** Orquesta Internacional de **(20)** Italia, que le acompañó durante todo **(21)** concierto.

(22) popularidad de José Carreras en Barcelona, su ciudad natal, no decae y **(23)** público respondió llenando **(24)** Avenida de María Cristina. Dos horas antes de **(25)** inicio, **(26)** 5.000 sillas instaladas para parte de **(27)** público ya estaban ocupadas. A **(28)** 22.00 horas, 50.000 personas llenaban ya **(29)** avenida.

En línea con el espíritu del concierto, **(30)** recinto acogió tenderetes donde **(31)** personas que asistieron a **(32)** concierto pudieron ofrecer donativos para **(33)** fundación y también inscribirse como donantes de **(34)** médula ósea (bone marrow).

El País

 ¡... Y EN MARCHA!

4 Lista de bodas – ¡doble!

Unas amigas vuestras son gemelas idénticas. Siempre han hecho todo igual y ahora se casan el mismo día, ¡claro! Claro, también, que tú y tus compañeros/as de clase vais a darles un regalo idéntico, y por eso tendréis que comprar dos regalos. Discutid entre vosotros las cosas (en plural) que les vais a regalar.

Ejemplo:

– *¿Por qué no les regalamos manteles para la mesa?*
– *Pues yo pienso que les gustarían bandejas.*
– *Yo les daría sábanas para las camas.*

Cuando lo hayáis discutido, cada uno hace una lista corta de las posibilidades (¡en plural, claro!)

5 Ambiciones

Discute con tus compañeros/as de clase lo que queréis ser después de terminar vuestros estudios. Podéis hacer algunas propuestas unos a otros, también.

Ejemplo:

– Yo quiero ser cartero.
– A mí me gustaría hacerme cirujana.
– ¿Por qué no te haces cantante de música pop?

6 Palabras no castizas

Con una selección de revistas y periódicos españoles trabaja con tus compañeros/as para encontrar palabras de origen extranjero, como, por ejemplo, *footing, software, web,* etc., y hacer una lista de ellas. Mirad primero los anuncios y las páginas sobre la música, la informática y los deportes, donde tienden a proliferar. Después comprobad su género con un diccionario moderno.

7 Geografía europea o mundial

Trabaja con un(a) compañero/a. Uno/a tiene que nombrar un país europeo o del mundo entero, y el/la otro/a cómo se llaman los habitantes, qué idioma(s) hablan y luego preguntar el género del país. Podéis utilizar un diccionario si queréis.

Ejemplo:

– Francia
– Los habitantes se llaman los franceses y hablan francés (algunos hablan bretón).
– ¿De qué género es Francia?
– Es femenina.

Al decir el idioma, escríbelo también para comprobar si necesita acento o no.

francés – sí

8 ¡Viva el Tipp-Ex!

Pide a tu profesor(a) una fotocopia de cualquier trozo de español. Con el Tipp-ex quita todos los artículos definidos e indefinidos. Vuelve a fotocopiar la hoja y da la segunda copia a un(a) amigo/a para que vuelva a rellenar los espacios en blanco que tú has hecho. Si prefieres, puedes trabajar en parejas para quitar los artículos, y dar la copia a otra pareja para que discutan los artículos que tienen que reemplazar.

3 Adjectives

MECANISMOS

An adjective describes a noun or a pronoun: 'a **red** bus', 'a **modern** one'.

3.1 The agreement of adjectives

In Spanish, adjectives agree in gender (masculine/feminine) and number (singular/plural) with the noun(s) or pronoun(s) they describe, as follows:

a) Adjectives ending in **-o**:

masc. singular	masc. plural	fem. singular	fem. plural
un coche blanc**o**	coches blanc**os**	una casa blanc**a**	casas blanc**as**

b) Adjectives ending in a consonant or **-e** are usually the same in the masculine and feminine singular; those ending in **-e** add **-s** for the plural, and those ending in a consonant add **-es**:

un coche gri**s**	coches gri**ses**	una casa gri**s**	casas gri**ses**
un coche verd**e**	coches verd**es**	una casa verd**e**	casas verd**es**

But there are some exceptions to the above rule:

• Some adjectives have a predictable masculine plural in **-es** but end in **-a** in the feminine singular and in **-as** in the feminine plural:

i) adjectives denoting nationality, region or place:

ingl**és**	ingl**eses**	ingl**esa**	ingl**esas**
catal**án**	catal**anes**	catal**ana**	catal**anas**
cordob**és**	cordob**eses**	cordob**esa**	cordob**esas**

ii) adjectives with the following endings: **-án, -ín, -ón, -or**:

charlat**án**	charlat**anes**	charlat**ana**	charlat**anas**
chiquit**ín**	chiquit**ines**	chiquit**ina**	chiquit**inas**
mand**ón**	mand**ones**	mand**ona**	mand**onas**
encantad**or**	encantad**ores**	encantad**ora**	encantad**oras**

(**charlatán** = talkative; **chiquitín** = tiny; **mandón** = bossy; **encantador** = charming)

17

But the pairs of comparative adjectives ending in *-or* behave normally (like *gris*, above): *mejor*, *peor*; *mayor*, *menor*; *exterior*, *interior*; *anterior*, *posterior*; *superior*, *inferior*; and also *ulterior*.

• Some adjectives end in *-a* regardless of gender, and add *-s* for the plural:

| *bel**ga*** | *bel**gas*** | *bel**ga*** | *bel**gas*** |

(*belga* = Belgian)

This includes all adjectives ending in *-ista*, of which there are many:

| *social**ista*** | *social**istas*** | *social**ista*** | *social**istas*** |

But *cada* (each) is invariable.

c) Adjectives still agree with the noun when used as the complement of the sentence, after *ser*, *estar*, *parecer* (to look/seem), *resultar* (to result/turn out), etc:

Las paredes *eran/parecían rojas.*   The walls **were/looked red**.

d) Certain nouns used as adjectives, such as colours where the name of a fruit or flower is used, do not change:

paredes **naranja**   **orange** walls   insectos **hembra**   **female** insects

e) Adjectives placed after more than one noun always take masculine plural agreement if at least one of the nouns is masculine:

profes**ores** y profeso**ras** ingles**es**   English teachers (m + f)

f) Adjectives placed before more than one noun tend to agree with the first noun:

con **una** fingid**a atención** y esmero   with feigned attention and care

g) Shortened ('apocopated') adjectives. Some adjectives used before the noun drop the final letter(s):

• in both genders, singular: *grande* becomes *gran*:

un **gran** hombre, una **gran** mujer   a great man, a great woman

• in masculine singular only: *bueno, malo, primero, tercero, alguno, ninguno*:

un **buen/mal** día, el **primer/tercer** ejercicio, **algún/ningún** problema
a good/bad day, the first/third exercise, some/no problem

• where *santo* is used as a title for a male saint, it becomes *San*:

San Pedro (except for those beginning with *Do-* or *To-*: *Santo* Domingo, *Santo* Tomás)

➡ **Exercises 1, 2**

3.2 The position of adjectives

a) In general, adjectives follow the noun, as in the examples in section 3.1a, b. Adjectives which commonly precede the noun are the shortened ones mentioned in section 3.1g. The adjective comes first at the start of a letter:

***Querida** Conchi:*
***Distinguido** Señor:*

There are certain other circumstances when the adjective may precede the noun, though it is not easy to make a clear definition of when and where. A feeling for this is something which will develop with experience. Suffice it to say at this stage of your progress in Spanish, that the most likely cases you will meet are when the preceding adjective describes an expected quality, and refers in general to all examples of a particular category, whereas the adjective placed after has a greater discriminating force and draws rather more attention to the quality.

> *Sobrevolábamos los **altos picos** y los **verdes prados** de Cantabria.*
> We were flying over the **high peaks** and **green meadows** of Cantabria.

That is, in general the peaks of Cantabria are known to be high and the meadows green. Although it can be argued that *los picos altos y los prados verdes* would mean the same thing, there could be an implication that you were flying over only the high (as opposed to the low) peaks and the green (and not e.g. the brown) meadows.

*los **magníficos esfuerzos** de los concursantes*
*los **esfuerzos magníficos** de los concursantes*
the **magnificent efforts** of the competitors

The first example assumes that it goes without saying competitors in any competition make magnificent efforts. The second version tends to imply that there was something more special about their efforts on this occasion.

b) Some adjectives vary their meaning according to their position:

	before noun	after noun
antiguo	*former, ancient*	*ancient*
cierto	*(a) certain*	*beyond doubt*
medio	*half*	*average, mean*
pobre	*poor (wretched)*	*poor (not rich)*
puro	*sheer*	*pure (clean)*
raro	*rare*	*strange, rare*
simple	*simple, mere*	*simple-minded*
varios	*several*	*assorted, various*

> *El **consumo medio** de aceite es **medio litro** por mil kilómetros.*
> The **average oil consumption** is **half a litre** per thousand kilometres.

> ***Cierto día** de **cierto año** el pobre hombre salió al encuentro de una **muerte cierta**.*
> On **a certain day** of **a certain year** the poor man went to meet **a certain death**.

Exercise 3

3.3 Qualifying nouns

Although English often uses nouns rather like adjectives to qualify other nouns, these expressions normally have to be explained in Spanish:

una camisa *de seda*	a **silk** shirt
un bolso *de piel*	a **leather** handbag
un bocadillo *de jamón*	a **ham** sandwich

However, you will encounter some expressions where a second noun qualifies another, often explaining or defining its purpose:

un carril *bus*	a **bus** lane
un hombre/una mujer *bomba*	a suicide **bomber** (lit. a bomb man/woman)

3.4 Using the pronoun *lo* with an adjective

This forms a kind of abstract noun, where it is not always easy to find an English equivalent.

Lo horroroso es que ...	**The horrific thing** is that ...
Eso es *lo importante*.	That is **what's important**.
Lo demás	**The rest, the remainder**

3.5 Making adjectives negative

Although the prefix *in-* is sometimes used in Spanish, there is no predictable equivalent to the English prefix 'un-' to reverse the meaning of an adjective. You can sometimes use *sin* with a verb infinitive:

*Es un método **sin probar**.*
It's an **untried** method.

But the most common way to do this is to use *poco*.

*Fue una película **poco interesante**.*
It was an **uninteresting** film./It **wasn't a very interesting** film.

¡PONTE A PUNTO!

1 Reunión en el aeropuerto

Vas a ir a trabajar a casa de una familia en España, a quien no conoces. Quieres mandar un e-mail dando una descripción de ti mismo/a. Escoge un adjetivo de los que vienen abajo para describir tu aspecto y tu ropa y hazlo concordar si hace falta.

Ejemplo:

piernas largas

---

aspecto: pelo, nariz, ojos, orejas, piernas, pies, camisa, blusa, pantalones, falda, anorak, zapatos, bolso, vaqueros, camiseta, gorra

adjetivos: corto, largo, puntiagudo, rojo, azul, blanco, amarillo, negro, verde, grande, pequeño, ligero, espeso, moderno, viejo, nuevo, brillante, luminoso, de lana, de algodón, de plástico, de piel, de moda, de béisbol

---

Puedes utilizar más de un adjetivo y más de una vez si quieres.

2 ¡Se busca criminal!

Rellena los espacios en blanco con un adjetivo escogido de los que aparecen abajo. ¡Deja que la concordancia te ayude en ciertos casos!

Ayer por la noche el anciano Federico Arenas Muñoz fue atracado en la calle de la Flor. Según su descripción el atracador tenía el pelo . . 1 . . y . . 2 . . con la cara . . 3 . . . Llevaba cazadora . . 4 . . con bolsillos . . 5 . . y pantalones . . 6 . . . . 7 . . y . . 8 . . . En los pies llevaba botas . . 9 . . . . 10 . . . Era bastante . . 11 . . , es decir, medía quizás 1m 80.

El Sr Arenas dijo que tenía las uñas muy . . 12 . . y hablaba con acento . . 13 . . , puesto que las . . 14 . . palabras que profirió fueron bastante mal . . 15 . . . Claro que la policía quiere que se coja a este criminal lo más pronto posible, puesto que puede ser . . 16 . . y los ciudadanos del barrio no se sienten . . 17 . . .

---

alto	azules	sucias	redonda	pronunciadas	moreno	de charol	marrón	pocas
vaqueros	seguros	desgarrados	peligroso	largo	grandes	extranjero	negras	

---

3 ¿Antes o después?

Vuelve a escribir las frases siguientes, utilizando el adjetivo entre paréntesis para describir el sustantivo en cursiva. ¡Cuidado! – porque tienes que decidir si el adjetivo viene *antes* o *después* del sustantivo.

1 Isabel vive en un *pueblo* del oeste de España. *(antiguo)*
2 En efecto, hay *pueblos* de este tipo en toda la región. *(varios)*
3 Comparada con otras partes del país, ésta es una *región*. *(pobre)*
4 En todos estos pueblos la *renta* de los habitantes es bastante baja. *(media)*
5 Sin embargo hay *ventajas* de vivir en las montañas con su *aire,* *(ciertas, puro)*
6 sin mencionar el *placer* de contemplar el magnífico paisaje. *(puro)*
7 Isabel vive a *kilómetro* del centro del pueblo. *(medio)*
8 En la casa al lado de la suya vive su *maestra* de escuela, ya jubilada. *(antigua)*
9 Pero una *cosa* es que al cumplir los 18 años, Isabel se marchará a la universidad. *(cierta)*

¡... Y EN MARCHA!

¡En todas estas actividades, no te olvides de la concordancia de los adjetivos!

4 ¡Mira en torno tuyo!

Con tus compañeros/as puedes jugar a *I spy*, pero tienes que dar dos letras iniciales, uno para el sustantivo y otro para el adjetivo.

Ejemplo:

– Yo veo *algo que empieza con* C.A. ⟶ *cortinas amarillas*
– Yo veo *algo que empieza con* E.E. ⟶ *enchufe eléctrico*

Si quieres, puedes permitir que tus compañeros/as adivinen el sustantivo primero antes que el adjetivo.

5 ¿Quién es?

Tienes que describir a tus compañeros/as a alguien que no está en el aula o el cuarto con vosotros. Puede ser un amigo o una amiga, una estrella de pop u otra personalidad. Tienes que describir su aspecto físico y su carácter, empleando tantos adjetivos como puedas.

6 ¿Qué es?

Has perdido algún objeto corriente. Tienes que describirlo a tu compañero/a, que es empleado/a de la oficina de objetos perdidos, describiendo su tamaño, su color, y diciendo de qué material está hecho.

7 Vendedor de chismes

Cada uno/a de la clase trae dos o tres cosas – por ejemplo: una percha, un martillo, una bomba de bicicleta, un chupete de bebé – y tiene que persuadir a sus compañeros/as a comprarlas. Claro que tienes que emplear adjetivos, además de explicar para qué sirve el objeto.

8 ¿Cómo fue?

¡Basta de colores, tamaños y materiales! Piensa en adjetivos abstractos para describir:

una película	una experiencia tuya
un personaje famoso	unas vacaciones
un programa de televisión	una filosofía
unas noticias	un examen
un partido de tenis/fútbol u otro deporte	una aventura
una guerra	una montaña

Trata de encontrar varios adjetivos para describir cada cosa, luego compara tu lista con la de tus compañeros/as. ¿Cuántos habéis encontrado en total?

Ejemplo:

La conferencia a la que asistí la semana pasada fue interesante, estimulante, informativa, religiosa, práctica, internacional, aburrida, poco animada, incomprensible, bien/mal organizada, desastrosa ...

Claro que te hará falta buscar palabras en el diccionario para lograr una buena gama de adjetivos abstractos.

4 Adverbs

MECANISMOS

We have looked at adjectives, which qualify nouns and pronouns. Adverbs qualify other parts of speech, most commonly:

- verbs: we finished it **quickly**;
- adjectives: we found the journey **amazingly** easy;
- other adverbs: we got there **amazingly** quickly.

Adverbs have two main forms:

a) Those which are single words in their own right. They can be, amongst other things, adverbs of degree: *muy* (very), *bastante* (quite), *mucho* (a lot), *poco* (little, not much); adverbs of time: *ya* (already), *todavía* (still, yet), *pronto* (soon), *tarde* (late); adverbs of place: *aquí* (here), *ahí, allí* (there).

b) Those which are formed from adjectives. Most adverbs are formed in English by adding '-ly' to an adjective, with or without minor spelling adjustments:
pretty ⟶ prettily, quick ⟶ quickly.

4.1 Formation of adverbs

In Spanish, most adverbs are formed by adding *-mente* to the feminine singular of the adjective, if this is different from the masculine singular:

absoluto ⟶ *absoluta* ⟶ *absolutamente*	absolutely
rápido ⟶ *rápida* ⟶ *rápidamente*	quickly
regular ⟶ *regularmente*	regularly
cortés ⟶ *cortésmente*	politely

✐ Note:
- The accent on the original adjective remains when *-mente* is added.
- You can't add *-mente* to all adjectives. Use those English ones to which you can't add '-ly' as a fairly reliable guide (you wouldn't normally say 'fatly' nor *gordamente*!).
- When you have two or more adverbs consecutively which would both end in *-mente*, the ending *-mente* appears only on the last adjective, though all adjectives will be in the feminine form: *lenta y cuidadosamente* – slowly and carefully.
- The adverbs corresponding to *bueno* (good) and *malo* (bad) are *bien* (well) and *mal* (badly), although you may come across *buenamente* and *malamente* in popular speech.

➡ **Exercises 1, 2**

24

4.2 Adverbial phrases

An adverbial phrase is a group of words which perform the function of an adverb.

For example, quite a number of adverbial phrases of more than one word are used in Spanish where English uses a one word adverb:

a menudo	often
muchas veces	often
en/por todas partes	everywhere
en cualquier parte	anywhere
en ninguna parte	nowhere
de prisa	quickly, hurriedly

Because some of the adverbs of the *-mente* type can be rather long (try *independientemente*!), an adverbial phrase is sometimes used, often with *con* or *sin* + the related noun:

> *Habló **con tristeza**.*
> (for ***tristemente***) He spoke sadly/with sadness.

> *Actuó **sin prisa**.*
> (for ***lentamente***) He acted slowly/without haste.

or with ***de un modo***, ***de una manera*** or ***de una forma***:

> *Actuó **de una manera extraña**.*
> He acted strangely/in a strange way.

This is simply expressing in modern Spanish what ***triste mente*** meant in the original Latin: 'with a sad mind'.

Many other adverbial phrases are possible, telling you when, where, how, etc:

hace tres semanas	three days ago
cada quince días	every fortnight
a cuatro kilómetros de aquí	four kilometres from here
con mucha dificultad	with great difficulty

4.3 Using an adjective

Sometimes you can use an adjective as an adverb:

*El tiempo pasó muy **rápido**.*
Time passed very quickly.

but be careful, if you don't like taking risks!

 Note: when **sólo** means 'only' and is the equivalent of **solamente** (an adverb), it has an accent; when it means 'alone' or '**solo**' (an adjective), it has no accent:

Sólo *(= solamente) tengo un hermano.*
I have **only** one brother.

*Vive **solo**.*
He lives **alone**.

➡ **Exercise 3**

 ## ¡PONTE A PUNTO!

1 Todo está en la mente

Haz adverbios de los adjetivos que vienen en cursiva.

1 Yo aprendo muy *lento*.
2 Nuestro profesor habla muy *rápido*.
3 Tú te comportas muy *estúpido*.
4 Todo esto sale muy *lógico*.
5 Estoy hablando *personal*.
6 Ocurre *regular*.
7 Ahora sabes hacerlo *correcto*.
8 Pues ¡hazlo *bueno*!

2 En viaje de negocios

Has estado en España en viaje de negocios, y aquí describes los éxitos y fracasos del viaje. Escoge un adverbio de los que aparecen abajo para contestar a cada pregunta. Algunos pueden servir para dos o más respuestas, pero trata de usar cada uno una vez solamente.

1 ¿Cuándo fuiste a España?
2 ¿Cómo conseguiste el billete de avión?
3 ¿Cómo te recibieron en la primera empresa que visitaste?
4 ¿Cómo llevaste las negociaciones sobre el precio de tu producto?
5 ¿Cómo contestaron al rechazar el producto?
6 ¿Cómo explicaste tu problema a tu jefe?
7 ¿Cómo reaccionó éste cuando le hablaste del fracaso?
8 ¿Cómo persuadiste a la segunda empresa a comprar el producto?
9 ¿Cómo recibió las mejores noticias tu jefe?
10 ¿Cómo dormiste aquella noche?

entusiasmadamente	atentamente	categóricamente	profundamente
recientemente	persuasivamente	diplomáticamente	difícilmente
fácilmente	airadamente		

3 Todavía en viaje de negocios

Empareja correctamente las frases adverbiales de la columna A con los adverbios de la columna B:

A		B	
1	con discreción	**a**	profundamente
2	con ahínco	**b**	diplomáticamente
3	con satisfacción	**c**	categóricamente
4	hace poco	**d**	airadamente
5	como un tronco	**e**	entusiasmadamente
6	sin dificultad	**f**	difícilmente
7	con enojo	**g**	persuasivamente
8	no sin problemas	**h**	atentamente
9	sin duda alguna	**i**	recientemente
10	con cortesía	**j**	fácilmente

 **¡… Y EN MARCHA!**

4 ¿Cómo lo hacen?

Trabaja con tus compañeros/as, empleando adverbios para describir los movimientos y acciones de varios animales, personas y objetos. Los otros/as tienen que adivinar lo que se describe.

Ejemplo:

– *Es un animal que se mueve lenta y pesadamente.*
– *Es un elefante.*

5 Un ejercicio inmensamente útil

Trabajando en parejas, uno tiene que pensar en un adjetivo y el otro en un adverbio que lo modifique. Luego los dos tenéis que inventar una frase que contenga esta combinación. Inventad diez combinaciones.

Ejemplos:

barato ⟶ *absurdamente* ⟶ *Estos zapatos eran absurdamente baratos.*
feliz ⟶ *sumamente* ⟶ *Los recién casados estaban sumamente felices.*

6 «Publiciadverbios»

Tú y tus compañeros/as trabajáis en una agencia de publicidad, y habéis decidido montar una campaña de «publiciadverbios», es decir, anuncios que lleven un adverbio que termine con -*mente*. Tenéis que discutir qué producto o mensaje iría mejor con algunos de estos publiciadverbios, y cómo presentaríais el anuncio (quizás dibujándolo si eres buen artista). Inventad un eslogan para cada adverbio.

Ejemplo:

¿Para qué serviría ¡DULCEMENTE!? ¿Quizás para anunciar una tableta de turrón o chocolate, una caja de caramelos? ¿Con un chico que se la ofrece a su novia o al revés? '¡Con nuestro turrón lo pasarás dulcemente!'

Ahora a ver qué pasa con:

¡Independientemente!	¡CLARAMENTE!	¡LOCAMENTE!
¡SINCERAMENTE!	¡PRIMERAMENTE!	¡Inesperadamente!
¡Imposiblemente!	¡Concretamente!	¡ENTERAMENTE!
¡CONFIDENCIALMENTE!	¡INNEGABLEMENTE!	¡IGUALMENTE!

5 Comparative of adjectives and adverbs

 **MECANISMOS**

There are various ways of comparing people and things: 'more ... than', 'less ... than', 'as ... as', 'not so ... as'.

5.1 Adjectives

5.1.1 More ... than

In English we either add '-er' to an adjective ('bigger', 'smaller') or use 'more' before the adjective ('more intelligent'). In Spanish you use *más* + **adjective** + *que*.

> *España es **más grande que** el Reino Unido.*
> Spain is **bigger than** the UK.

> *El japonés es **más difícil que** el español.*
> Japanese is **more difficult than** Spanish.

The exceptions are *mejor* (better), *peor* (worse), *mayor* (older), *menor* (younger).

> *El tren de las 11.01 es **mejor que** el de las 10.47.*
> The 11.01 train is **better than** the 10.47.

> *Manuel es **mayor que** Conchita.*
> Manuel is **older than** Conchita.

There is no need to express 'than' when there is no follow-up to the comparison:

> *Este tren es bueno pero el otro es **mejor**.*
> This train is good but the other is **better**.

5.1.2 Less ... than

In Spanish, use *menos ... que*.

> *Calatayud es una ciudad **menos importante que** Burgos.*
> Calatayud is a **less important** town **than** Burgos.

5.2 Adverbs

5.2.1 Adverbs can be compared in exactly the same ways as the adjectives above:

*Mi colega trabaja **más/menos rápidamente** que yo.*
My colleague works **more/less quickly** than I (do).

*Este libro explica el problema **más claramente**.*
This book explains the problem **more clearly**.

*Hablas castellano **mejor que** nosotros.*
You speak Spanish **better than** we (do).

Mejor and *peor* are also the comparatives of *bien* and *mal*: *mejor* (better), *peor* (worse).

5.2.2 *Cuanto más … más* ('the more … the more') and *cuanto menos … menos* ('the less … the less').

***Cuanto más** trabajas, **más** cobrarás.*
The more you work, **the more** you'll earn.

***Cuanto menos** trabajas, **menos** cobrarás.*
The less you work, **the less** you'll earn.

***Cuanto más** trabajo, **menos** cobro.*
The more I work, **the less** I earn.

5.3 Equality

a) Use *tan* + adjective or adverb + *como* (not *que*) where English uses 'as' + adjective/adverb + 'as':

*Este tren es **tan bueno como** el otro.*
This train is **as good as** the other.

*Hablas castellano **tan bien como** nosotros.*
You speak Spanish **as well as** we do.

Notice that 'as much/as many as' in Spanish is: *tanto(s)/tanta(s) como* (not *tan mucho*!):

*Siempre tiene **tanta suerte**.*
He always has **so much luck**./He's always **so lucky**.

b) You can also use these phrases negatively in the sense of 'not as … as, not as much/many … as':

*El problema **no es tan sencillo como** parece.*
The problem is **not as simple as** it looks.

*No tenemos **tantos problemas como** Vds.*
We don't have **as many problems as** you.

c) *Tan … que* and *tanto … que* are used with a clause of result:

*Es **tan listo que** sus profesores no saben cómo tratarle.*
He's **so clever (that)** his teachers don't know how to deal with him.

*Hablaba **tan rápidamente que** no la entendíamos.*
She was speaking **so fast (that)** we couldn't understand her.

*Llovió **tanto que** tuvimos que volver a casa.*
It rained **so much (that)** we had to go back home.

➤ **Exercises 1, 2**

5.4 Comparison with a number

When used with a number, *más* and *menos* are followed by *de* (not *que*):

*Había **más/menos de cien** personas en el auditorio.*
There were **more/fewer than a hundred** people in the auditorium.

However, you say *no más que* meaning 'only':

***No** tengo **más que** tres euros.*
I've **only** got 3 euros.

5.5 Comparison with a clause

When the comparison is of quantity with a clause containing a noun or pronoun, use *más del/de la/de los/de las que*, depending on the noun referred to.

*Vinieron cien personas **más de las que esperábamos**. (**las** refers back to **personas**)*
A hundred **more** people **than** (those whom) **we were expecting** came.

If there is no noun or pronoun to compare, use *de lo que*:

*Es **menos** importante **de lo que** pensaba originalmente.*
It's **less** important **than** I originally thought.

➤ **Exercise 3**

¡PONTE A PUNTO!

1 ¿Qué sabes de Latinoamérica?

¡Todo mentiras! Las siguientes observaciones sobre Latinoamérica son todas incorrectas. Corrígelas, usando una forma del comparativo: *más ... que, menos ... que, (no) tan ... como, (no) tanto ... como.*

1 Brasil es menos grande que Chile.
2 No llueve tanto en las selvas de Brasil como en el desierto de Atacama en Chile.
3 Más personas hablan portugués que español en Latinoamérica.
4 Hay más capitalistas en Cuba que en el resto de Latinoamérica.
5 Acapulco está más contaminada que la Ciudad de Méjico.
6 El Río Grande es más largo que el Río Orinoco.
7 Hace más frío en Caracas que en la Tierra del Fuego.
8 No hay tantos galeses en Gales como en Patagonia.
9 Más ingleses que norteamericanos visitan los países de Sudamérica.
10 Los habitantes de las Islas Malvinas hablan más español que inglés.

2 Geografía europea

Usando las diferentes formas del comparativo, haz frases que comparen los sitios, etc., que se ponen aquí abajo. Quizás te haga falta un mapa de Europa.

Ejemplo:

Madrid y Córdoba

Madrid es más grande/ruidosa/cosmopolita que Córdoba.
Córdoba es menos importante/estratégica/moderna que Madrid.
Madrid (no) es tan interesante/histórica/antigua/turística como Córdoba.
Córdoba no tiene tanto tráfico/tantos habitantes como Madrid.
Se llega a Madrid más fácilmente/rápidamente/difícilmente que a Córdoba.

1 Luxemburgo y Rusia
2 El río Rin y el río Támesis
3 Los Picos de Europa y los Cotswolds
4 España y Portugal
5 Suiza y Holanda
6 Islandia y Malta
7 Los ferrocarriles franceses y los españoles
8 Londres y París
9 El idioma catalán y el castellano
10 Tu ciudad o pueblo y una ciudad o pueblo que conozcas en otro país europeo

3 Lo entiendo, ¡más o menos!

En las frases que siguen a continuación tienes que escoger entre *que, de, de lo que, del que, de los que, de la que,* o *de las que.*

1   En mi clase hay menos ... diez estudiantes.
2   Son menos estudiantes ... yo pensaba al matricularme en el curso.
3   En una clase tan pequeña, estudio mejor ... he podido estudiar antes.
4   En efecto, estoy seguro que hago mejores progresos ... hacía antes.
5   Yo creo que ahora trabajo mejor ... mis compañeros.
6   Si hubiera más ... diez estudiantes sería difícil conseguir suficiente práctica oral.
7   Desgraciadamente mi trabajo escrito es peor ... yo quisiera.
8   ¡Parece que tengo mucho más suerte ... tuve el año pasado!
9   Y ¡creo que voy entendiendo este problema de *que* y *de* mejor ... lo entendía antes de empezar este ejercicio!

 ¡... Y EN MARCHA!

4 ¡Yo soy más perfecto/a que tú!

Cambia observaciones (¡o quizás insultos!) con tus compañeros/as de clase sobre vosotros mismos.

Ejemplo:

– Yo soy más jóven/guapo(a)/inteligente/alto(a) que tú.
– Tú no eres tan guapo/a como yo./No tienes tanta edad como yo.

5 ¡No es igual!

Haz comparaciones entre lo que se ve en la calle donde vives y otra calle más importante, como Oxford Street en Londres.

Ejemplo:

En la calle donde vivo hay más tranquilidad pero menos comodidades.

6 Superlative of adjectives and adverbs

 **MECANISMOS**

6.1 The superlative of adjectives

a) The superlative in English ends in '-est' ('biggest', 'smallest'), or we use 'most' before the adjective ('most important'). For the negative superlative we use 'least' with all adjectives. In Spanish you use the noun with its article followed by *más* or *menos* and the adjective – the definite article is not repeated.

la ciudad más importante   the **most important** city

📝 Note: this is unlike French where the definite article is repeated: *La ville la plus importante*.

b) The following superlatives are exceptions worth noting:

el/la mayor (the biggest/the eldest)   *el/la menor* (the youngest)
el/la mejor (the best)   *el/la peor* (the worst)

> *Esta carretera es la peor.*
> This road is **the worst**.

c) The superlative is normally followed by *de* if a direct comparison is made:

> *Barcelona es la ciudad más importante de Cataluña.*
> Barcelona is the most important city **in** Catalonia.

d) With a possessive, the superlative of the adjective does not take the article:

> *El «Guernica» es su obra más famosa.*
> 'Guernica' is **his most famous** work.

➡ **Exercise 1**

6.2 The superlative of adverbs

To form the superlative of adverbs, again use *más* or *menos* without the definite article. Although this is the same as the comparative, the context will usually give the sense of the superlative:

> *Ana trabaja **más de prisa**.*
> Ana works **fastest**.

> *Pedro escribe **mejor**.*
> Pedro writes **best**.

The comparative form will usually be followed by *que* (than):

> *Pedro escribe **mejor que** todos/ninguno/nadie.*
> Pedro writes **better than** everyone/anyone.

6.3 Emphasis

To say 'very, very', 'extremely', you can add *-ísimo* to most adjectives.

> *un profesor **aburridísimo***
> an **extremely boring** teacher

> *La comida fue **riquísima*** (note *qu* spelling change)
> The food was **very good indeed**.

You can also add *-mente* to this form to make an adverb (see Chapter 4):

> *Hablaba **rapidísimamente**.*
> She was speaking **very, very quickly**.

Exercise 2

¡PONTE A PUNTO!

1 Más sobre España

Empleando un superlativo con *más* o *menos*, haz frases completas de las palabras siguientes.

Ejemplo:

Barcelona – puerto – importante – costa mediterránea

Barcelona es el puerto más importante de la costa mediterránea.

1   La Rioja – autonomía – pequeña – toda España
2   El vino – producto – importante – la Rioja
3   Las drogas – problema – preocupante – la juventud española
4   Pedro Almodóvar – director de cine – conocido – la actualidad española
5   Torrelavega – ciudad – turística – Cantabria
6   El AVE – tren – rápido y moderno – la RENFE
7   El turismo – factor – imprescindible – la economía española
8   El autobús – modo de viajar – cómodo – todos
9   El Ebro – río – largo – España
10 Granada – ciudad – con influencia árabe – toda Andalucía

2 ¡Un restaurante estupendísimo!

Contesta a las declaraciones siguientes, añadiendo un superlativo.

Ejemplo:

– Las fresas están muy frescas, ¿verdad?

– Sí, están fresquísimas.

1   El gazpacho está muy frío, ¿verdad?
2   Estos manteles son muy lindos, ¿verdad?
3   Estas gambas son muy ricas, ¿verdad?
4   Estos restaurantes son muy buenos, ¿no?
5   La camarera es muy simpática, ¿verdad?
6   Los postres son muy grandes, ¿no te parece?
7   La salsa es muy sabrosa, ¿no?
8   El personal trabaja mucho, ¿no?
9   Estás contenta de la comida, ¿no?
10 Te sirven muy rápidamente, ¿verdad?

 **¡... Y EN MARCHA!**

3 El concejo

Con tus compañeros/as estás seleccionando representantes para el concejo de tu curso escolar. Empleando superlativos, haz comentarios sobre tus compañeros/as.

Ejemplo:

Ana es la más lista, Pablo es el menos amable, Linda y Juan son los más populares del curso.

He aquí unos adjetivos para ayudarte:

descarado	inteligente	educado	perezoso	aplicado	sabio
informado	honrado*	difícil	simpático	conflictivo	hablador
socarrón	positivo	gracioso*	joven	ingenuo*	persuasivo
vital*	soñador	idealista	realista	izquierdista*	derechista*

* ¿Sabes exactamente lo que significan estas palabras? ¡Quizás valga la pena comprobarlas en el diccionario!

4 Titulares

Estás produciendo un periódico escolar en español, y te hacen falta titulares impresionantes o chocantes. Con la ayuda de un periódico cualquiera, español o inglés, inventa titulares para algunos de los reportajes, usando superlativos. Discute tus titulares con tus compañeros/as.

Ejemplo:

La basura – el problema más apremiante de nuestras calles

La Señora X – ¡la profesora menos comprendida del colegio!

7 Demonstrative adjectives and pronouns

MECANISMOS

a) Demonstrative adjectives and pronouns, as their name implies, are used to demonstrate or pinpoint whatever is being referred to. Because they refer to nouns, there are masculine and feminine, singular and plural forms to match the nouns they describe.

- *Este/esta* (this) and *estos/estas* (these) are used to describe something close to you.
- *Ese/esa* and *esos/esas* are used for 'that' and 'those', usually when the thing in question is near the person you are talking to.
- *Aquel/aquella* (that) and *aquellos/aquellas* (those) are used to describe something further away from you, especially to distinguish it from *este* and *ese*. As you can see, Spanish is unusual in having three levels of demonstration or comparison:

este ... (this), *ese* ... (that), and *aquel* ... (the ... over there).

> *Este chico es más alto que ése.*
> **This** boy is taller than **that one**.

> *Esta chica es menos inteligente que aquélla.*
> **This** girl is less intelligent than **that one**.

> *Esos perros son más ruidosos que aquéllos.*
> **Those** dogs (near you) are noisier than **those over there**.

b) They can all be used as adjectives, either placed in front of a noun, or as pronouns, standing alone to represent a noun. As pronouns, they carry an accent on the first *e* to distinguish them from the adjectives.

este/éste	ese/ése	aquel/aquél
esta/ésta	esa/ésa	aquella/aquélla
estos/éstos	esos/ésos	aquellos/aquéllos
estas/éstas	esas/ésas	aquellas/aquéllas

c) There are also three special neuter forms of the pronouns (which do not have an accent):
esto, *eso* and ***aquello***.

These are used to describe a general idea or to refer to something whose gender is not known.

> *¿Qué es **esto**?*
> What's **this**?

They are often used as in the following examples to express an idea.

> ***Esto** es algo que no me gusta nada.*
> **This** is something I don't like at all.

> *Nunca había oído hablar de **eso**.*
> I had never heard of **that**.

> *¿Qué piensas de todo **aquello**?*
> What do you think of all **that**?

d) The pronoun forms *éste* and ***aquél*** are often used in the sense of the English 'the latter' and 'the former'.

> *Londres es más grande que Madrid, pero **ésta** tiene más problemas con el tráfico que* ***aquélla***.
> London is larger than Madrid, but the **latter** has more traffic problems than the **former**.

➡ **Exercise 1**

 ¡PONTE A PUNTO!

1 ¡El profesor criticón!

Rellena los espacios en blanco con adjetivos o pronombres adecuados de los que se ven arriba.

El señor don Eutiquio Deberes es profesor en . . **1** . . instituto. Enseña Historia en . . **2** . . aula, pero a veces tiene que pasar a . . **3** . . , que está al lado de la biblioteca. . . **4** . . buen señor, que suele estar de mal humor y que es muy criticón, habla de sus alumnos mientras escribe sus informes.

'A ver, a . . **5** . . chico le voy a dar un cinco. Y a . . **6** . . le daré un cuatro, porque trabaja aun menos que . . **7** . . . La verdad es que todos . . **8** . . chicos son unos vagos. No estudian tanto como mis compañeros y yo; . . **9** . . generación parece que no quiere progresar como . . **10** . . . No me gusta nada todo . . **11** . . . Y las chicas son iguales. . . **12** . . chicas de hoy no son tan formales como . . **13** . . , las de mi generación. Sobre todo la Concha y la Juanita: . . **14** . . , parece que no sabe nada, y . . **15** . . no quiere saber nada. Nunca hubo jóvenes tan perezosos como . . **16** . . !'

Nota: ¡No te olvides de hacer concordar los adjetivos y pronombres con los sustantivos!

39

 **¡... Y EN MARCHA!**

2 ¡Qué cliente más pesado/a!

Trabajas en una tienda de ropa deportiva y tu compañero/a de clase es un(a) cliente: él/ella pide toda una serie de prendas, pero todo es demasiado grande/largo/caro… . En cada caso, tú le ofreces otra cosa, ¡y continúas así!

Ejemplo:

Cliente: *Quiero un suéter, pero éstos son demasiado grandes para mí. ¿No tiene Vd uno más pequeño que aquéllos?*

Tú: *Claro, este suéter es más pequeño que aquéllos.*

3 Don Sabelotodo

Cuentas a un(a) amigo/a una noticia tuya, pero – ¡ya la sabe, ya lo ha hecho, ya lo ha visto todo!

Ejemplo:

Tú: *Ayer fui a ver la nueva película de Antonio Banderas.*
Sabelotodo: *¡Ya vi esta película la semana pasada!*
Tú: *¿Sabes que Loli va a casarse con Manuel?*
Sabelotodo: *Sí, sí. Ya sabía esto.*

4 El concurso de Crufts en España

Tú y tus compañeros/as sois jueces en un concurso para perros o gatos. Tenéis que comparar los perros o gatos que han pasado a la etapa final para decidir cuál de los animales va a ganar.

Ejemplo:

A: *Este perro es más inteligente que aquél, ¿verdad?*
B: *Sí, pero ese perro de la derecha tiene la cara más bonita que aquéllos.*
C: *Pues yo prefiero los perros con el rabo largo como aquél.*

5 Niños mimados

Llevas a un(a) niño/a mimado/a a un almacén grande para comprarle un regalo. Pero el/la niño/a, que también es travieso/a y rebelde, se opone a todo lo que le ofreces y propones. (Tu amigo/a es el/la niño/a.)

Ejemplo:

Tú:	*¿Quieres un paquete de estos caramelos?*
Niño/a:	*¡Ya sabes que nunca compro aquéllos!*
Tú:	*Bueno, ¿por qué no vamos a mirar los DVDs?*
Niño/a:	*¡Porque no me interesa nada hacer eso!*

6 ¡El contrario!

Has invitado a un(a) amigo/a a tu casa, y le ofreces varias cosas. En cada caso, él/ella no quiere aquella cosa, sino otra.

Ejemplo:

Tú:	*¿Quieres un vaso de este vino?*
Amigo/a:	*No, gracias, prefiero aquél.*
Tú:	*¿Te gustaría escoger uno de estos pasteles?*
Amigo/a:	*Ay, no. ¡No puedo comer éstos! ¡No quiero engordar! Prefiero aquello.*

7 El vendedor

Imagina que trabajas en una tienda y que das una descripción por hablado o por escrito de varios productos del mismo tipo, dando sus méritos y características.

Ejemplo:

Bueno, este aspirador funciona muy bien, y tiene un motor más potente que aquél. Pero éste es más caro que aquéllos que tenemos allí.

8 Possessive adjectives and pronouns

 **MECANISMOS**

8.1 Possessive adjectives

Possession can be expressed in many different ways, most commonly by means of an adjective. As with other adjectives, Spanish possessive adjectives have to agree with the nouns they describe, so they have more than one form:

mi/mis	my
tu/tus	your = belonging to *tú*
su/sus	{ your = belonging to *usted* his, her, its
nuestro/nuestra/nuestros/nuestras	our
vuestro/vuestra/vuestros/vuestras	your = belonging to *vosotros*
su/sus	{ your = belonging to *ustedes* their

As you can see, only **nuestro** and **vuestro** have four forms, for masculine and feminine, singular and plural:

nuestro coche/nuestra madre/ *nuestros tíos/nuestras amigas* }	our car/mother/uncles (and aunts)/friends
vuestro padre/vuestra comida/ *vuestros discos/vuestras tías* }	your father/meal/records/aunts

Mi, **tu** and **su** have only one singular and one plural form – the same form is used for masculine and feminine, in both singular and plural:

mi libro	my book	*mis cartas*	my letters
tu perro	your dog	*tus gatos*	your cats
su casa	his/her/its/their/your house	*sus pisos*	his/her/its/their/your flats

✎ Note: **su** is used for 'his', 'her', 'its', 'their' and for the formal forms of 'your' (of **usted** and **ustedes**).

➡ **Exercise 1**

42

Note also that all these possessive adjectives agree with the noun in the same way as other adjectives – that is, they agree with the **thing owned**, not with the owner. A common error is to think that *su* means 'his/her/its/your (*de usted*)', and that *sus* means 'their/your (*de ustedes*)'; instead, both *su* and *sus* can mean all of these, but while *su* is used for a singular possession, *sus* is used for plural possessions.

8.2 Use of *de*

To answer the question ¿*De quién es esto?* 'Whose is it?', Spanish uses *de* + person:

*Es **de** Miguel.*
It is Miguel's.

*Es la casa **de** Fernando.*
It is Fernando's house.

*Son las hermanas **de** Maribel.*
They are Maribel's sisters.

*Aquélla es la **de** ella.*
That one is hers.

This structure is sometimes used to avoid ambiguity after one of the various uses of *su*.

*Vi a José y a Teresa con su madre **de ella**.*
I saw José and Teresa with her mother.

*Oiga, por favor, ¿es su coche **de usted**?*
Excuse me, is this your car?

➤ **Exercise 3**

8.3 Possessive pronouns

To convey the sense of 'mine', 'yours', 'hers' and so on, that is, to express possession without repeating the nouns, the following possessive pronouns are used:

mine	mío	mía	míos	mías
yours (tú)	tuyo	tuya	tuyos	tuyas
his/hers/its/yours (usted)	suyo	suya	suyos	suyas
ours	nuestro	nuestra	nuestros	nuestras
yours (vosotros)	vuestro	vuestra	vuestros	vuestras
theirs/yours (ustedes)	suyo	suya	suyos	suyas

These possessive pronouns can be used as in the following examples.

- No article is used when these possessives are used with **ser**:

  *Este libro es **mío**, aquél es **tuyo**.*
  This book is **mine**, that one is **yours**.

- No article is used when the possessive pronoun is used in an adjectival way in the sense of '… of mine':

  *Ayer visité a unos tíos **míos** que viven en Granada.*
  Yesterday I visited an uncle and aunt **of mine** who live in Granada.

- The article is used when a possessive pronoun is needed to replace a noun:

  *Mi casa es más grande que **la tuya**, pero tus padres son más ricos que **los míos**.*
  My house is bigger than **yours**, but your parents are richer than **mine**.

➡ **Exercises 2, 3, 4**

8.4 Reflexive used to express possession

With parts of the body and clothes, as in cases such as 'he washed his face', possession is not expressed by using a possessive adjective as in English, but by the use of a reflexive construction (see Chapter 16 on reflexive verbs used to express possession).

Me *lavé la cara.*
I washed **my** face.

Se *limpian los dientes después de comer.*
They clean **their** teeth after eating.

The same structure is used, for example, for 'he put on his hat', where the subject puts on an item of clothing.

Me *puse el sombrero.*
I put **my** hat on.

*Vamos a poner**nos** el abrigo.*
We'll put **our** coats on.

Notice the singular **abrigo** – only one coat each!

✐ Note: this is similar to the use of the indirect object pronoun to express possession, e.g. **le vendé el dedo** – I bandaged his finger.

¡PONTE A PUNTO!

1 Los poseedores

Tu amigo trata de averiguar de quién es/son varios objetos dejados en el club; dejó un mensaje para ti con varias preguntas. Tienes que contestarlas como en el ejemplo.

Ejemplo:

La raqueta es de Julio, ¿verdad? Sí, es su raqueta.

1 Éstos son los zapatos de María, ¿no?	No, ...
2 Este CD es de Ramoncín, ¿no?	Sí, ...
3 La chaqueta de cuero es de Pepe, ¿verdad?	No, ...
4 ¿Las zapatillas rojas son de Conchi?	Sí, ...
5 ¿De quién son los monopatines? ¿De Pilar?	Sí, ...
6 No sé si el MP3 es de Marcos o no...	No, ...
7 Si no es de Marcos, ¿es tu MP3?	Sí, ...
8 Creo que los naipes son de Cris: es así, ¿no?	Sí, ...
9 ¿Éstas son mis gafas?	No, ...
10 ¿Crees que el vídeo es nuestro?	Sí, ...
11 Los carteles son nuestros, ¿verdad?	No, ...
12 Es mi DVD, ¿no?	Sí, ...

2 ¿De quién son?

Estáis en la oficina de objetos perdidos del colegio. El bedel quiere saber de quién son varios objetos perdidos. Contesta a las siguientes preguntas según lo que viene en paréntesis.

1 ¿De quién es este bolígrafo? (Marcos)
2 ¿De quién es esta corbata? (Ángel)
3 ¿De quién es aquella radio? (Anita)
4 ¿De quién es el diccionario? ¿Es del profesor de inglés? (Sí, ...)
5 ¿De quién es aquella carta? ¿Es tuya? (Sí, ...)
6 ¿De quién es ese diario? ¿Es mío? (Sí, ...)
7 ¿De quién es aquel balón? ¿Es vuestro? (Sí, ...)
8 ¿De quién es la toalla? ¿Es nuestra? (Sí, ...)
9 ¿De quién son esos cuadernos? (Miriam González)
10 ¿De quién son las fotos? (Pablo Picazo)
11 ¿De quién son estas naranjas? ¿Son tuyas? (Sí, ...)
12 ¿De quién son los mapas? ¿Son del profesor de geografía? (Sí, ...)
13 ¿De quién son aquellas gafas? ¿Son de tu madre? (Sí, ...)
14 ¿De quiénes son estos sombreros? ¿Son de las cocineras? (Sí, ...)
15 ¿De quiénes son los bolígrafos rojos? ¿Son de ustedes? (Sí, ...)
16 ¿De quiénes son estas bebidas? ¿Son vuestras? (Sí, ...)

3 Tu casa y la mía

Acabas de recibir esta carta de un amigo tuyo – español – que ha pasado un mes contigo. Hace una comparación entre vuestras respectivas familias, casa, ciudades, y escuelas. Pero ha omitido todos los posesivos. ¿Sabrás rellenar los espacios con el posesivo más apropiado? ¡Suerte!

Madrid
2 de mayo

¡Hola!

Ya estoy otra vez en . . 1 . . casa después de estar un mes en . . 2 . . . . . 3 . . padres dicen que tengo que volver a darles las gracias a . . 4 . . .

Ya sabes que . . 5 . . familia es más pequeña que . . 6 . . ; . . 7 . . madre dice que . . 8 . . tiene mucha suerte. Además, . . 9 . . casa es más pequeña que . . 10 . . . Y también, en Inglaterra todas . . 11 . . casas tienen jardín, mientras que aquí la mayoría de . . 12 . . no lo tienen.

. . 13 . . ciudad tiene más espacios abiertos que . . 14 . . , pero . . 15 . . tiene más parques que . . 16 . . en Inglaterra. . . 17 . . ciudades grandes suelen tener más embotellamientos que . . 18 . . .

Lo que me parece muy interesante es que . . 19 . . clase sea más pequeña que . . 20 . . ¡Me parece también que . . 21 . . compañeras de clase son tan simpáticas como . . 22 . . ! Una cosa más: si encuentras unas zapatillas blancas, ¡son . . 23 . . ! Creo que las dejé en . . 24 . . dormitorio.

Un abrazo,

Felipe

4 Mensajes conflictivos

Imagina que un día, en clase, tú y tus compañeros/as de clase os mandáis mensajes unos/as a otros/as mientras el profe no está mirando. Estáis haciendo comparaciones y contradicciones. Así, tienes que escribir una respuesta a los mensajes de tus amigos/as.

1 Mi moto es más rápida que la tuya, ¿verdad?
2 Tu novio/a es más feo/a que el mío/la mía, ¿no?
3 Nuestra abuela es más vieja que la vuestra.
4 Tus tíos son más simpáticos que los míos.
5 Oye, mi perro es más feroz que el suyo, ¿verdad?
6 Ya sabes que tu amiga es más tonta que la mía.
7 Mi móvil costó más dinero que el tuyo.
8 Nuestros deberes son más difíciles que los suyos, ¿verdad?
9 Vuestro profesor es mejor que el nuestro.
10 Los mensajes que mandan ellos por e-mail son más aburridos que los nuestros, ¿no?

 **¡... Y EN MARCHA!**

5 El cleptómano

Uno/a a uno/a, hacéis el papel de un cleptómano: el cleptómano roba todo lo que pueda a sus compañeros. Éstos tienen que pedirle que se lo devuelva, usando los posesivos como en los ejemplos siguientes.

Cleptómano:	*Ay, ¡que me gusta mucho esta cartera! Creo que es mía.*
Víctima:	*Huy no, no puede ser. Es mi cartera ... Sí, sí, es mía.*
Compañero/a:	*¡Tiene razón! Es suya, no es tuya.*
Otro/a compañero/a:	*¡No es tuya, imbécil! Es de Sarah. La tuya es más pequeña.*

6 Juego de memoria

Un(a) voluntario/a sale de vuestra aula. Cada miembro de vuestra clase pone un objeto distinto en el pupitre del profesor, o en cualquier mesa o pupitre. Llamáis al/a la voluntario/a, que tiene que adivinar de quién son los artículos.

Ejemplo:

Profe:	*¿De quién es este libro?*
Voluntario/a:	*¿Es de Julián?*
Clase:	*No, no es suyo.*
Voluntario/a:	*¿Es del profesor?*
Profe:	*No, no es mío tampoco.*

7 En la oficina de objetos perdidos

Perdiste tu paraguas, o lo dejaste en el autobús. En la oficina de objetos perdidos te hacen varias preguntas sobre el color, el tamaño y otras características de tu paraguas. ¡También puedes 'perder' otros artículos, hasta a tu hermano o un animal doméstico!

Ejemplo:

Tú:	*Perdí mi paraguas. Creo que lo dejé en el autobús ayer.*
Empleado/a:	*Bueno, tenemos varios. ¿Cómo era el suyo?*
Tú:	*El mío era de color naranja.*
Empleado/a:	*¿Es éste?*
Tú:	*No, no es mío. El mío era más largo ...*

8 Y tú, ¿qué vas a tomar?

Invitas a varios/as amigos/as, o sea, a la clase entera, incluso/a tu profesor(a), a tomar algo. Cada uno/a pide una cosa distinta. Cuando llega el/la camarero/a, te pregunta de quién es cada bebida: tú tienes que contestarle, ¡si recuerdas todos los detalles!

Ejemplo:

Camarero/a:	*¿De quién es el café solo?*
Tú:	*Es de Simón.*
Camarero/a:	*Y la cerveza, es de esta señorita, ¿no?*
Tú:	*No, no es suya. Es suya el agua mineral. La cerveza es de mi profesor.*

9 ¡Novios ideales!

En una página de una revista para jóvenes, la Tía Angustias publica cartas de sus lectores, dándoles consejos y sugerencias para ayudarles a resolver sus problemas. Escribes una carta a la Tía Angustias en la cual describes a tu novio/a con todas sus cualidades y defectos.

Luego tienes que imaginar que eres la Tía Angustias. Contestas, comparando al/a la novio/a de la carta con el/la novio/a ideal, pero recordando a tu lector(a) que tiene que aceptar a su novio/a tal y como es.

Ejemplo:

Lectora:	*Mi novio no es muy generoso, pero siempre me da un regalo para mi cumpleaños.*
Tía Angustias:	*El novio ideal ofrece más regalos que el tuyo, y es más generoso, pero el tuyo, por lo menos, siempre recuerda tu cumpleaños.*

9 Numerals

MECANISMOS

9.1 Cardinal numbers

1 uno	11 once	21 veintiuno	31 treinta y uno
2 dos	12 doce	22 veintidós	32 treinta y dos
3 tres	13 trece	23 veintitrés	40 cuarenta
4 cuatro	14 catorce	24 veinticuatro	45 cuarenta y cinco
5 cinco	15 quince	25 veinticinco	50 cincuenta
6 seis	16 dieciséis	26 veintiséis	60 sesenta
7 siete	17 diecisiete	27 veintisiete	70 setenta
8 ocho	18 dieciocho	28 veintiocho	80 ochenta
9 nueve	19 diecinueve	29 veintinueve	90 noventa
10 diez	20 veinte	30 treinta	100 cien

101 ciento uno	1.000 mil
102 ciento dos	2.000 dos mil
127 ciento veintisiete	5.000 cinco mil
198 ciento noventa y ocho	10.000 diez mil
200 doscientos/as	1.000.000 un millón
300 trescientos/as	2.000.000 dos millones
400 cuatrocientos/as	
500 quinientos/as	
600 seiscientos/as	
700 setecientos/as	
800 ochocientos/as	
900 novecientos/as	

987.654.321 *novecientos ochenta y siete millones*, *seiscientos cincuenta y cuatro mil*, *trescientos veintiuno*.

a) *Uno*, including numbers ending with it, drops the *-o* ('**apocopates**') to become *un* before a masculine noun, and becomes *una* before a feminine one:

*un euro, trescientos **veintiún** euros*
*una libra, cincuenta y **una** libras, trescientas **veintiuna** libras*

b) From 200 upwards, the 'hundreds' have masculine and feminine forms:

*doscient**os** euros*
*cuatrocient**as** libras*

c) 100 is *cien* when counting, or when saying 'a hundred (+ noun)':

cien libras	**a hundred** pounds
cien habitantes	**a hundred** inhabitants

Ciento is used when followed by a number (when you say 'a hundred and ...'):

ciento tres	**a hundred** and three
ciento ochenta y dos	**a hundred** and eighty-two

There is no *y* after hundreds:

ciento dos	**a hundred** and two

d) The *y* comes between tens and units after 16, though it is usually written as *-i-* within the word in the teens and twenties:

*ciento diecisiete, doscientos veinticinco, trescientos treinta **y** tres, quinientos ochenta **y** cuatro*

e) When expressing numbers of thousands, *mil* does not change:

*tres **mil***	three **thousand**

However, 'thousands of ...' – *miles de ...*

f) One million – *un millón de ...* , two million – *dos millones de* ...

9.2 Ordinal numbers

1st	primero	7th	sé(p)timo
2nd	segundo	8th	octavo
3rd	tercero	9th	noveno/nono
4th	cuarto	10th	décimo
5th	quinto	11th	undécimo
6th	sexto	12th	duodécimo

a) Ordinal numbers tell you the order things come in. They are adjectives and therefore must agree with their noun:

*la tercer**a** planta*	the third floor
*la reina Isabel Segund**a***	Queen Elizabeth the Second
*las primer**as** flores*	the first flowers

b) The ordinal numbers are usually only used up to 10th (occasionally 12th). Thereafter, although in theory the appropriate ordinal numbers exist, the cardinal number is almost invariably used, placed after the noun:

*el siglo **doce***	the **twelfth** century
*Alfonso **Décimo*** (but *Alfonso **Trece***)	Alfonso the **Tenth** (**Thirteenth**)

c) *Primero* and ***tercero*** lose the final ***-o*** before a masculine singular noun:

*su **primer** empleo*	her first job
*el **tercer** ejercicio*	the third exercise

Exercise 1

¡PONTE A PUNTO!

1 Jugando con números

a) Escribe en palabras o dicta en voz alta a un(a) compañero/a los números siguientes.

24	43	65	92
51	101	112	148
187	202	342	405
466	503	513	673
772	821	954	1.001
1.234	2.378	8.743	12.876
59.483	83.689	1.000.001	4.986.523
56.409.004	452.694.570		

b) Y también estas frases.

Isabel I de Inglaterra
el papa Pablo VI
el rey Alfonso X
el 5 aniversario
su 8 cumpleaños
su 15 cumpleaños

c) Y además …

tu número de teléfono
la edad de tu abuelo/a
el año en que naciste
tu edad
el año en que estamos
la fecha de hoy

 ¡... Y EN MARCHA!

2 ¿Eres buen matemático?

A ver si sabes sumar, restar, multiplicar y dividir.

Ejemplo:

¿Cuántos son doce más trece? Son veinticinco.
¿Cuántos son trece menos siete? Son seis.
¿Cuántos son tres multiplicados por cuatro? Son doce.
¿Cuántos son quince divididos por tres? Son cinco.

Haz preguntas similares a tus compañeros/as, inventando problemas cada vez más difíciles.

Ahora pregunta a tus compañeros/as acerca de los cuadrados, los cubos y las raíces cuadradas y cúbicas de algunos números.

Ejemplo:

¿Cuál es la raíz cuadrada de 81? Es 9.

3 ¡No eres buen matemático!

Estás trabajando de camarero/a en un restaurante español, pero tienes problemas en sumar las cuentas de los clientes. Trabaja con un(a) compañero/a, alternando el papel de camarero/a y cliente/a. Presentas una cuenta incorrecta a tu cliente, que, claro, protesta.

Emplead las cuentas que vienen abajo y luego inventad otras vuestras si queréis.

Restaurante Europa Cuenta	
2 x gambas a 3.50€	8.50€
1 x solomillo a 5.60€	5.60€
1 x merluza a 7.20€	7.20€
2 x postre a 2.20€	4.50€
2 x café a 0.50€	1.10€
Total	27.90€

Restaurante Europa Cuenta	
3 sopa a 2.70€	9.00€
1 pescado a 6.80€	6.80€
2 ternera a 5.05€	11.10€
3 postre a 2.10€	7.30€
3 coñac a 0.75€	2.50€
Total	38.70€

4 ¿A qué distancia?

Mira un mapa del mundo. Estima a qué distancia y a cuántas horas varias ciudades están unas de otras.

Ejemplo:

Caracas está a cuatro mil quinientos sesenta y cinco kilómetros de Madrid. Está a siete horas en avión. Está a cuatro días en barco.

10 Measures and dimensions

10.1 Length, breadth, depth, height, thickness, area, capacity

The most common way to express dimensions in Spanish is to say:

(El objeto) tiene 20 centímetros de largo/longitud
ancho/anchura
profundo/profundidad
alto/altura
espeso/espesura.
(The object) is 20 centimetres **long/wide/deep/tall/thick**.

You can also say:

un objeto largo
ancho
profundo ⎱ *de 20 centímetros*
alto
espeso
an object 20 centimetres long/wide/deep/high/thick

*El cuarto **tiene/mide 6 metros por 5**.*
The room **is/measures 6 metres by 5**.

*Mi hermana **mide 1 metro 55** y **pesa 45 kilos**.*
My sister **measures 1.55 metres** and **weighs 45 kilos**.

*La casa **tiene 200 metros cuadrados**.*
The house **is 200 square metres**.

10.2 Shapes

un cuadrado	square	*un rectángulo*	rectangle	*un triángulo*	triangle
un círculo	circle	*un óvalo*	oval	*un polígono*	polygon
un pentágono	pentagon	*un cubo*	cube	*un cilindro*	cylinder
un romboide	rhomboid				

redondo, circular	round, circular	*triangular*	triangular
oval	oval	*cilíndrico*	cylindrical
cuadrado	square	*cúbico*	cubic, cube-shaped
rectangular	rectangular, oblong		

10.3 Measures

un milímetro	un centímetro	un decímetro	un metro	un kilómetro
un mililitro	un centilitro	un decilitro	un litro	
un miligramo	un centigramo	un gramo	un kilo(gramo)	

10.4 Percentages

El/Un 34 por ciento *de los habitantes no son de origen vasco.*
34% of the inhabitants are not of Basque origin.

 Exercise 1

 **¡PONTE A PUNTO!**

1 Medidas necesarias

Describe la forma y toma las medidas (exactas, de ser posible) de:

a   el cuarto en que estás
b   la mesa en que trabajas
c   una de las ventanas del cuarto
d   tu lápiz o bolígrafo
e   este libro

f   el cajón de una mesa o un escritorio
g   el material que cubre el suelo, sea alfombra u
   otra cosa
h   el reloj de la pared o tu reloj de pulsera
i   una moneda de 50 peniques

 ¡... Y EN MARCHA!

2 Puzzle líquido

Tienes tres jarros, A, B y C, cuya capacidad es respectivamente ocho, cinco y tres litros. Necesitas tener un litro exactamente, pero no tienes un cuarto jarro. Vertiendo de un jarro a otro, **sólo dos veces**, tienes que quedarte con un solo litro en uno de los tres jarros. ¿Cómo vas a hacerlo? Discute el problema con tus compañeros/as. Necesitarás la expresión: **Me/Nos quedará(n) ...** (I/We shall have ... left).

	Jarro A	**Jarro B**	**Jarro C**
Capacidad:	8 litros	5 litros	3 litros
Contenido:			

La solución está en la página 282.

3 Estadísticas vitales

Con una báscula comprueba cuánto pesa en kilos cada miembro de tu clase. ¡A ver si tu profesor(a) se deja pesar! Cuando sepas el peso de cada uno en kilos, convierte éstos en libras, o mejor, *stones* y libras, inglesas. Para ayudarte: hay 453 gramos en una libra, y 14 libras en un *stone*. Es preferible que uses tu cerebro más que una calculadora, pero cualquiera que sea tu método, ¡comenta tus cálculos en voz alta en español!

Ahora mide la altura de cada uno. ¿Cuánto mides? ¿Un metro sesenta (1,60)? ¿Más? ¿Menos? Convierte esto a pies con pulgadas. (Hay 2,54 centímetros en una pulgada y doce pulgadas en un pie.)

4 La casa nueva

Trabaja con un(a) compañero/a. Estás haciendo construir una casa nueva en un terreno que has comprado en la Costa Blanca en España. Estás discutiendo los planes preliminares de la casa con tu arquitecto/a. Dibujáis primero el terreno mismo, y decidís dónde precisamente vais a construir la casa. Luego dibujáis la casa, con todas las dimensiones exteriores e interiores. ¡No os olvidéis de la altura y la forma que van a tomar la casa y las habitaciones! ¿Cómo quieres que sea?

5 Exportaciones

a) Estás trabajando en una empresa que exporta sus productos a España. Primero tienes que describir a un(a) compañero/a (el/la jefe/a de compra de una empresa española) *unos* productos de la empresa, por ejemplo: minicalculadoras, relojes digitales, ordenadores, destornilladores, raquetas de tenis. Detalla sus dimensiones, material, colores posibles, uso y precio.

Puede que tu profesor(a) te dé más objetos a vender.

b) Más tarde estás al teléfono, hablando con la empresa en España, comprobando los precios en moneda británica y europea. Primero comprueba en un periódico corriente el tipo de cambio del euro a la libra esterlina.

Ejemplo:

Si una libra vale 1.40 euros, £20.35 son 28.49 euros (veintiocho euros con cuarenta y nueve céntimos).

| £7.89 | £11.45 | £45.98 | £67.90 | £78.75 | £342.99 | £5674.42 |

c) Luego convierte los precios al peso mejicano (digamos que una libra vale 20 pesos), puesto que tu compañía está aumentando sus exportaciones a Méjico.

¡Si el Reino Unido adopta el euro durante la vida de este libro, puedes adaptar este ejercicio cambiando euros a pesos mejicanos!

11 Times, dates, weather and *tener* expressions

 **MECANISMOS**

11.1 Time of day

¿Qué hora es?
What's the time?

¿A qué hora ...?
At what time?

Es la una.
It's one o'clock.

Son las dos/siete.
It's two/seven o'clock.

A las cinco.
At five o'clock.

As in English, there are two ways of stating the time, the 'conversational' and the 'digital' or timetable style.

las ocho y media (de la mañana) half past eight (in the morning/a.m.)	*las ocho treinta* eight thirty a.m.
las tres y cuarto (de la tarde) a quarter past three (in the afternoon/p.m.)	*las quince quince* three fifteen p.m.
las diez y veinte (de la noche) twenty past ten (at night/p.m.)	*las veintidós veinte* ten twenty p.m.
las doce menos cuarto (de la mañana) a quarter to twelve (a.m.)	*las once cuarenta y cinco* eleven forty-five a.m.
las doce menos cinco (de la noche) five to twelve (at night/p.m.)	*las veintitrés cincuenta y cinco* eleven fifty-five p.m.

Note:

- All hours except one o'clock take a plural verb: ***son las tres***; ***es la una***.
- This applies of course in all tenses: ***eran las siete*** (it was seven o'clock); ***será la una*** (it will be/it must be one o'clock); ***daban las once*** (it was striking eleven).
- In 'digital' style you don't normally put ***y*** between hours and minutes.
- In conversational style you can add ***de la mañana*** up to about 1 p.m., thereafter ***de la tarde*** until dark, and then ***de la noche***. Times in the 'small hours' can be referred to as ***de la madrugada*** – up to about 5 a.m.
- When no time is expressed, you say ***por la mañana/tarde/noche*** for 'in the morning/afternoon/at night'.

11.2 Words for 'time'

a) *El tiempo* = the general concept of 'time':

*¡Cómo vuela **el tiempo**!*
How **time** flies!

*¿**Cuánto tiempo** vas a pasar en la costa?*
How long (= how much time) are you going to spend on the coast?

Otherwise, *tiempo* usually means 'weather' (see section 11.4): ***tuvimos buen tiempo*** means 'we had good weather', not 'a good time', which would be ***lo pasamos bien***.

b) *La vez* = time = occasion:

una vez	once	*dos veces*	twice
muchas veces	lots of times, often	*¿cuántas veces?*	how many times?
a veces, algunas veces	sometimes		how often?

c) *La hora* = time of day; see section 11.1.

d) *La época* = period of time:

en <u>la época</u> de Franco   in Franco's **time**
<u>la época</u> de la vendimia   grape harvest **time**

11.3 Days and dates

The days and months are:

lunes	Monday	*enero*	January
martes	Tuesday	*febrero*	February
miércoles	Wednesday	*marzo*	March
jueves	Thursday	*abril*	April
viernes	Friday	*mayo*	May
sábado	Saturday	*junio*	June
domingo	Sunday	*julio*	July
		agosto	August
		se(p)tiembre	September
		octubre	October
		noviembre	November
		diciembre	December

¿Qué fecha es?
¿A cuánto estamos?
What's the date?

Es jueves, primero de mayo.
Estamos a domingo, siete de enero.
It's Thursday, 1st May/Sunday, 7th January.

 Notes:

- Days and months are spelt with a small letter.
- **Lunes** to **viernes** have no separate plural form.
- 'On Monday', i.e. next Monday, is simply **lunes** or **el lunes**; 'on Tuesdays' is **los martes**.
- '(On) Thursday morning/afternoon/evening' is (**el**) **jueves por la mañana/tarde/noche**;
  '(on) Saturday morning**s**/afternoon**s**/evening**s**' is **los sábados por la mañana/tarde/noche**
  (i.e. you make the **day** plural).
- 'Next Sunday' is **el domingo que viene** or **el domingo próximo**.
- 'In' a month is **en**: **en abril** 'in April'.
- For dates use **el primero** for the first of the month; for other dates use cardinal numbers:
  primero de abril, **dos de mayo**.
- You put **de** between both the date of the month and the month of the year:
  el doce de noviembre de dos mil doce 'the twelfth of November, 2012'.
- You can't 'short-cut' years as in 'nineteen ninety-nine', you have to say the year in full:
  mil novecientos noventa y nueve. It gets easier and shorter from 2000 for a century or so!

Exercise 1

11.4 The weather

*¿Qué **tiempo** hace/hacía?*
What is/was the **weather** like?

a) Many weather expressions are introduced by **hace** in the relevant tense:

hace/hacía/hizo/va a hacer:	the weather (it) is/was/is going to be:
(mucho) frío	(very) cold
(bastante) calor	(quite) hot
bueno/buen tiempo	fine
malo/mal tiempo	bad
(poco) sol	(not very) sunny
(mucho) viento	(very) windy
veinte grados	it/the temperature is 20 degrees

b) Some, usually visible, conditions are introduced by **hay** in the relevant tense:

hay/había/va a haber:	it is/was/will be:
(mucha) niebla	(very) foggy
neblina	misty
(muchas) nubes	(very) cloudy
escarcha/heladas	frosty

Note: after **hace** and **hay**, 'very' is **mucho/mucha**, agreeing because **frío** and the other weather words are nouns.

c) **Estar** is also used in some expressions with a gerund, past participle or adjective:

está/estaba lloviendo	it is/was raining
está/estaba nevando	it is/was snowing
está/estaba (muy) cubierto	it is/was (very) overcast
está/estaba (muy) nublado	it is/was (very) cloudy

d) Learn carefully these weather verbs, which are radical-changing (group 1, in present only) and note the often small difference with the corresponding noun!

verb infinitive		present indicative		noun	
llover	to rain	llueve	it rains	la lluvia	the rain
nevar	to snow	nieva	it snows	la nieve	the snow
helar	to freeze	hiela	it freezes	la helada	the frost
tronar	to thunder	truena	it thunders	el trueno	the thunder

Exercise 2

11.5 Feelings

a) The weather can make you feel hot or cold, and when you talk about yourself in this way you use *tener*. As *calor/frío* are nouns you again use *mucho* for 'very':

> *Teníamos mucho calor en esos suéteres.*
> **We were very hot** in those sweaters.

> *Si tienes frío puedes poner la calefacción.*
> If **you are cold** you can turn on the heating.

b) Other useful expressions using *tener* with a noun are:

tener (mucha) hambre	to be (very) hungry
tener (mucha) sed	to be (very) thirsty
tener (mucho) sueño	to be (very) sleepy
tener (mucho) miedo	to be (very) afraid/frightened
tener (mucho) cuidado	to be (very) careful
tener (mucho) éxito	to be (very) successful
tener (mucha) suerte	to be (very) lucky
tener (mucha) prisa	to be in a (great) hurry
tener razón	to be right
tener ganas de + infinitive	to feel like (doing)

 **Exercises 3, 4**

 ¡PONTE A PUNTO!

1 Horas, días, fechas y años

Lee en voz alta o escribe en su forma completa las siguientes horas y fechas. Entonces lee las horas en su forma 'conversacional'.

1 23.59, viernes 31-12-1999
2 00.01, sábado 1-1-2000
3 19.05, jueves 20-8-1998
4 07.30, martes 29-2-2000
5 11.45, lunes 14-2-1972
6 15.35, domingo 25-5-1997
7 23.40, viernes 28-12-1945
8 11.00, lunes 11-11-1918
8 17.15, miércoles 10-9-2008
10 03.50, lunes 12-10-2009

2 ¿Qué tiempo hará mañana?

Vuelve a escribir este boletín meteorológico, empleando solamente expresiones que contengan *hace*, *hay*, o un verbo en tercera persona.

El cielo estará nuboso a primeras horas en el norte de Galicia, *con alguna lluvia débil* en toda Galicia. Por la tarde *saldrá el sol*, *con una subida de temperaturas*. *Cielo nuboso* en el norte de Castilla y León. *Cielo despejado* en el resto del centro. En las costas este y sur *las temperaturas serán altísimas*; en la región de Almería *las temperaturas serán de unos 42 grados*. *Nieblas y temperaturas más frescas* en los Pirineos. *No corre riesgo de nieve* en ningún sitio.

Ejemplo:

El cielo estará nuboso: Habrá nubes.

3 El tiempo que hace y sus problemas

Empareja las circunstancias que se describen en las dos secciones para que hagan el mejor sentido.

1 Sudábamos la gota gorda.
2 Me mojé hasta los huesos.
3 Decidimos que era prudente no quedarnos debajo de unos árboles.
4 Tuve que proteger las plantas delicadas en mi terraza.
5 Decidí llevar mi impermeable y paraguas.
6 Tuve que conducir con mucho cuidado porque no veía por dónde iba.
7 Tuvimos que excavar una salida de la casa.
8 Las tejas se desprendían de los tejados y un árbol cayó a unos metros en la calle.
9 Me extrañaba de que no se hubiera puesto a llover.
10 Como me quemo tan fácilmente me quedé en la sombra de los árboles.

a El cielo había estado muy cubierto durante toda la mañana y ahora estaba casi oscuro a las cuatro de la tarde.
b ¡Qué viento hizo anoche!
c Habían avisado en la radio que la lluvia sería muy fuerte.
d Aunque no hacía un calor excepcional, el cielo estaba despejado y el sol brillaba con claridad.
e Nos había sorprendido una tormenta violenta.
f ¡Qué escarcha hubo la semana pasada!
g Con el calor que hacía en el bus …
h ¡No había previsto que llovería tanto!
i Durante la noche cayó casi un metro de nieve.
j Estaba en carretera volviendo del trabajo cuando me metí en una niebla espesa.

4 ¿Qué tenías?

Tienes que reaccionar a cada una de estas observaciones con una de las expresiones con *tener* utilizada en un tiempo pasado.

1 Te encontraron temblando y al borde de la hipotermia.
2 Acababas de ganar un campeonato de tenis.
3 Te caíste mientras estabas esquiando, deslizándote muchos metros hacia abajo, pero no te hiciste daño.
4 Pasaste dos semanas en el sur de España en agosto cuando hacía unos cuarenta grados cada día.
5 Te dormiste en clase de español.
6 Sentías que se te secaban por completo la boca y la garganta, tanto que casi no podías hablar.
7 Tu amigo/a te había invitado a salir, pero preferías quedarte en casa a leer un libro.
8 Te parecía tu estómago un hueco sin fondo, como si hiciera un mes que no tuviera nada que digerir.
9 En el examen, te quedaban cinco minutos para terminar tu redacción de español ¡y tres párrafos por escribir!
10 Nadie quería creerte, pero te pusiste firme y por fin todos tuvieron que aceptar lo que decías.

¡... Y EN MARCHA!

5 El programa para la banda municipal

La banda municipal de tu ciudad hermana va a hacer una visita y va a tocar en varios sitios de la ciudad. Tú tienes que discutir con el jefe de la banda (tu compañero/a de clase) el itinerario que seguirá la banda por la ciudad y tenéis que decidir la hora exacta en que tocará en todos los sitios clave de la ciudad y cuánto tiempo se quedará allí.

Ejemplo:

La banda deberá reunirse en el polideportivo a las diez y media, donde tocará durante media hora hasta las once. Entonces ...

Después de la discusión puedes escribir todos los detalles para que los invitados españoles sepan lo que tienen que hacer.

6 El programa del próximo año

Un(a) profesor(a) español(a) visita tu colegio para saber más del sistema educativo en este país. Te ha pedido que le expliques el calendario de tu colegio, con todos los sucesos que van a tener lugar con sus fechas.

7 Un poco de historia

Explica a tu compañero/a de clase los acontecimientos principales en la historia de tu ciudad, pueblo, colegio, club, familia, o lo que sea. Luego escribe unas diez de las fechas más importantes, explicando lo que ocurrió.

8 ¿Qué tiempo hará mañana?

En tu trabajo tienes que escribir el boletín meteorológico para mañana de tu propio país para una página web de Internet destinada a los turistas españoles en ese país.

9 ¿Por qué estabas así?

Este ejercicio es un poco como el Ejercicio 4 hecho al revés. Trabaja con un(a) compañero/a de clase. Uno/a tiene que anunciar una condición utilizando una de las expresiones con *tener*, y el/la otro/a otra tiene que explicar las circunstancias que llevaron a la condición. Damos como ejemplo una adaptación del número 1 del Ejercicio 4, pero es de esperar que inventaréis circunstancias nuevas y originales.

Ejemplo:

– Tenías mucho frío.
– Sí, claro, porque me había caído por un agujero en el hielo que había encima del estanque y salí temblando y al borde de la hipotermia.

12 Pronouns

MECANISMOS

Pronouns are words which replace nouns; there are several types of pronoun, corresponding to the different functions these words can have.

12.1 Subject pronouns

First and foremost are subject pronouns, used to denote who or what carries out an action, i.e. the subject of the verb.

I	yo	we	nosotros/as
you (familiar singular)	*tú	you (familiar plural)	*vosotros/as
he, it	él	they	ellos/ellas
she, it	ella		
you (formal singular)	usted	you (formal plural)	ustedes

*The familiar forms *tú* and *vosotros* are increasingly widely used in Spain, and the formal forms are generally only used now in addressing strangers older than yourself. In Latin America, *ustedes* is used as both the formal and informal plural form. In some countries, notably Argentina, *vos* is used instead of *tú*. This has its own verb forms, e.g. *vos hablás* (you speak).

In Spanish, subject pronouns are usually unnecessary in verb constructions because there are different endings for each person, and these are clearly distinguishable in both spoken and written Spanish (see Chapter 14). The subject pronouns listed above are, however, used where emphasis is required or to avoid ambiguity. They can also be used standing alone, for example in answer to the question *¿Quién ... ?*

Yo voy al parque, *tú* vas al instituto y *ellos* van al trabajo.
I'm going to the park, **you** are going to school and **they** are going to work.

La rompió **él**.
He broke it./**He** was the one who broke it.

Alguien llama a la puerta. Voy a ver quién es. ¿ **Tú***?*
Someone's knocking at the door. I'll go and see who it is. **You**?

¿Quién comió mi helado? – **Yo***.*
Who ate my ice-cream? – **I** did.

Yo voy al bar, ¿y *tú*? – ¡*Yo* no!
I'm going to the bar. What about **you**? – **I**'m not!

¿Quién, **yo***?*
Who, **me**?

In the last three examples the sense of the verb is understood, and the **yo** is therefore used on its own.

➡ **Exercise 1a**

12.2 Direct object pronouns

There are two types of object pronoun – direct and indirect – though for some persons the same form is used for both. Here are the direct object pronouns.

me	me	*us*	nos
you (familiar singular)	te	*you (familiar plural)*	*os
him, it	le/lo	*them*	les/los/las
her, it	la		
you (formal singular)	le/lo/la	*you (formal plural)*	les/los/las

These pronouns are used when the person is the object of the verb; usually they come immediately before the verb, but they can be added to the end of an infinitive or present participle/gerund (optional), and to the end of a positive command (compulsory). Note the accents which are added to keep the stress on the same syllable.

*Mi amigo **me** vio en el parque.*
My friend saw **me** in the park.

*Tu madre **te** llama desde el salón.*
Your mother is calling **you** from the lounge.

*¡Cóme**lo** todo!*
Eat **it** all!

*¡Levánte**las**!*
Lift **them** up!

*¡Míra**me**!*
Look at **me**!

*¡Voy a castigar**os**!/¡**Os** voy a castigar!*
I am going to punish **you**.

*Estoy mirándo**las**./**Las** estoy mirando.*
I am looking at **them** (fem.).

*¡Ya **lo** he hecho!*
I've already done it!

These pronouns cannot go between one verb and an infinitive, gerund or participle.

✎ Note: while many people use **le** for 'him', in some parts of Spain and in Latin America in general, **lo** is used for 'him' instead.

Here is a simple rule which will help you to avoid problems:

Use *le* for 'him' and add *-s* for plural (*les* 'them' – people).
Use *lo* for 'it' (masculine) and add *-s* for plural (*los* 'them' – things).

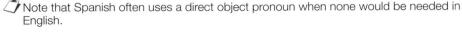 Note that Spanish often uses a direct object pronoun when none would be needed in English.

*¡Ya **lo** sé!*
I already know (**it**)!

*Me dicen que es inteligente, pero ¡no **lo** es!*
They tell me that he is intelligent, but he isn't!

➡ **Exercise 1b**

12.3 Indirect object pronouns

These are used to denote 'to me/us/him/them' etc., i.e. the person on the receiving end of the action, but not the actual 'victim'.

to me	me	to us	nos
to you (familiar singular)	te	to you (familiar plural)	os
to him, to her, to it	le	to them	les
to you (formal singular)	le	to you (formal plural)	les

a) The rules for positioning these indirect object pronouns are the same as for the direct object pronouns.

*Tu hermano **le** dio un caramelo.*
Your brother gave **him** a sweet.

***Les** doy el periódico.*
I give **them** the newspaper.

***Nos** mandaron una postal desde Málaga.*
They sent **us** a postcard from Malaga.

*Vamos a ofrecer**les** dinero./**Les** vamos a ofrecer dinero.*
We are going to offer **them** some money.

*¡Dé**nos** las joyas!*
Give **us** the jewellery!

*¡Dad**les** una limosna!*
Give **them** a donation!

*¡Díga**me**!*
Speak to **me**./Tell **me**.

b) When two object pronouns are used together, the indirect object pronoun comes first.

Te los daré esta tarde.
I will give **them to you** this afternoon.

Nos lo robaron en la calle.
They stole **it from us** in the street.

Note: if both are third person, the indirect pronoun changes to *se* to avoid two pronouns beginning with *l-* being used together: *se lo doy*.

Se lo mandó con la carta.
He sent **it to her** with the letter.

No se las voy a ofrecer.
I won't offer **them to him/her/you**.

c) If there is any risk of confusion where *le* or *les* could refer to more than one of the persons used in the sentence, add *a él*, *a ella*, *a Vd*, *a ellos/ellas*, *a Vds*.

Le dio el dinero a ella.
He gave the money **to her**.

Les mandé el paquete a ellos.
I sent the parcel **to them**.

Les hablaré a ustedes de los problemas de sus hijos.
I will talk **to you** about your children's problems.

d) Spanish commonly uses *le(s)* with the verb even when there is a clear indirect noun object after it, thus duplicating the indirect object.

Le di un regalo a mi amiga.
I gave a present **to my girlfriend**.

Exercise 1c

12.4 Reflexive pronouns

Reflexive pronouns are used with reflexive verbs, conveying the idea of 'self'. For their use and other relevant aspects, see Chapter 16 on reflexive verbs. You will notice from the table below that most are the same as object pronouns (*se* being the only exception).

myself	me	*ourselves*	nos
yourself (familiar singular)	te	*yourselves (familiar plural)*	os
himself/herself/itself	se	*themselves*	se
yourself (formal singular)	se	*yourselves (formal plural)*	se

 Exercise 1e

12.5 Prepositional pronouns

These pronouns (sometimes called disjunctive pronouns) are used after prepositions such as *con*, *para*, *cerca de*.

*Se sentó delante **de mí**.*
He sat down in front **of me**.

*Vive cerca **de nosotros**.*
He lives near **us**.

*Irá al cine **con ellas**.*
He will go to the cinema **with them**.

*Esta carta **es para ti**.*
This letter **is for you**.

- For most persons the subject pronoun is used; however, *yo* and *tú* have special forms – *mí* and *ti* respectively.
- The form *sí* exists for all third person cases (*él*, *ella*, *usted*, *ellos*, *ellas*, *ustedes*), but is only used when the pronoun refers back to the person who is the subject of the verb; otherwise the subject pronoun is used as explained above.

me	mí	us	nosotros
you (fam sing)	ti	you (fam plur)	vosotros
him	él	them (masc)	ellos
her	ella	them (fem)	ellas
(reflexive form)	sí	(reflexive form)	sí
you (formal sing)	usted	you (formal plur)	ustedes

Note: *sí* is not often used for *usted/ustedes*; instead *usted/ustedes* are used after the preposition.

*Este paquete es para **ella**.*
This parcel is for **her**.

*María tenía el paquete delante de **sí**.*
Maria had the parcel in front of **her**.

*Compré este billete para **usted**.*
I bought this ticket for **you**.

*Ustedes tendrán que comprarlos para **ustedes** mismos.*
You will have to buy them for **yourselves**.

- Note the common form of *mí* and *ti* used in combination with the preposition *con*: *conmigo* and *contigo*.

*¿Quieres ir **conmigo**?*
Do you want to go **with me**?

*Tienes que llevar el pasaporte **contigo**.*
You have to take your passport **with you**.

- Less common and only used in a truly reflexive situation is ***consigo***.

   Ustedes sabrán que es mejor llevar las cosas de valor ***consigo***.
   You will know that it is best to take your valuables **with you**.

   Virginia llevó a su hijo ***consigo***.
   Virginia took her son **with her**.

But:

   Voy con ***ella***.
   I'm going with **her**. (i.e. somebody else)

➡ **Exercises 1d, 2, 3**

12.6 Table of pronouns

	Subject	**Direct object**	**Indirect object**	**Reflexive**	**Prepositional**
I	yo	me	me	me	mí
you	tú	te	te	te	ti
he	él	le/lo	le*	se	él (*refl.* sí)
she	ella	la	le*	se	ella (*refl.* sí)
it		lo	le*	se	ello (*neuter*)
you	usted	le/la	le*	se	usted (*refl.* sí)
we	nosotros/as	nos	nos	nos	nosotros/as
you	vosotros/as	os	os	os	vosotros/as
they	ellos	les/los	les*	se	ellos (*refl.* sí)
they	ellas	las	les*	se	ellas (*refl.* sí)
you	ustedes	les/los/las	les*	se	ustedes (*refl.* sí)

*__se__ when followed by a third person direct object pronoun.

¡PONTE A PUNTO!

1 ¿De quién hablamos?

Sustituye los nombres o las palabras subrayadas con el pronombre adecuado.

a) **Subject pronoun**
1   Oye, <u>Juan</u> tiene un coche nuevo.
2   <u>Los señores Ramírez</u> no tienen hijos.
3   <u>Tú y yo</u> somos amigos, ¿no?
4   ¿Qué te parece <u>el novio de Mari-Carmen</u>?
5   <u>Aquella chica</u> es un poco tonta, ¿verdad?

b) **Direct object pronoun**
6   La profesora pidió <u>mis deberes</u>.
7   Pobre Susana: ¡ayer nuestro gato mató <u>su conejo</u>!
8   ¿Dónde encontraste <u>estas revistas</u>?
9   Vamos a ver, ¿compraste <u>el diario</u> o no?
10 ¿Sabes a qué hora nos traerá <u>nuestra cena</u>?

c) **Indirect object pronoun**
11 Por favor, ¿puedes pasar el pan <u>a mis amigas</u>?
12 ¡No deberías decir tonterías <u>al director</u>!
13 Vamos a mandar un crismas <u>a Doña Mariana Iturbe</u>.
14 Sabes contar chistes <u>a los niños</u>, ¡a que sí!
15 ¿Por qué no dijiste nada <u>a tu chico</u>?

d) **Prepositional/disjunctive pronoun**
16 Vaya, ¡no le digas nada a <u>tu novia</u>!
17 ¿Sabes por qué no vamos a visitarles a <u>nuestros hijos</u>?
18 María y Juan vinieron con <u>tu madre y conmigo</u>.
19 Siéntate al lado de <u>tu papá</u>; quiero hablar contigo.
20 Vamos a viajar en el coche de <u>mi amigo</u>.

e) **Reflexive pronoun**
Contesta a estas preguntas usando el verbo con el pronombre reflexivo apropiado, según la(s) palabra(s) subrayada(s).

Ejemplo:

Por favor, lava <u>a los niños</u>.

No, ellos pueden lavar<u>se</u>.

1   José, baña <u>a tus hijos</u>. No, …
2   Chicos, vamos a pasear <u>al perro</u>, ¿vale? No, …
3   <u>Señores</u>, ¿quieren sentar<u>se</u> aquí? Sí, …
4   <u>Marita</u>, ¿quieres duchar<u>te</u>? Sí, …
5   <u>Vosotros</u> tenéis mucho sueño, ¿verdad? Sí, vamos a …

2 ¡Frases rellenas!

Rellena los espacios en blanco con el pronombre más adecuado para cada caso.

1   ... y ... , vamos a bailar juntos, ¿no?
2   No, ... no podemos quedar más tiempo; tendrás que quedar ... .
3   ¿Quiénes van a lavar los platos? Pues los van a lavar ... .
4   Oye, ¿ ... vas a prestar tu coche?
5   Fui a comprar unos libros, y ... llevé a casa de mis abuelos.
6   Manuel y Juan, ... quiero ver en mi despacho a las tres.
7   ... vamos a mandar una carta a nuestros amigos.
8   Quiero ofrecer ... un regalo para tu cumpleaños.
9   Ayer ... presté mi disco favorito a mi hermana.
10 Pepe ... lavó en el cuarto de baño.
11 Concha, ¿ ... vas a levantar hoy, o no?
12 Vamos a bañar ... en la piscina.
13 Mi novia se sentó al lado de ... .
14 Señores, ¿puedo viajar con ... ?
15 Cuando volvimos a casa, mi padre llegó cinco minutos después de ... .

3 Los anónimos

Vuelve a escribir este cuento, reemplazando todos los nombres con los pronombres más apropiados.

El jueves pasado fueron las bodas de plata de Angela y Nicolás. **Nicolás** le regaló **a Angela** un anillo de plata, y **Angela** le dio un reloj **a Nicolás**. Sus hijos, Marián y Miguel, les regalaron **a Angela y a Nicolás** dos copas plateadas.

Por la mañana Nicolás le llevó el desayuno **a Angela** a la cama. Se levantaron, y Marián y **Angela** fueron a comprar un vestido nuevo para Angela. Mientras tanto, **Nicolás y Miguel** dieron un paseo en el parque. Por la tarde, **Angela y Nicolás** fueron a visitar a los padres **de Angela**, don Rodrigo y doña Blanca. Don Rodrigo les sirvió algo de beber, y **Nicolás** ayudó a su madre a preparar la cena.

Después de la cena, todos – **Nicolás, Angela, don Rodrigo y doña Blanca** – fueron a su bar favorito para celebrar el aniversario.

4 El ligón

Rellena los espacios en blanco con el pronombre más apropiado.

El sábado pasado, salí con dos chicas a la vez. ¡A que no me crees!

Pues primero fui a buscar a Maribel, y . . **1** . . llevé a la discoteca. Allí . . **2** . . reunimos con Juanita y José; . . **3** . . di cuenta de que tenía una cita con Ana, entonces sin decir . . **4** . . nada, . . **5** . . dejé con . . **6** . . y fui al Bar Manchego. Allí encontré a Ana y tomamos una cerveza. Luego fuimos al parque, donde vimos a mis amigos del cole. . . **7** . . dejé con . . **8** . . y volví a la discoteca a buscar a Maribel, a Juanita y a José. . . **9** . . encontré en la puerta: salían para ir a dar un paseo en el parque. ¡Madre mía, qué lío! Afortunadamente, aunque allí . . **10** . . reunimos todos con Ana y con mis amigos, ni Ana ni Maribel . . **11** . . dieron cuenta de lo que pasaba. Pero . . **12** . . gustó mucho Juanita, y al final, ¡ . . **13** . . fui con . . **14** . . !

 **¡... Y EN MARCHA!**

5 Los santos

Estás de vacaciones con tu familia y dos amigos. Después de un día en la playa, tus padres vuelven a vuestra casa alquilada. Tú, tus hermanos y vuestros amigos habéis hecho varios quehaceres para ayudarles, ¡y se quedan bastante sorprendidos! Imagina sus preguntas ... y vuestras respuestas.

Ejemplo:

– ¿Quién lavó los platos?
– Los lavé yo.
– ¿Y quién cortó el césped, tu hermana o tú?
– Lo cortó ella.

6 Los demonios

Esta vez, lo que encuentran tus padres en la casa no es bueno: ¡todo está roto, arruinado, estropeado! Imagina lo que se dice.

Ejemplo:

–¿Qué ha pasado con los vasos?
– Los rompieron mis amigos.
– Y ¿la mesa del comedor?

7 El/La sospechoso/a

Ha habido un robo. Tu compañero/a de clase es policía, y te sospecha a ti de ser el ladrón. Registrando tu casa, encuentra varios objetos robados. Te acusa de haberlos robado, y tú tienes que negarlo todo.

Ejemplo:

Policía: Robaste este teléfono móvil, ¿no?
Tú: ¡Qué va! No lo he visto en mi vida.
Policía: ¿De dónde obtuviste este anillo de diamantes? ¿Lo robaste?
Tú: Pues no, lo compré en la Calle de Goya.

8 ¡Qué generoso/a!

Tu madre te pregunta sobre los regalos que vas a comprar para toda la familia, ya que pronto llega Navidad. Tú le contestas.

Ejemplo:

Madre: ¿Qué le vas a regalar a tu hermana?
Tú: Le voy a dar un CD.
Madre: Y ¿a tu hermano/abuelo/a?

9 El ciego

Para este juego, un(a) voluntario/a tiene que salir del aula, y volver con los ojos vendados. Mientras tanto, los demás habéis cambiado de sitio. Al volver a entrar, 'el ciego' tiene que adivinar dónde están todos, contestando a vuestras preguntas sin usar los nombres.

Ejemplo:

Chico/a: ¿Dónde está Penny?
Ciego/a: Está al lado de ti.
Chico/a: Y, ¿dónde está Pete?
Ciego/a: Está detrás de ella.

10 ¡Inventa tú!

Inventa tú mismo/a unos ejercicios comunicativos parecidos a los que ya has hecho. Trata de inventar uno para cada tipo de pronombres. Para cada uno, escribe un cuento de unas diez frases, tratando de usar un pronombre distinto en cada una. Luego puedes ofrecer el mismo ejercicio a tus compañeros/as de clase. Esto se puede hacer por hablado o por escrito.

Ejemplo:

A. Un día por la mañana, el líder de una expedición científica usa el pronombre del sustantivo para darles órdenes a los miembros de la expedición, cuando se preparan para empezar su viaje.

  – Tú vas a preparar el desayuno.
  – Él irá a buscar agua.
  – Ella va a ayudaros.

B. Usáis el pronombre reflexivo para hablar de la moda.

  – Me visto muy bien, pero tú te vistes mal. Ella ...

13 Infinitives

MECANISMOS

13.1 General notes

- In Spanish, infinitives are very helpful when you are getting to know how to handle and manipulate verbs. Each regular verb belongs to one of three conjugations or families, with its own 'surname' – ending in *-ar*, *-er* or *-ir*.
- The infinitive form is the one you will find in a dictionary or vocabulary list, so that even with an unfamiliar verb, you can work out its forms according to the family it belongs to.
- Regular verbs in each family behave in the same way and share family characteristics. Once you know how a model verb in each of these families behaves, you can work out the forms for other regular members of the same family. Every part of a verb in every tense is based on the infinitive.
- In most tenses, the stem, root or basic part to which you add the tense endings can be found by removing the *-ar*, *-er* or *-ir* ending from the infinitive. In the future and conditional tenses, most verbs use the whole of the infinitive as their stem. When working out the forms of an unfamiliar verb, it is always safest to work through the infinitive. Equally, when you come across any form of a new verb, e.g. when reading, you need to work out the infinitive form before looking for it in the dictionary.

If you know the infinitive, you will know the verb!

- There are, of course, irregular verbs, or verbs which are partially irregular, but even they follow many of the same patterns as regular verb families.

13.2 Use of the infinitive

a) Infinitives are often used in Spanish where English would use a verb form ending in '-ing'; this is a sort of noun form of the verb.

*Me gusta **bailar**.*
I like **dancing/to dance**.

***Ver** es **creer**.*
Seeing is **believing**.

(See other uses of the infinitive after different verbs and prepositions.)

b) Infinitives are often used after an adjective, as in the following examples.

*Es muy difícil **ir** allí sin coche.*
It is very difficult to get there without a car.

*Es mejor no **saber** nada.*
It is best to know nothing.

Note the difference in use, emphasis and meaning between the following two examples:

*El inglés es **difícil de comprender**.*
English is difficult to understand.

*Es **difícil comprender** el inglés.*
It is difficult to understand English.

In the second example, the infinitive is the subject of the verb, i.e. 'to understand English is difficult'.

c) Infinitives are also used after auxiliary verbs (except ***estar***, for ***seguir/continuar*** see section **h)** below), some of which in English would instead be followed by '-ing' or the infinitive form with or without 'to', as in the following examples. (See also Chapters 25 and 27.)

*Mis amigos no saben **nadar**.*
My friends don't know how to swim.

*No puede **comprar** nada sin dinero.*
He can't buy anything without money.

*Olvidé **traer** mi pasaporte.*
I forgot to bring my passport.

*Querían **hablar** con su amiga.*
They wanted to talk to their friend.

*Empezó a **trabajar**.*
He began to work.

*Dejaré de **estudiar** después de los exámenes.*
I shall stop studying after the exams.

*Tengo que **irme** en seguida.*
I have to go straight away.

Some of these constructions need ***a***, some ***de***, and others nothing between the auxiliary verb and the infinitive. A couple take ***que***. (See Chapter 27.)

d) The infinitive is used in two expressions which, in a way, have the force of separate verb tenses:

- *ir a* + infinitive is used to convey the sense of the immediate future.
- *acabar de* + infinitive is used for the immediate past – for something which has **just** happened.

*Van a **tomar** algo.*
They are going to have something (to drink).

*Voy a **hablar** con mi madre.*
I am going to speak to my mother.

*Acabo de **oír**lo.*
I have just heard it.

*Acabamos de **llegar**.*
We have just arrived.

➥ **Exercise 3**

e) Infinitives are also commonly used after prepositions, especially those referring to time: indeed, the infinitive is the only part of the verb that can be used after a preposition.

***Antes de irme**, me despediré.*
Before going, I will say goodbye.

***Después de llegar**, fue a ver al director.*
After arriving, he went to see the headmaster.

*Lo hice **sin querer**.*
I did it **without meaning to**.

*Te llamo **para decirte** algo.*
I'm calling you **to tell you** something.

Note also the use of *al* + infinitive:

***Al abrir** la puerta, vio a su hermana.*
On opening/When he opened the door, he saw his sister.

(See Chapter 27 on prepositions and the infinitive.)

f) They are also often used to express warnings and instructions, notably in recipes.

*No **fumar**.*
Do not smoke/No smoking.

***Abrir** con cuidado.*
Open with care.

***Cortar** los tomates en trozos pequeños.*
Cut the tomatoes into small pieces.

➥ **Exercise 2**

g) The infinitive is used in certain other expressions.

- **A** or **de** + infinitive is used to express the idea of 'if':

  De saberlo, no me hubiera ido.
  If I had known, I would not have gone.

- The infinitive is used after **que** in various expressions such as the following:

  No tenemos **nada que ver**.
  We haven't **anything to see**.

  Me queda **mucho que hacer**.
  I have **a lot** still **to do**.

- After verbs of needing, requesting or searching, use **para**:

  Buscamos algo **para comer**.
  We are looking for something to eat.

  Necesita algo **para beber**.
  He needs something to drink.

  Pidieron algo **para leer**.
  They asked for something to read.

h) There are some expressions in which the infinitive is not used when you might expect it. Two examples are **seguir** and **continuar**.

  Siguieron **cantando**.
  They went on/continued singing/to sing.

  Continuó **hablando**.
  He carried on/continued speaking/to speak.

 **¡PONTE A PUNTO!**

1 Explicaciones

Tu amigo quiere saber por qué haces o no haces varias cosas. Usa una de las siguientes expresiones que aparecen en la caja a continuación o cualquier otra expresión adecuada para explicárselo.

Ejemplo:

– ¿Por qué pasas tanto tiempo jugando al fútbol?
– Porque me gusta jugar al fútbol.

1 ¿Por qué vas al cine todos los días?
2 ¿Vas al bar?
3 ¿Vas a ver la televisión?
4 ¿Por qué gastas tanto dinero en comprar CDs?
5 ¿Conque compras otro vestido/traje nuevo?
6 ¿Estás estudiando todavía?
7 ¿Por qué tienes tantos libros de medicina?
8 ¿Vas a comer todas esas manzanas?
9 ¿Por qué vas al club?
10 Compraste un billete para el teatro – ¿por qué?
11 ¿Por qué vas a ayudar a tu abuela con sus quehaceres?
12 ¿Cómo es que puedes llevar a tu hermano al cole en el coche de tus padres? (saber …)
13 ¿No vas al concierto?
14 ¿No quieres escuchar mi nuevo CD?
15 ¿No lees este libro?
16 ¿No vas a hacer tus deberes?
17 ¿Quieres ir al parque conmigo?
18 ¿Por qué llevas tanto dinero?
19 No quieres ser profesor(a), ¿verdad?

me gusta	me encanta	me interesa	me apetece	prefiero	quiero	puedo
sé	pienso	necesito	deseo	espero		

2 El nuevo trabajo

Empiezas un nuevo trabajo. Tu jefe te da una serie de instrucciones: tienes que hacer varias cosas durante tu primer día en este restaurante. Apuntas todo lo que tienes que hacer, empleando el infinitivo.

Ejemplo:

Limpia la cocina.
Limpiar la cocina.

1   Limpia las mesas.
2   Prepara las legumbres.
3   Pon las mesas.
4   Fríe la carne.
5   Haz la sangría.
6   Ponte el uniforme.
7   Sirve las comidas.
8   Lava los platos.
9   Barre el suelo del restaurante.
10 Escribe los menús para mañana.

3 Tu amigo, Tomás

Un amigo tuyo no se fía de ti: tienes que asegurarle de todo lo que vas a hacer.

Ejemplo:

– Mañana, jugarás al fútbol, ¿verdad?
– Sí, voy a jugar.

1   Esta tarde, me prestarás este DVD, ¿no?
2   Oye, ¿me vas a llevar al club?
3   ¿Me prometes que me ayudarás con los deberes?
4   Me contarás lo que pasó, ¿verdad?
5   ¿De verdad me vas a dejar tu moto?

4 Entrevista con el psiquiatra

El psiquiatra quiere analizar tus problemas, pues necesita saber algo de tus costumbres, y tú contestas a sus preguntas.

Ejemplo:

–¿Por qué hablas contigo mismo?
– Porque no me gusta hablar con los demás.

1   ¿Por qué comes demasiado?
2   ¿Por qué te comes las uñas?
3   ¿Por qué te vistes siempre de colores fuertes?
4   ¿Por qué no olvidas tus problemas?
5   ¿Por qué no vas a ver a otro psiquiatra?

 **¡... Y EN MARCHA!**

5 El futuro

Habláis del futuro, y cada miembro de la clase explica algo de sus ambiciones, empleando expresiones tales como las siguientes.

Ejemplo:

Quisiera trabajar en la informática.
Me gustaría ser mecánico.
Pienso buscar un puesto como psicólogo en un hospital.

6 Consejos para un(a) futuro/a universitario/a

Escribe una serie de recomendaciones para un(a) amigo/a que pronto va a ir a la universidad. Tiene que estudiar mucho, pero a la vez tiene que mantener sus intereses para tener una vida equilibrada. Al mismo tiempo, va a vivir solo/a por primera vez.

Ejemplo:

Debes leer muchos libros.
Deberías seguir jugando al golf.
Tendrás que lavar tus propias camisas.

7 ¿Cómo se hace?

Se puede expresar el método de hacer algo mediante el uso del infinitivo. Cada miembro de la clase tiene que explicar un procedimiento, por sencillo que sea, y el resto de la clase tiene que adivinar qué es.

Ejemplo:

Echar el contenido del paquete en un plato. Echar un poco de azúcar encima.
Añadir leche. Comer inmediatamente.
Solución: Desayunas copitos de maíz, y los comes rápidamente para que estén crujientes.

Después podéis hacer algo parecido usando *Hay que ...,* *Es necesario ...,* *Tienes que ...,* *Se debe ...,* *Se tiene que ...* u otras expresiones parecidas.

Ejemplo:

Hay que echar un poco del contenido del tubo en el cepillo, hay que abrir la boca y cepillar bien los dientes con el cepillo.
Solución: Te limpias los dientes.

8 ¡Peligro!

Podéis inventar una serie de avisos y amonestaciones en español, usando el infinitivo en forma positiva y negativa. Si no se os ocurren cosas sensatas y normales, podéis inventar cosas más bien absurdas y ridículas. Además de utilizar sólo el infinitivo, se pueden usar otras expresiones seguidas del infinitivo, a veces en forma negativa.

Ejemplo:

Cruzar la calle con los ojos cerrados es muy peligroso.
No echar salsa de tomate en una taza de té.
¡No se debe dar la comida del perro al canario si no quieres que te muerda!

14 Present tense

 MECANISMOS

14.1 Uses

a) The present tense in Spanish is used to convey the idea of an action taking place in present time and can be translated into English in two ways: 'he eats' and 'he is eating'. Both of these can be rendered by the present tense in Spanish.

- to describe what is going on at the moment:

  *Javier **habla** con sus amigos.*
  Javier **is talking** to his friends.

- to describe what happens regularly or repeatedly, or something which is true or valid at the moment: a general statement of a verb covering 'now', but not limited to 'now' (i.e. a general statement valid in the past and the future as well as at present):

  *Julián **habla** español, francés e inglés.*
  Julian **speaks** Spanish, French and English.

b) In addition, the present tense can be used to denote an action in the immediate future, as in English.

  *Mamá **llega** en el tren de las 14.00 horas.*
  Mum **arrives** on the two o'clock train.

c) It can also be used to describe actions in the past in a dramatic way, to give added immediacy; this is known as the historic present.

  ***Voy** a casa de mi amigo, y le **digo** que no **salgo** con él.*
  I go (went) to my friend's house and tell (told) him that I am (was) not going out with him.

d) Finally, it can be used to indicate how long you **have been** doing something, where English uses a past tense; note that this only applies if the action is still going on at the time of speaking. (See also Chapter 43).

  ***Espera** desde hace diez minutos./Hace diez minutos que **espera**.*
  He **has been waiting** for ten minutes. (and is still waiting)

The same idea can also be expressed by using the structure ***llevar*** + gerund in the present tense (see Chapter 28):

  ***Llevo** dos horas **trabajando**.*
  I have been working for two hours.

14.2 Formation

a) The present tense of regular verbs is formed as follows:

hablar	comer	subir
hablo	como	subo
hablas	comes	subes
habla	come	sube
hablamos	comemos	subimos
habláis	coméis	subís
hablan	comen	suben

The obvious patterns across the three verb types or families are easy to observe:

- the similarities in the endings for each person of the verb;
- the dominant **a** in the endings for the **-ar** verb;
- the dominant **e** in those for **-er** and **-ir** verbs.

In each case, the basic part of the word – the stem or root – consists of the infinitive but with the **-ar**, **-er** or **-ir** removed. The various forms are then made by adding a special ending to that basic part; each is distinct from the others in both spoken and written form. You will see that the **nosotros** and **vosotros** forms always have the vowel of the infinitive ending.

Note that these forms can all stand alone: there is no need for a subject pronoun because the endings are clear in both written and spoken Spanish. The subject pronoun is only used where clarity or emphasis is needed. (See Chapter 12 on pronouns.)

b) Spanish has a number of verbs in which spelling changes occur in some forms, but which are otherwise mostly regular.

- Two verbs (**dar** and **estar**) have a first person singular in the present tense ending in **-oy** (like **soy** from the verb **ser** and **voy** from the verb **ir**), but are otherwise regular:

dar: ***doy***, *das, da, damos, dais, dan*
estar: ***estoy***, *estás, está, estamos, estáis, están* (note the accent)

- A number of verbs have a **-g-** in the first person singular, but are otherwise regular within their verb group:

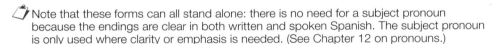

caer: caigo, caes ...   *salir: salgo, sales ...*
hacer: hago, haces ...   *traer: traigo, traes ...*
poner: pongo, pones ...   *valer: valgo, vales ...*

- A few have this change and are also radical-changing (see Chapter 15):

decir: ***digo***, *dices, dice, decimos, decís, dicen*
oír: oigo, oyes, oye, oímos, oís, oyen
tener: tengo, tienes, tiene, tenemos, tenéis, tienen
venir: vengo, vienes, viene, venimos, venís, vienen

- A group of verbs ending in **-ecer**, **-ocer**, **-ucir** have a change to **-zc-** in the first person singular of the present tense and forms based on it, but are otherwise regular:

*conocer: cono**zc**o, conoces …*   *parecer: pare**zc**o, pareces …*

- Note also **saber** and **ver**, which have an irregular first person but are otherwise regular:

*saber: **sé**, sabes, sabe …*   *ver: **veo**, ves, ve …*

- Verbs with infinitives ending in **-uir** take a **-y-** in all of the singular forms and in the third person plural:

*huir: hu**y**o, hu**y**es, hu**y**e, huimos, huís, hu**y**en*

Other verbs like this include **concluir**, **construir**, **destruir**, **incluir** and **sustituir**.

- Certain verbs need an accent on a weak **-i-** or **-u-** of the stem in all of the singular and the third person plural forms:

criar: crío, crías, cría, criamos, criáis, crían
continuar: continúo, continúas, continúa, continuamos, continuáis, continúan

c) The following verbs are totally irregular.

ir: voy, vas, va, vamos, vais, van
ser: soy, eres, es, somos, sois, son
haber: he, has, ha*, hemos, habéis, han
[***hay** when it means 'there is/are']

➡ **Exercises 1, 2**

 ¡PONTE A PUNTO!

1 Pavo relleno

Rellena los espacios en las frases siguientes con la forma correcta del presente del verbo cuyo infinitivo viene en paréntesis.

1   ¡Ya … ([nosotros] estar) en agosto, y ya … ([nosotros] estar) de vacaciones!
2   En este momento, mi padre … (mirar) los mapas y … (preparar) la ruta.
3   Mi madre … (buscar) sus gafas de sol.
4   Mis hermanos y yo … (sacar) la ropa que … (querer) llevar con nosotros.
5   Hoy … ([nosotros] tener) que ir a las tiendas a comprar trajes de baño.
6   En efecto, … ([nosotros] ir) a pasar dos semanas en Paignton, en el condado de Devon.
7   Cerca de allí … (encontrarse) muchas playas bonitas y pueblos interesantes.
8   Nos … (decir) que hace bastante buen tiempo allí, aunque … (llover) mucho.
9   Si … (hacer) mal tiempo, … ([nosotros] poder) ir a un museo, o a un gran polideportivo que … (haber) en Torquay.
10   ¡Por lo menos en Devon no … ([nosotros] necesitar) hablar idiomas extranjeros!

2 Caja de las sorpresas

Rellena los espacios en este artículo con la forma correcta de un verbo escogido de la lista
que se ofrece debajo. ¡Cuidado, porque tienes que usar algunos más de una vez, y
además sobran verbos!

La región del sur de Devon se . . **1** . . los South Hams. Esta zona . . **2** . . varios
pueblos bastante pequeños, o sea de unos diez mil habitantes cada uno. Los más
conocidos . . **3** . . Totnes, Dartmouth y Kingsbridge. Aparte de éstos, . . **4** . .
también muchos pueblos más pequeños. En esta región se . . **5** . . muchos
productos agrícolas, sobre todo fruta y trigo. También se . . **6** . . vacas y ovejas,
siendo ésta una región que se . . **7** . . por sus productos lácteos.

Sin embargo, la actividad económica más importante de la región . . **8** . . el
turismo: con sus muchas playas bonitas, sus calas pintorescas y pueblos antiguos,
. . **9** . . a muchos turistas; se . . **10** . . hacer excursiones a Dartmoor, y se . . **11** . .
ir en barco sobre el río Dart; en efecto mucha gente . . **12** . . vela por aquí. Los
turistas . . **13** . . no sólo de Gran Bretaña, sino también de todos los países del
oeste y del norte de Europa. Sobre todo se . . **14** . . coches noruegos, suecos,
alemanes, holandeses y franceses. En total, la zona de los South Hams . . **15** . . ser
una de las regiones más amenas de nuestro país.

atraer	deber	querer	comprar	decidir	ser	conocer	haber	venir
contener	hacer	ver	criar	llamar	visitar	cultivar	poder	volar

¡... Y EN MARCHA!

3 Ahorita mismo

Describe lo que haces tú y lo que hacen tus amigos y familiares. Tus compañeros/as de
clase pueden hacer preguntas, si queréis.

Ejemplo:

A: *¿Qué haces en este momento?*
B: *¡Hablo español, claro!*
C: *Y, ¿qué hace el profesor ahora?*
B: *Pues, trabaja.*

Después puedes escribir unas 100 palabras para resumirlo todo.

4 En general

Esta vez habláis de cosas más generales, o sea de la vida en general.

Ejemplo:

A: *Oye, ¿qué hace tu madre para ganarse la vida?*
B: *Es cocinera en este colegio.*
C: *¿Y tu hermana?*
B: *Trabaja de dependienta en Fat Face.*

Otra vez, puedes escribir un resumen de lo que dices y oyes.

5 Esta tarde

¿Vais a salir esta tarde? Usando el presente para expresar actividades en el futuro, hablad de lo que pensáis hacer esta tarde.

Ejemplo:

A: *Esta tarde vamos al café después de las clases, ¿no?*
B: *Sí, y luego cenamos en casa de Brian, ¿vale?*

6 Los artistas

¿Sabéis dibujar? Si no sabéis, podéis dibujar monigotes como los niños. Tú tienes que dibujar una escena, como por ejemplo el patio de recreo del cole. Luego la describes para tu colega, que sin mirar tu dibujo tiene que dibujarlo según lo que vayas describiendo. Después, comparad los dos dibujos!

Ejemplo:

A la izquierda, unos chicos juegan al fútbol, mientras dos chicas charlan en el rincón ...

7 El artículo

Tienes que escribir un artículo para la página web de una agencia de viajes, en el cual hay que describir no sólo tu pueblo, sino también las actividades que se puedan observar en la calle principal en un día típico.

15 Radical-changing verbs

 MECANISMOS

15.1 Types and patterns

a) Radical-changing verbs (sometimes known as root-changing or stem-changing verbs) feature a spelling change in the stem or root of the verb.

b) The stem or root of these verbs contains a vowel – **o**, **u** or **e** – which changes according to whether or not it bears the stress. When stressed, the vowel 'stretches' or changes, but when unstressed it goes back to normal: you could think of these vowels as 'elastic' vowels. You can see the pattern of changes in the model verbs given below.

Type 1			Type 2		Type 3
o → ue	u → ue	e → ie	e → ie	o → ue	e → i
volver	**jugar ***	**pensar**	**preferir**	**dormir**	**pedir**
vuelvo	juego	pienso	prefiero	duermo	pido
vuelves	juegas	piensas	prefieres	duermes	pides
vuelve	juega	piensa	prefiere	duerme	pide
volvemos	jugamos	pensamos	preferimos	dormimos	pedimos
volvéis	jugáis	pensáis	preferís	dormís	pedís
vuelven	juegan	piensan	prefieren	duermen	piden

* **Jugar** is the only **u** ⟶ **ue** verb.

c) You will see that there are three different types grouped according to their behaviour: Type 1 has a consistent change pattern of **o** to **ue**, **u** to **ue**, or **e** to **ie**. Type 2 is similar – **e** to **ie** or **o** to **ue** – but has added changes in the gerund and in the third person singular and third person plural forms of the preterite (see Chapters 21 and 28, and see below). Type 3 has a different type of change – **e** to **i** in the present tense, gerund and third person singular and plural forms of the preterite.

15.2 Tenses

Apart from the spelling changes shown above, most radical-changing verbs behave normally. Indeed, apart from those detailed below, changes do not occur in any tense other than the present tense and the present subjunctive, because verb forms in all other tenses have the stress on the verb ending, not on the stem.

15.2.1 Present tense

Because of the structure of the present tense, the change occurs only in the first, second, third persons singular and the third person plural, where the stem is stressed. You may find it useful to think of these verbs as '1 – 2 – 3 – 6 verbs' in order to remember which parts change. Equally, if you were to set them out as in this diagram, you could refer to them as 'boot' verbs; the singular forms and the third person plural are 'inside the boot' and the first and second persons plural are outside it.

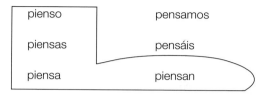

pienso	pensamos
piensas	pensáis
piensa	piensan

➡ **Exercises 1, 2**

15.2.2 Gerund

The gerunds for the verbs listed above are as follows:

volviendo, jugando, pensando, prefiriendo, durmiendo, pidiendo

✎ Note that the only radical-changing verbs which have a spelling change in the gerund are those with infinitives in *-ir*. In these cases *o* changes to *u* and *e* to *i*. The commonest are: ***durmiendo***, ***prefiriendo***, ***sintiendo***, ***viniendo***.

15.2.3 Present subjunctive

All of the spelling changes affecting the present indicative of these verbs also affect the present subjunctive (see Chapter 32). But note the irregular forms ***durmamos*** (***dormir***) and ***sintamos*** (***sentir***).

15.2.4 Preterite

- Most radical-changing verbs are regular in the preterite (see also Chapter 21). Since the stress never falls on the stem, there is no change in spelling except with *-ir* verbs (third person singular and plural forms only):

  durmió, durmieron; prefirió, prefirieron; pidió, pidieron

- Those radical-changing verbs which are irregular (e.g. ***tener***, ***venir***, ***querer***) are in the ***pretérito grave*** family (see Chapter 21), and so have their own special stems for this tense: ***tuve***, ***vine***, ***quise***.

15.2.5 Imperfect subjunctive

- Because the imperfect subjunctive is based on the third person of the preterite (see Chapter 32), *all* forms of the imperfect subjunctive of the *-ir* verbs above have the same change. Thus:

  durmiese/durmiera; prefiriese/prefiriera; pidiese/pidiera

- The imperfect subjunctive forms of the irregular radical-changing verbs are based on their preterite stems (***pretérito grave***):

  tuviera/tuviese, viniera/viniese, quisiera/quisiese

15.3 Other related spellings

These spelling changes affect other words too, according to the same rules of stress. Examples include:

la cuenta (account) < *contar* (to count)
la vuelta (return) < *volver* (to return)
ciento – centenario
nueve – noventa

These changes occur where what would have been an *e* or *o* is stressed.

 ¡PONTE A PUNTO!

1 ¡Salud!

a) Pon el verbo en la forma correcta en cada caso.

Hoy en día, muchas personas (tener) problemas de salud porque no se cuidan bien. No (pensar) mucho en lo que comen y beben, y (preferir) preparar algo que sea fácil y rápido; se (volver) perezosos en todo lo que hacen: (empezar) a coger el coche en lugar de ir a pie, y en sus horas de ocio, en lugar de hacer algo activo, (sentarse) a ver la televisión; no (querer) hacer nada que necesite esfuerzo físico, y no (esforzarse) en hacer deporte. También (acostarse) muy tarde, y por eso no (dormir) lo suficiente. Cuando el médico les (contar) como deberían cuidar de su salud, (cerrar) el oído y no (encontrar) nada anormal en su modo de ser, o no (entender) lo que les dice. Luego, al darse cuenta de la verdad, ya no (poder) cambiar su estilo de vida.

b) Ahora, vuelve a escribir este párrafo, hablando de 'nosotros'. Tendrás que cambiar varias palabras, empezando así.

Hoy en día, muchos tenemos problemas de salud porque no nos cuidamos bien.

2 Huecos

Rellena los espacios en blanco con la forma correcta del verbo. ¡Ten cuidado porque algunos son verbos radicales, algunos no!

1 Mi madre ... que todos los chicos son tontos. (pensar)
2 Nuestros amigos ... mucha influencia en nosotros. (tener)
3 ¿... tú y Marisa cenar conmigo esta tarde? (querer)
4 ¿Por qué no te ... al lado de Jorge? (sentarse)
5 ¿Qué dices, que Jorge ... mal? (oler)
6 Oye, ... la puerta cuando entres. (cerrar)
7 Como usted sabe, ... almorzar en este hotel o en un restaurante. (poder)
8 Mi profesor de español siempre ... dos o tres vasos de vino por la tarde. (beber)
9 Los profesores siempre ... bien después de beber vino. (dormir)
10 ¿Sabes qué tipo de flores ... mamá? (preferir)

 ¡... Y EN MARCHA!

3 ¿Qué piensas tú?

Imagina que estás ayudando a tu profesor(a) a organizar un intercambio. Tienes que ayudarle a hacer las parejas de participantes. Por eso tienes que hacerle preguntas a un(a) compañero/a tuyo/a que quiere participar para saber algo de sus gustos y preferencias.

a) Usando los verbos *preferir, querer, poder, pensar, tener (¿Qué opinión tienes?), entender (¿Entiendes bien el español hablado?)*, tu profesor(a) te preguntará qué te gusta en la vida, y qué opinión tienes de varias cosas específicas.

Ejemplo:

– *¿Prefieres la música pop o clásica?*
– *Prefiero ...*

b) Ahora haz las mismas preguntas a tu compañero/a, y cuenta a tu profesor(a) todo lo que te dijo. (Si quieres, puedes apuntar sus respuestas.)

Ejemplo:

Juan prefiere la música pop ...

c) Imagina que queréis estar en la misma casa tú y tu compañero/a, y que tú estás de acuerdo con todo lo que dice él/ella: cuenta a tu profesor(a) lo que opináis los/las dos.

Ejemplo:

Juan y yo preferimos ...

4 ¡Volver a empezar!

a) Estás grabando un mensaje en cassette para mandar a un(a) amigo/a español(a) que espera pasar las vacaciones contigo. Cuéntale cómo pasas el día, tratando de emplear todos los verbos siguientes: *empezar, encontrar(se), volver, cerrar, acostarse, dormir.* Luego imagina que hablas de toda la familia, y vuelve a contárselo todo utilizando la forma de *nosotros*.

b) Ahora, cuéntale lo que hiciste ayer, o lo que hacías el año pasado/cuando eras más jóven.

5 ¡Viva la democracia!

a) Pronto habrá elecciones en tu país, y tú tendrás el voto por primera vez. En la misma cassette, trata de explicarle a tu amigo/a:

- las principales diferencias entre los partidos políticos de tu país (por ejemplo los conservadores, laboristas y liberal-demócratas)
- lo que entienden por democracia
- qué piensan de varios aspectos de la vida contemporánea.

Ejemplo:

La enseñanza ...
La seguridad social ...
La defensa ...
Los sindicatos ...

Usa los verbos *entender, pedir, poder, preferir, querer,* etcétera.

b) Luego, dile cómo vas a votar y por qué.

16 Reflexive verbs

MECANISMOS

16.1 What are reflexive verbs?

16.1.1 Reflexive verbs

a) Reflexive verbs are verbs in which the subject and object are the same, or, looked at another way, where the action reflects back on the subject. English reflexives are easy to spot because they always involve a 'self' word. Many verbs are used in reflexive form in Spanish but not in English. These actions are usually ones which are done by the subject to or for himself/herself.

> *El chico **se** lava.*
> The boy washes/is washing **himself**.

> ***Me** llamo Manuel.*
> I am called Manuel. (I call **myself** ...)

> *Queremos pasear**nos**.*
> We want to go for a walk. (literally, 'take **ourselves** for a walk')

b) The fact that a verb is reflexive does not affect the way the verb forms are made up: being reflexive simply means that the verb is accompanied by a (reflexive) pronoun. This is so even when the verb has a subject pronoun with it.

> *Tú **te** lavas en el cuarto de baño, ¿verdad?*
> You wash (**yourself**) in the bathroom, don't you?

16.1.2 Reflexive pronouns

a) The pattern of the reflexive pronouns is as in these examples:

levantarse *(to get up)*		vestirse *(to get dressed)*	
me levanto	*I get up*	me visto	*I dress myself*
te levantas	*you get up (familiar)*	te vistes	*you dress yourself (familiar)*
se levanta	*he/she/it gets up*	se viste	*he/she/it dresses him/her/itself*
(Vd) se levanta	*you get up (formal)*	(Vd) se viste	*you dress yourself (formal)*
nos levantamos	*we get up*	nos vestimos	*we dress ourselves*
os levantáis	*you get up (familiar)*	os vestís	*you dress yourselves (familiar)*
se levantan	*they get up*	se visten	*they dress themselves*
(Vds) se levantan	*you get up (formal)*	(Vds) se visten	*you dress yourselves (formal)*

b) Normally, reflexive pronouns come just in front of a finite verb:

Se vistió despacio.
He got dressed slowly.

But they come at the end of a positive command; they also come at the end of an infinitive or a gerund but this is optional.

¡Levántate!
Get up!

Voy a ducharme./Me voy a duchar.
I'm going to have a shower.

Están bañándose./Se están bañando.
They are bathing.

They are always attached to the infinitive form of a reflexive verb:

Quiero sentarme.
I want to sit down.

Note that, like all pronouns, they cannot be placed between a verb and an infinitive or gerund.

c) Note that most of the reflexive pronouns are identical to the (direct/indirect) object pronouns. Only *se* (himself/herself/itself/themselves) is different.

d) In addition, the reflexive pronoun can have a 'direct object' function (e.g. *me lavo* 'I wash myself') and also an 'indirect object' function (e.g. *se compró un coche* 'he bought himself a car').

16.1.3 Common reflexive verbs

The following is a list of some common reflexive verbs, some of which are not reflexive in English. This is not an exhaustive list, but gives the flavour of these verbs:

acostarse	to go to bed	*irse*	to go away
afeitarse	to shave (oneself)	*lavarse*	to wash (oneself)
bañarse	to bathe, have a bath	*levantarse*	to get up
calzarse	to put on (shoes, etc.)	*pasearse*	to go for a walk
conocerse	to get to know (each other)	*peinarse*	to comb one's hair
		ponerse	to put on, begin to
cortarse	to cut oneself	*preocuparse*	to worry
despertarse	to wake up	*quitarse*	to take off
dormirse	to go to sleep	*romperse*	to break
ducharse	to have a shower	*vestirse*	to get dressed
emborracharse	to get drunk		

Exercises 1, 2

16.2 Uses

a) The reflexive form is often used in the plural with a reciprocal sense, i.e. doing the action to each other, as in the following examples.

Se amaban mucho.
They loved **each other** very much.

¿Dónde os conocisteis?
Where did **you** meet?

Nos vemos a menudo.
We see **each other** often.

Se miraron nerviosamente.
They looked at **each other** nervously.

b) An apparent reflexive form is often used to avoid the passive (see Chapter 31). This is usually only possible with inanimate objects, which cannot, logically, do things to themselves.

Aquí se habla inglés.
English is spoken here.

La puerta se cerró.
The door closed.

c) The reflexive form is used to express possession in self-inflicted actions, and the possessive adjective is not used.

Se rompió la pierna.
He broke his leg.

Nos ponemos el abrigo.
We put on our coats.

➡ **Exercises 1, 2**

d) There are other expressions such as *irse* (to go away) which use the reflexive form.

Me voy mañana.
I'm going (away) tomorrow.

e) Colloquial Spanish often uses a reflexive pronoun for emphasis.

Se lo comió todo.
He ate it all up.

Me lo sé de memoria.
I know it all by heart.

16.3 Expressions of 'becoming'

The various verbs used to describe the notion of 'becoming' are all reflexive in form; they differ from one another in shades of meaning.

- ***hacerse*** + noun or adjective (to become)
  This is usually used where there is voluntary effort on the part of the subject:

  Nos hicimos *amigos el año pasado.*
  We **became** friends last year.

  Quiero ***hacerme*** *médico.*
  I want **to be/become** a doctor.

- ***ponerse*** + adjective (to become, to get …)
  This is used to refer to a change of mood, appearance or physical condition:

  Al saberlo, ***se puso*** *contenta.*
  When she found out, **she became** happy.

  Comieron tanto que ***se pusieron*** *demasiado gordos.*
  They ate so much that **they got** too fat.

- ***volverse*** + adjective (to become, to go …)
  This is used to convey the idea of involuntary psychological or mental change, and can only be used for people or animals:

  *¿****Te has vuelto*** *loco, o qué?*
  Have you gone mad, or what?

- ***convertirse en*** + noun (to become/turn into/change into)
  This is often used where a fundamental change takes place:

  Madrid ***se ha convertido*** *en una ciudad muy moderna y atractiva.*
  Madrid **has become** a very modern and attractive city.

- ***quedarse*** (to become + adjective)
  This is often used where some sort of loss is implied:

  Después del accidente ***se quedó*** *sordo.*
  He became deaf after the accident.

➡ **Exercises 1, 2**

16.4 Reflexives which modify meaning

A few verbs have slight variations in meaning or emphasis when used in the reflexive form. Here are a few examples.

- a) ***morir***   to die (accidental or deliberate death)
  b) ***morirse***   to die (natural death, e.g. through illness)

  a) Su hermano ***murió*** *en un accidente de tráfico.*
  His brother **died** in a traffic accident.

94

b) La mujer **se murió** de una enfermedad contagiosa.
The woman **died** of a contagious illness.

- a) **encontrar**   to find, meet
  b) **encontrarse**   to find something (by chance)/to be situated

a) **Encontramos** al cura en la iglesia.
We found/met the priest in the church.

b) **Se encontraron** unos artefactos muy antiguos.
They found some very old artefacts.

- a) **olvidar**   to forget (intentionally)
  b) **olvidarse (de)** to forget (accidentally)

a) ¡Sería mejor **olvidar**le!
It would be best **to forget** him.

b) **Se olvidó** de lo que había prometido.
He forgot what he had promised.

- a) **reír**   to laugh
  b) **reírse (de)**   to laugh (at …)

a) El que **ríe** el último **ríe** el mejor.
He who **laughs** last **laughs** longest.

b) El profesor **se rio** de su alumno.
The teacher **laughed** at his pupil.

 Exercise 3

 # ¡PONTE A PUNTO!

1 ¡Qué día más caótico!

He aquí la descripción del día más caótico de mi vida. Lo hice todo al revés y, además, al escribir este resumen en mi diario ¡dejé todos los verbos en la forma del infinitivo! Usando el pretérito, pon los verbos de cada frase en la forma correcta y en el lugar más apropiado.

Esta mañana, *afeitarse* en mi dormitorio, *despertarse* en el cuarto de baño, luego *bañarse* delante del espejo. Antes de tomar el desayuno *sentarse* en el dormitorio, luego *vestirse* en la cocina para desayunar. Como hacía buen tiempo, decidí *ponerse* en el parque, pues *pasearse* el abrigo antes de salir. Allí, con mi móvil, *encontrarse* en contacto con mi novia, y *ponerse* media hora después delante del estanque. A las once *tomarse* en la terraza de un café y *sentarse* un chocolate y unos churros. *Dirigirse* a mediodía, y después de *levantarse* un rato *pasearse* de mi novia, y *despedirse* a mi casa. Por la tarde, *divertirse* en casa, y *quedarse* viendo la tele. Bastante cansado, *acostarse* a las diez, y *ducharse* en mi dormitorio a las once. De repente, *volverse* cuenta de que había sido un día de trabajo … ¡y de que *darse* loco!

2 El virus

El autor de este ejercicio tiene un gran problema: ¡su ordenador tiene un virus! ¡Todos los verbos reflexivos de las siguientes frases han caído al pie del ejercicio, y se han convertido en la forma del infinitivo! Selecciona el verbo que mejor convenga para cada frase, y adáptalo según el significado de la frase. ¡Y no te olvides de los pronombres reflexivos!

1 ¡Este chico huele mal, pues no … nunca!
2 Tenemos que … antes de … en la piscina.
3 Los domingos, muchos madrileños … en el Parque del Retiro.
4 A Miguel no le gusta … , pues por eso tiene barba.
5 A la reina le gustaba … en su espejo mágico.
6 Muchos españoles hacen el taekwondo para … en buena forma.
7 Los fines de semana, muchos granadinos … en la Sierra Nevada.
8 España … en una situación económica mucho más fuerte que hace cuarenta años.
9 A la edad de veinte años, Rebeca … guardia municipal.
10 ¡Con tanto trabajo, el autor … loco y … a vivir en un manicomio!

afeitarse	encontrarse	mantenerse	bañarse	hacerse	mirarse
divertirse	irse	pasearse	ducharse	lavarse	volverse

3 ¿Reflexivo o no?

Cambia los verbos de este relato a la forma correcta, pero cuidado, porque no hemos incluido los pronombres reflexivos de los verbos que son reflexivos: tú tienes que decidir en cada caso si se trata o no de un verbo reflexivo, y si se necesita un pronombre reflexivo.

¡Madre mía, qué horror tener que viajar en tren! Ayer (volver) a casa en tren – un viaje de siete horas. (Llegar) temprano a la estación, y (dirigir) al andén número 11. Al llegar, (dar) cuenta de que (necesitar) ir a los servicios, pero (decir) que sería mejor esperar la llegada del tren. Hacía mucho frío y llovía, y (quedar) de pie … Luego anunciaron que el tren iba a llegar tarde: (empezar) a preocuparme, y (sentir) incómodo. Después de media hora ya (tener) muchas ganas de ir al lavabo, pero no (querer) perder el tren. Veinte minutos después, ¡ya no (poder) más, y cuando (oír) que el tren llevaba más de una hora de retraso, (decidirse) a ir a buscar los servicios. Casi no (poder) andar, y el lavabo estaba en otro andén, por lo cual (tener) que subir y bajar escaleras, pero por fin (sentir) mucho mejor. (Volver) al andén número 11, y diez minutos más tarde (subir) al tren ¡por fin! (Sentar) y (empezar) a trabajar. Pero no (tener) mucho espacio ni para escribir ni para usar mi ordenador portátil, porque un señor muy grande vino a sentarse al lado de mí. Como no (poder) trabajar, al final (dormir).

 ¡… Y EN MARCHA!

4 El marciano

Imagina que tu compañero/a de clase es marciano. No tiene mucha experiencia de la vida terrestre … y te hace una serie de preguntas sobre la rutina diaria (¡empleando verbos reflexivos, naturalmente!)

Ejemplo:

Marciano:	¿Qué tienes que hacer para arreglarte por la mañana?
Tú:	Bueno, primero me despierto y me levanto, naturalmente.
Marciano:	¿Qué haces con la cara/el pelo/los dientes/la barba?

5 La cadena

Tenéis que inventar un cuento, por ejemplo 'La vida de Narciso'. El/La profesor(a) empieza, y cada miembro de la clase tiene que añadir una frase entera, por ridícula y absurda que sea. Cada frase tendrá un verbo reflexivo; pero si resulta demasiado difícil, sólo una de cada dos frases tiene que contener un verbo reflexivo.

Ejemplo:

Profesor:	Un día, Narciso decidió ir al baile.
Alumno 1:	Primero se lavó la cara, las manos y los pies.
Alumno 2:	Luego se puso un sombrero negro ...

6 Querido diario

Escribe un relato detallado, contando lo que hiciste ayer. Trata de usar verbos reflexivos, y usa el plural cuando puedas.

Ejemplo:

Ayer fui a la playa con mis amigos. Nos bañamos por la mañana y luego nos paseamos un poco por la playa ...

Después podéis escribir cada uno/a vuestra propia versión del relato de un(a) vecino/a, cambiando los verbos a la tercera persona.

Ejemplo:

Ayer, Juan fue a la playa con sus amigos. Se bañaron por la mañana y luego se pasearon un poco por la playa ...

7 Metamorfosis

Inventa una serie de frases originales usando cada uno de los verbos siguientes.

hacerse	volverse	quedarse	ponerse	convertirse en

Ejemplo:

Mi amiga quería hacerse azafata.
Se puso muy contenta al recibir una carta de la línea aérea.
Pero su novio se volvió loco de envidia.

17 Future tense

17.1 Uses

a) The future tense is used to indicate future events, whether in the near future or the distant future.

> **Compraré** la carne en la carnicería, luego **iré** al hipermercado.
> **I'll buy/I'm going to buy** the meat at the butcher's, then **I'll go** to the hypermarket.

> El año que viene, **pasaré** mis vacaciones con mis padres, pero cuando tenga veinte años, **iré** con mis amigos.
> Next year **I shall spend** my holidays with my parents, but when I'm twenty **I shall go** with my friends.

b) The future tense is also sometimes used to indicate suppositions or approximations (often involving numbers).

> ¿Dónde **estará**?
> I wonder where **he is**.

> ¿Dónde está papá? **Estará** en la cocina.
> Where is Dad? **He's probably** in the kitchen.

> ¿Cuántos años tiene el abuelo? **Tendrá** unos setenta años.
> How old is grandad? **He must be** about seventy.

➡ **Exercises 1a, 2**

17.2 Formation

There are two main ways in Spanish of describing actions in the future.

17.2.1 Future simple

a) The true future tense, sometimes referred to as the future simple, has a special set of endings. With most verbs, these endings are added to the whole of the infinitive.

-ar	-er	-ir
hablar	**comer**	**vivir**
hablar**é**	comer**é**	vivir**é**
hablar**ás**	comer**ás**	vivir**ás**
hablar**á**	comer**á**	vivir**á**
hablar**emos**	comer**emos**	vivir**emos**
hablar**éis**	comer**éis**	vivir**éis**
hablar**án**	comer**án**	vivir**án**

NB: all endings are stressed and all have a written accent except the first person plural.

b) Verbs which are irregular in the future are simply ones which have an irregular stem, but all the stems end in **-r**; the endings are the same as for regular verbs. Thus the irregularity is always in the stem, and never in the ending. Here is a list of the most important irregular verbs.

caber:	*cabré*	*querer:*	*querré*
decir:	*diré*	*saber:*	*sabré*
haber:	*habré*	*salir:*	*saldré*
hacer:	*haré*	*tener:*	*tendré* (and compounds)
poder:	*podré*	*valer:*	*valdré*
poner:	*pondré* (and compounds)	*venir:*	*vendré* (and compounds)

17.2.2 *Ir a*

The future can also be expressed as in English, simply by taking the appropriate part of the present tense of the verb *ir* 'to go' and adding *a* + the infinitive of the main verb.

Voy	*a hablar*	*con tus padres.*
I am going	to speak	to your parents.

Vamos	*a ir*	*al restaurante.*
We are going	to go	to the restaurant.

(See also Chapter 13.)

➡ **Exercise 1b**

As can easily be deduced from these examples, this structure is used to describe an action which is immediately about to happen: it is often referred to as the future immediate.

17.3 Using the present

The idea of the future can also be expressed by means of the present tense, as in English.

*Esta tarde **van** al Corte Inglés a comprar un regalo para su madre.*
This afternoon they **are going** to Corte Inglés to buy a present for their mother.

*El tren **sale** a las diez y media.*
The train **leaves** (will leave) at ten thirty.

(See also Chapter 14.)

 ¡PONTE A PUNTO!

1 Mañana

a) ¿Por qué se debe hacer hoy lo que se puede hacer mañana? Contesta a estas órdenes según el siguiente ejemplo.

– *Oye, ¡limpia tus zapatos en seguida!*

– *Los limpiaré mañana.*

1	¡Arregla tu dormitorio!	8	¡Ve a visitar a tu abuela!
2	¡Lava estas camisas!	9	¡Pon tu bicicleta en el garaje!
3	¡Haz tus deberes!	10	¡Vuelve a la biblioteca!
4	¡Friega los platos!	11	¡Compra unos huevos!
5	¡Barre el patio!	12	¡Busca tu reloj!
6	¡Limpia la alfombra!	13	¡Escribe a tu novia!
7	¡Lee este libro!	14	¡Llama a tus amigos!

b) Ahora vuelve a hacer el ejercicio usando *ir a* + infinitivo.

– *Voy a limpiarlos en seguida.*

2 La boda

He aquí lo que escribió un novio (Andrés) el día después de su boda. Cuenta todo lo que sucedió en la boda. Usando este modelo, imagina que tienes que hacer tus planes para tu propia boda. Puedes hacerlo desde el punto de vista del novio o de la novia. Tienes que basarlo sobre este cuento, pero cambia los verbos al futuro.

La víspera de la boda, salí por la tarde con unos amigos. Tomamos unas copitas, luego fuimos a cenar a un restaurante. Después ... bueno, no lo recuerdo bien, ¡ni quiero recordarlo!

El día de la boda, me levanté a las ocho, y desayuné con el padrino de boda, que llegó a las ocho y pico. Los dos salimos a dar un paseo al lado del río, y a las diez volvimos a casa a vestirnos para la boda.

Llegamos a la iglesia a las doce menos cuarto; muchos parientes y amigos ya estaban allí, y otros llegaron después de nosotros. El cura entró a las doce en punto y, por fin, llegó Juanita con su padre. ¡Qué hermosa estaba! Con ella llegaron también las damas de honor, mis sobrinas Mariana y Sara. Ellas también estaban muy guapas. La ceremonia duró un poco menos de una hora, y después se hicieron las fotos delante de la iglesia.

A las dos fuimos todos al hotel, donde almorzamos, bailamos, y nos divertimos. Por fin, Juanita y yo nos despedimos de todos, y nos pusimos en camino para nuestra luna de miel. ¡Y ya no escribo más!

 ## ¡... Y EN MARCHA!

3 ¡Estos niños se meten en todo!

Estás a punto de salir – tal vez con tu novio/a o con unos amigotes. Mientras te arreglas, tus hermanos/as menores te hacen una serie de preguntas. Tus compañeros/as de clase harán el papel de tus hermanos/as: contéstales usando el futuro. No necesitas decir la verdad en tus respuestas. ¡A veces hay que usar alguna mentirilla sarcástica con los hermanitos que se meten en todo!

Ejemplo:

– Oye, ¿por qué te estás vistiendo así?
– Bueno, ¡porque vamos a ir a la discoteca, tonta!
– Y, ¿qué vais a hacer en la discoteca?
– ¡Vamos a cenar, idiota!

4 Encuentro con la justicia

¡Qué inocentes sois! Tú y tus amigos/as vais al centro de la ciudad a divertiros, pero se para al lado de vosotros un coche de patrulla. Uno de los policías – el/la profe – os hace una serie de preguntas para saber adónde vais y qué vais a hacer.

Ejemplo:

– *Decís que vais al cine pero está cerrado hoy. ¿Qué vais a hacer, entonces?*
– *Iremos al bar a tomar algo.*
– *¿Qué haréis después?*
– *A lo mejor volveremos a casa de Juan, y veremos un vídeo.*

¡Otra vez, vuestras respuestas podrían contener unas mentiras o tonterías!

5 El nuevo conductor

a) Cuenta a tus amigos/as cuándo, cómo y por qué vas a aprender a conducir, y describe tu coche ideal. En todos los verbos, usarás el futuro, incluso cuando quieras describir cómo será tu coche probablemente …

Ejemplo:

Voy a empezar a aprender a conducir el día de mi cumpleaños. Tardaré dos o tres meses en aprender, y después de hacerme el carnet de conducir …

b) Escribe una carta a un(a) amigo/a español/a, contándole todo lo que acabas de decir a tus compañeros/as.

6 Ambiciones – juego de memoria

Cada miembro de la clase explica sus ambiciones para el futuro, y los demás le escuchan pero sin apuntar nada.

Luego cada miembro tiene que explicar las ambiciones de otro – el/la profesor(a) tiene que nombrar una víctima para cada alumno/a. A ver si acertáis todos a recordar los planes de los otros. Igualmente, el/la profe, u otro alumno, puede hacer preguntas tales como:

¿Qué va a hacer Ricardo? o bien *¿Qué dice que hará después de los exámenes?*

7 Predecir el futuro

Eres adivina en un parque de atracciones. Tienes que estudiar la cara, la mano o los naipes de tus compañeros/as y decirles lo que les va a pasar en el futuro … pero ¡tienen que pagarte con una moneda de plata!

Igualmente, imagina que eres quiromántico/a. Tus compañeros/as tienen que mandarte cada uno/a una fotocopia anónima de sus palmas: tienes que predecirles el futuro, por escrito. También puedes tratar de decir de quién es la mano. ¡Suerte!

18 Conditional tense

MECANISMOS

18.1 Uses

a) The conditional tense is used by and large where in English we use the word 'would' (but see section 18.4 below). Its name reflects one of its uses: to express the result of a condition 'if', but see also Chapter 38).

> **Podría** irse si terminase sus deberes a tiempo.
> He **would be able** to go if he finished his homework in time.

b) Its main uses are as follows.

* to indicate an implied condition:

> **No** me **gustaría** hacerlo.
> I **wouldn't like** to do it.

> **Sería** una buena idea.
> It **would be** a good idea.

* to express suppositions or approximations in the past (often involving numbers):

> ¿Dónde estaba papá en aquel momento? **Estaría** en la cocina.
> Where was dad at that moment? He **was probably** in the kitchen.

> ¿Cuántos años tenía la abuela entonces? **Tendría** unos setenta años.
> How old was grandma at the time? She **must have been** about seventy.

* to express the future in the past, especially in reported speech:

> Dijo que el año siguiente **iría** a la universidad.
> He said that the following year he **was going/would go** to university.

> **Compraría** el pan en la panadería, luego **iría** al mercado.
> I **was going to/I would buy** the bread at the baker's, then **was going/would go** to the market.

* to express rhetorical questions:

> ¿Quién **haría** tal cosa?
> Who **would do** such a thing?

➡ Exercises 1, 2, 3

18.2 Formation

a) The conditional tense in Spanish is formed by taking the stem of the future tense (which is the infinitive for most verbs) and adding to it the **-ía** (imperfect tense) endings (see Chapter 19). This applies both for regular and irregular verbs.

-ar	-er	-ir
hablar	comer	vivir
hablaría	comería	viviría
hablarías	comerías	vivirías
hablaría	comería	viviría
hablaríamos	comeríamos	viviríamos
hablaríais	comeríais	viviríais
hablarían	comerían	vivirían

b) Those verbs with irregular stems in the future tense (see Chapter 17) have the same irregular stems in the conditional. For example:

hacer	poner
haría	pondría
harías	pondrías
haría	pondría
haríamos	pondríamos
haríais	pondríais
harían	pondrían

18.3 Replacing the conditional

- The conditional tense is often replaced by the imperfect, especially in conditional sentences in colloquial language:

  Si ganara el Gordo, **no necesitaba** *trabajar más.*
  If I won the jackpot, **I wouldn't need** to work any more.

- The conditional tense is often replaced by the imperfect subjunctive **-ra** form; this is especially so with the verbs **querer**, **haber** and **deber**, but often occurs with others:

  Quisiera *tener mucho dinero.*
  I **would like** to have lots of money.

  Hubiera querido *ir a casa de mi abuela.*
  I **should have liked** to go to my grandmother's house.

  Debiera *haber ido.*
  He **should** have gone.

(See also Chapter 38 'If …' clauses.)

18.4 Other meanings of 'would'

- Be careful with the English words 'would' and 'wouldn't' when they refer to someone's willingness (or otherwise) to do something. They need to be rendered using the verb *querer* in the imperfect or preterite form.

  *Quería oírla, pero ella **no quería/quiso** cantar.*
  I wanted to hear her but she **wouldn't** sing.

- Always take care when 'would' in English actually means 'used to'; when this is the case, use either the imperfect or *soler* + infinitive. (See also Chapter 19.)

  *Cuando éramos jóvenes, a menudo **íbamos** juntos al bosque.*
  When we were young, **we would** often **go** to the woods together.

  *Hace muchos años, la gente **no solía bañarse** mucho.*
  Years ago, people **did not** often **take baths**.

- 'Could' in English is often not conditional, in which case it is best translated by the imperfect form of *poder*. This is certainly true if it can be replaced with 'was/were able to …', but the preterite is needed in some cases (see also Chapter 25).

  *Dije que **podía** ir.*
  I said that he **could (was able to)** go.

  ***No pude** repararlo.*
  I **could not (was not able to)** repair it.

 ¡PONTE A PUNTO!

1 Fantasía

¿Quién sabe lo que podría traer el futuro de este mundo nuestro? Imagina que un día tus padres te mandan a hacer varias tareas domésticas. Mientras las haces, piensas en el futuro y en los robots especiales que todos tendríamos para hacerlo todo. Inventa una respuesta para cada orden. (Algunas respuestas podrían ser un poco ridículas …)

Ejemplo:

– *¡Limpia tus zapatos en seguida!*

– *En el futuro, los limpiaría mi robot.*

1	¡Limpia tu dormitorio!	6	¡Pon la mesa!
2	¡Lava el coche!	7	¡Lleva tu bicicleta al garaje!
3	¡Friega los cacharros!	8	¡Seca estos vasos!
4	¡Barre el suelo de la cocina!	9	¡Búscame un huevo en la nevera!
5	¡Prepara la cena!	10	¡Corta el césped!

2 La boda

Hé aquí un e-mail escrito por una novia dos o tres semanas antes de su boda. Lo mandó a la chica que iba a ser su dama de honor, diciéndole lo que tendría que hacer el día de la boda.

¡Hola!

Te escribo para decirte cómo será el día de la boda y lo que tendrás que hacer.

La víspera de la boda, tendrás que llegar a mi casa a las ocho; Sara ya estará allí. Prepararemos varias cosas para la boda, luego saldremos a cenar con unas amigas mías.

El día de la boda, nos levantaremos a las ocho, y después del desayuno iremos a la peluquería. A las diez y cuarto volveremos a mi casa a vestirnos para la boda. ¡Todas estaremos guapísimas!

Iremos con mi padre a la iglesia y llegaremos a las doce y pico: ¡la novia tiene que llegar un poquito tarde! Los parientes y amigos ya estarán allí, pues seremos los últimos en llegar. Al entrar, tú y Sara andaréis detrás de mí. El cura te dirá lo que tienes que hacer durante la ceremonia: la ceremonia durará un poco menos de una hora, y después se harán las fotos delante de la iglesia.

A las dos iremos todos al hotel, donde almorzaremos, bailaremos y nos divertiremos. Por fin, Andrés y yo nos despediremos de todos vosotros y nos pondremos en camino para nuestra luna de miel.

Llámame por teléfono o mándame un e-mail si se te ocurre algo más que necesites saber.

¡Hasta pronto!

Un beso,

Juanita

Imagina que tú fuiste la dama de honor, y después de recibir el e-mail, escribes otro e-mail a una amiga, contándole todo lo que te había dicho Juanita.

Ejemplo:

Juanita me dijo que la víspera de la boda tendría que ...

3 ¡Ojalá!

¿Qué harías si ganaras el Gordo en la Lotería Nacional? He aquí unas sugerencias: sólo tienes que expresarlos usando la forma correcta del condicional.

Ejemplo:

comprar – castillo – España

Compraría un castillo en España.

1 comprar – coche – elegante
2 buscar – chalet – cerca de la playa
3 regalar – algo muy precioso – madre
4 ayudar – hermano – a comprar un negocio
5 venir – a visitar amigo – en España
6 dar mucho dinero a …
7 casarse con …
8 tener muchos …
9 no trabajar más excepto …
10 ir de vacaciones a …

Ahora, cambia los verbos para decir lo que haríais tú y un(a) amigo/a tuyo/a.

 # ¡... Y EN MARCHA!

4 ¡El invento!

Un(a) compañero/a de clase hace el papel de tus padres. Están hartos de los quehaceres que tienen en casa. Como buen(a) chico/a, les ayudas, y dices que un día inventarás una máquina para hacerlo. Quieren saber más, y tú tienes que explicárselo todo (usando el condicional): cómo sería el aparato, cómo funcionaría y qué haría. Cada miembro de la clase tiene que inventar varios chismes y explicárselos a los demás.

Ejemplo:

Papá: *Oye, ¿quieres limpiarme los zapatos? No tengo tiempo, y no quiero mancharme la camisa.*
Tú: *Claro. Pero un día voy a inventar una máquina para hacerlo.*
Papá: *¿Cómo funcionaría?*
Tú: *Bueno, tendría un motor eléctrico y un cepillo automático: meterías los zapatos en un agujero, y saldrían limpios.*

5 En el año 2050

En el siglo 20, la tecnología hizo unos progresos tremendos; ¿y qué pasará en el siglo que acaba de empezar? Con tanto progreso ¿todavía tendríamos necesidad de trabajar? Imagina una serie de cambios fundamentales en la vida y en el trabajo y, usando el condicional, cuéntalos a tu clase.

Ejemplo:

Para mí, no creo que tendríamos que trabajar más. Me parece que las fábricas funcionarían automáticamente, y la administración sería hecha por ordenadores ...

Después de escuchar a tus compañeros/as, escribe un resumen de 150 palabras sobre cómo sería el año 2050, según la clase.

6 El loco del volante

a) Acabas de aprender a conducir y, desgraciadamente, acabas de tener tu primer accidente. Pero todo fue culpa de un loco del volante que causó el accidente y luego se escapó. Tienes que describirlo al policía que llega después para ayudarle a encontrar al delincuente. Describe el coche, al conductor, y su manera de conducir ... pero no estás seguro/a de nada, por lo tanto utilizas el condicional para expresarte.

Ejemplo:

Pues, era un coche deportivo – sería un Ferrari o un Porsche. No le vi muy bien al conductor – tendría unos treinta años, pero iría a unos cien kilómetros por hora, ¡como si fuera Michael Schumacher!

b) Ahora, como es natural, tienes que preparar una declaración por escrito para la policía.

c) A ver si tú y tus amigos sabéis imaginar otros accidentes y siniestros para hacer descripciones parecidas de ellos y de los culpables.

7 Lo sabía todo

Imagina a un sabelotodo que expresa su reacción a varios hechos y acontecimientos recientes o históricos. Al oír lo que pasó, siempre dice que ya sabía lo que pasaría. El sabelotodo puede existir hoy o en el pasado.

Ejemplo:

Profesor(a):   *Cristóbal Colón se fue hacia el oeste porque creía que la Tierra era redonda, y por eso ...*

Sabelotodo: *¡Ya sabía Colón que encontraría tierras nuevas!*

Tú: *Hubo un incendio en nuestro pueblo anoche, ¿sabes? Se incendió el ayuntamiento.*

Sabelotodo: *¡Ya sabía yo que habría un incendio, y que se arrasaría el ayuntamiento!*

19 Imperfect tense

MECANISMOS

The main point about the imperfect is that it is the tense that tells you what used to happen or what was happening at some point in the past. We are not concerned about when the action began or ended. If you say **Tomaba el desayuno cuando vino el cartero,** all that matters is that the action going on when the postman came was you having breakfast; we're not concerned when you started it, or even if you finished it!

19.1 Uses

The imperfect tense has three main uses:

a) to indicate what **used** to happen, such as habitual or repeated happenings:

*Cuando **vivíamos** en Barcelona, **teníamos que** hablar catalán.*
When we **lived (used to live)** in Barcelona, we **had to (used to have to)** speak Catalan.

Note that the corresponding English verbs 'lived', 'had to' are expressed in the simple past in this example but these are definitely ongoing or habitual actions, so use the imperfect in Spanish.

b) description:

*Antes del siglo XVI Madrid no **era** más que un pueblo sin importancia situado en un río que **quedaba** vacío lo más del año.*
Before the XVIth century Madrid **was** only an unimportant village situated on a river which **stayed** dry for most of the year.

➡ **Exercises 1, 2**

c) to say what was happening at a particular time:

***Hablaba** al teléfono.*
I was talking on the phone.

***Arreglaba** mi cuarto.*
I was tidying my room.

Note: the imperfect is often used in conjunction with the preterite to indicate what was going on when something else happened. In this case, you can also use the 'continuous' form (see Chapter 20), with the imperfect of **estar** and the gerund, as in English:

***Estaba hablando** por teléfono cuando llamaron a la puerta.*
I was talking on the phone when someone knocked at the door.

See also Chapter 22 on the use of the imperfect and preterite together.

➡ **Exercise 3**

19.2 Formation

a) The imperfect tense has two sets of endings, one for **-ar** verbs and the other for **-er** and **-ir** verbs:

trabajar	*to work*	comer	*to eat*	vivir	*to live*
trabaj**aba**		com**ía**		viv**ía**	
trabaj**abas**		com**ías**		viv**ías**	
trabaj**aba**		com**ía**		viv**ía**	
trabaj**ábamos**		com**íamos**		viv**íamos**	
trabaj**abais**		com**íais**		viv**íais**	
trabaj**aban**		com**ían**		viv**ían**	

b) The verbs **ser** and **ir** are irregular:

ser	*to be*	ir	*to go*
era		iba	
eras		ibas	
era		iba	
éramos		íbamos	
erais		ibais	
eran		iban	

Note that the verb **ver** adds the **-ía** endings to the stem **ve**: **veía**. There are no other irregularities of formation.

¡PONTE A PUNTO!

1 La bisabuela

Cambia los verbos entre paréntesis al imperfecto.

Nunca conocí a mi bisabuela, porque murió antes de que yo naciera, pero según mi madre (ser) una mujer pequeña, que siempre (llevar) un sombrero en la calle y muchas veces en la casa. (Vivir) en una casa vieja que (tener) siempre una aspidistra en la ventana del salón. Todos los domingos (ir) a la iglesia y luego (almorzar) con mis abuelos, porque mi bisabuelo ya (estar) muerto y ella se (encontrar) sola. A mi madre le (gustar) las visitas de su abuela – es decir, mi bisabuela – porque ésta siempre le (traer) un regalito o le (dar) una moneda de un duro – ¡cinco pesetas (comprar) bastantes cosas en aquellos días! Después de casarse mi madre no (ver) tanto a su abuela, pero la (querer) mucho hasta que murió un poco antes de nacer yo.

2 En la época de Franco

Cambia los verbos al imperfecto.

Durante los años franquistas por lo general (prohibirse) hablar catalán. También en esa época (haber) censura y la prensa no (poder) imprimir todo lo que (querer). Muchos de los periódicos y revistas que disfrutamos hoy no (existir) aún, aunque hacia finales de la dictadura ya (empezar) a aparecer revistas como *Cambio 16*. Sin embargo (decirse) que la gente (leer) 'entre líneas' y, por ejemplo, cada vez que los periódicos (negar) que hubiese huelgas en Cataluña o el País Vasco, y cuanto más la prensa franquista (insistir) en que no, tanto más la gente (darse) cuenta de lo que (estar) ocurriendo. También la censura (restringir) las películas que se (poder) ver en los cines.

3 ¡Caos en casa!

Una madre fue un día a la ciudad a hacer la compra. Aquí habla de la situación que encontró en casa al volver. Cambia los verbos entre paréntesis al imperfecto.

Cuando llegué a casa, lo que (pasar) era horroroso. Los niños (jugar) a la corrida en el comedor, el gato (trepar) por las cortinas, el perro (roer) un hueso sobre la alfombra. Mi marido (dormir) en una butaca en la sala de estar y su cigarrillo (quemar) la butaca. La radio (estar) puesta lo más alto posible ¡y el programa (tratar) de la vida familiar! En la cocina el agua (escaparse) del grifo y (desbordarse) sobre el suelo. En el jardín nuestros dos conejos (correr), (saltar) y (comer) las verduras. El vecino (cortar) un árbol y las ramas (caer) sobre mis flores. Cuando les pregunté a todos qué (pensar) que (hacer), me respondieron «Nosotros (cuidar) la casa mientras tú (ir) de compras ». Pensé que lo (soñar) todo, ¡pero (ser) la verdad!

 # ¡... Y EN MARCHA!

4 Recuerdos

Piensa en cuando tenías diez años, y describe tu vida de entonces. ¿Cómo eras? ¿Dónde vivías? ¿A qué colegio ibas? ¿Qué hacías allí y cómo eran tus profesores y tus compañeros de clase? ¿Cuáles eran tus intereses? Cuenta a tus compañeros/as de clase actuales todo lo que recuerdas de aquellos tiempos.

5 ¡Al ladrón!

En tu colegio desapareció ayer una videocámara. El/La director(a) está haciendo pesquisas. ¿Dónde estabas tú, y qué hacías a la hora en que desapareció el aparato? ¿Y tus compañeros/as? Discutid vuestras actividades y uno/a hace de reportero/a.

6 La vida es sueño

a) Anoche, todos soñasteis unos con otros. Cada estudiante tiene que decir lo que hacía otro miembro del grupo en su sueño. ¡Podéis imaginar acciones algo absurdas si queréis, ya que ésta es una oportunidad para emplear vuestra imaginación!

Ejemplo:

¡Anoche soñé que Sam escribía una redacción en español!
¡Y yo tuve un sueño en el que Julia nos compraba unas cervezas!
Anoche soñé contigo, Isabel. ¡Nadábamos en el mar de una isla tropical!

(*NB: to dream of* = soñar con)

b) Ahora escribe un párrafo describiendo (en el imperfecto, claro) por lo menos seis acciones de los personajes de tu sueño.

7 En aquella época

Escoge una época de la historia que te interesa o que has estudiado, sea de la historia española, británica o de otro país, y cuéntala a tus compañeros de clase. Describe, por ejemplo, las circunstancias políticas, sociales, culturales, militares, económicas. Es decir, empleando el imperfecto, evocarás el ambiente más que los acontecimientos de la época.

Luego escribe una corta redacción sobre lo que acabas de describir.

MECANISMOS

20.1 Continuous actions

As you saw in Chapter 14, the present tense in Spanish is used to convey the idea of an action taking place in present time in two ways: 'he reads' and 'he is reading', for example. Whilst the first version refers to a general truth, the latter describes what is going on at the moment:

*Javier **lee** muchos libros.*
Javier **reads** lots of books.

*Javier **lee** un libro en este momento.*
Javier **is reading** a book at the moment.

Although the verb itself is the same, the idea of the action is entirely different. Normally in Spanish, the context of the verb will make it quite clear which of these ideas is being conveyed.

20.2 The present continuous

Spanish also has a separate tense to express ongoing actions more vividly: the present continuous. This tense is used where there is special emphasis on the ongoing nature of the action. It is not used as often as its equivalent in English for the simple reason that the ordinary present tense is usually quite enough.

Note: you cannot use this tense for the immediate future; the ordinary present tense is used instead.

¿Qué haces esta tarde?
What are you doing this evening?

It is formed in very much the same way as in English by using the appropriate form of the present tense of ***estar*** followed by the gerund (see Chapter 28).

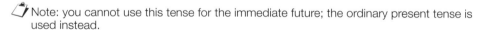

estoy *hablando*	I am speaking
estás *hablando*	you are speaking
está *hablando*	he/she is speaking, you (*usted*) are speaking
estamos *hablando*	we are speaking
estáis *hablando*	you (plural) are speaking
están *hablando*	they are speaking, you (*ustedes*) are speaking

➡ **Exercise 1**

20.2.1 Gerunds

a) The gerund of regular **-ar** verbs ends in **-ando**, and those of **-er** verbs and **-ir** verbs in **-iendo**:

hablar ⟶ habl**ando**   comer ⟶ com**iendo**   vivir ⟶ viv**iendo**

b) Note the spelling change in the gerund of verbs such as the following:

construir ⟶ constru**y**endo   leer ⟶ le**y**endo   oír ⟶ o**y**endo
caer ⟶ ca**y**endo   creer ⟶ cre**y**endo

This also applies to other verbs ending in **-uir**.

c) Note also that most radical-changing verbs do not undergo any spelling change to their gerund:

volver ⟶ volviendo   jugar ⟶ jugando   pensar ⟶ pensando

The exceptions are those with infinitives in **-ir**. In these cases **o** changes to **u** and **e** to **i** (see also Chapter 15):

dormir ⟶ d**u**rmiendo   pedir ⟶ p**i**diendo   reñir ⟶ r**i**ñendo

Others in this group are:

preferir ⟶ pref**i**riendo   sentir ⟶ s**i**ntiendo   venir ⟶ v**i**niendo

Note: verbs with infinitives ending in **-ñer**, **-ñir** or **-llir** lose the **i** of the gerund ending, e.g.:

tañer ⟶ tañ**e**ndo, reñir ⟶ riñ**e**ndo, zambullirse ⟶ zambull**é**ndose

20.3 The imperfect continuous

There is a similar tense which is used to describe ongoing actions in the past: the imperfect continuous. The imperfect itself is usually quite adequate to describe such actions, but this continuous tense is used where extra emphasis is required to stress the ongoing nature of the action.

This tense is similar to the present continuous; instead of the present tense of **estar**, it uses the imperfect of **estar**, but the gerund is the same.

estaba hablando	I was speaking
estabas hablando	you were speaking
estaba hablando	he/she was speaking, you (usted) were speaking
estábamos hablando	we were speaking
estabais hablando	you (plural) were speaking
estaban hablando	they were speaking, you (ustedes) were speaking

Exercise 2

20.4 Other continuous tenses

You may come across 'continuous' forms of other tenses. They are all formed as you might expect, with the appropriate tense of *estar* followed by the gerund. They are easy to translate:

*¿Qué **estarán haciendo** ahora?*
What **will they be doing** now? (future, but expressing probability)

*¿Por qué **estaría cantando**?*
Why **would he/she be singing**? (conditional)

20.5 Other continuous expressions

The gerund may also be used with *ir* and *venir* to express similar 'ongoing' actions or notions of progression:

*Los días **iban alargándose**.*
The days **were growing longer**.

*La gente **venía gritando** por la calle.*
The people **were coming** along the street **shouting**.

 ¡PONTE A PUNTO!

1 El espía

He aquí un relato en el que el Señor X nos cuenta lo que hace todos los días cuando va al trabajo. Imagina que eres espía industrial o detective, y que tienes que espiarle. Un día le observas clandestinamente en camino de su lugar de trabajo. Tienes un teléfono móvil con el cual cuentas a un colega todo lo que está haciendo el Señor X. Claro, tienes que utilizar el presente continuo. Empieza así:

Son las nueve y está saliendo de casa.

Salgo de casa a las nueve y pico. Cruzo la calle y espero el autobús. Cuando llega, subo y pago el billete. Bajo delante del ayuntamiento, y tomo la calle de Toledo. Luego subo la avenida de Burgos, y entro en el edificio de la empresa donde trabajo. Normalmente llego a las nueve y media. Cojo el ascensor al cuarto piso, salgo y me dirijo a mi despacho. Saludo a mi secretaria, y me siento detrás de mi escritorio. Empiezo a abrir el correo y comienzo a redactar mis respuestas a las cartas. Poco después, entra mi secretaria con una taza de café, y se prepara para tomar unos apuntes. Llamo por teléfono a mi jefe, y luego entra un colega para mostrarme unos dibujos. A mediodía los dos salimos, y vamos al bar que se encuentra enfrente de la oficina, y tomamos un aperitivo. Luego vamos al restaurante Salamanca y nos sentamos cerca de la ventana. Pedimos algo de comer y una botella de vino tinto. A veces charlamos con el camarero. Después de tomar café, volvemos al trabajo.

2 El novio celoso

Eres un(a) entrometido/a. Ayer viste a la novia de José María en varios sitios. Él quiere saber qué hacía la chica ¡y con quién! Completa las frases siguientes para decir lo que estaba haciendo la novia:

1 Ayer a las diez de la mañana vi a Concha en el parque y …
2 A las diez y media la vi en la biblioteca y …
3 A las once la vi en el café Chinchón y …
4 A mediodía la vi salir de la panadería y …
5 A la una la vi entrar en el Restaurante Zeluán y …
6 A las dos la vi en la playa y …
7 A las cuatro la vi en la Calle Mayor y …
8 A las siete la vi entrar en la Discoteca Marisol y …
9 A las nueve la vi en Bodegas Muñoz-Rivas y …
10 A medianoche la vi volver a casa y …

 # ¡… Y EN MARCHA!

3 ¿Qué profesión?

Tienes que escoger una profesión u oficio. Los demás tienen que hacerte preguntas para adivinar qué es. Para ayudarles, tienes que representar tu profesión con gestos apropiados.

Ejemplo:

Eres carpintero: haces como para cortar un trozo de madera con tu sierra.

– ¿Estás boxeando?	– No.
– ¿Estás cortando carne?	– No.
– ¿Estás cortando madera?	– Sí.
– ¿Eres leñador?	– No.
– ¿Eres carpintero?	– Sí.

4 ¡Al ladrón!

Ha habido un atraco en un banco de Bogotá donde estáis de vacaciones. Un transeúnte vio a los atracadores entrar en vuestro hotel. Por coincidencia, en todos los aspectos se os parecen. Uno/a de tus compañeros/as hace el papel del policía que os está interrogando. Os pregunta a cada uno dónde estabais y qué estabais haciendo.

Al terminar el interrogatorio, cada miembro de la clase tiene que preparar su declaración escrita, y el 'policía' escribe su relato para el comisario.

5 El reportaje

Imagina que eres periodista. Asistes a un concierto muy importante, a un accidente espectacular, a un partido de fútbol, a la boda de una persona famosa, o a otro acontecimiento importante. Utiliza el imperfecto continuo para escribir una descripción de lo que estaban haciendo todos los participantes. Escribe unas 120 palabras.

21 Preterite tense

MECANISMOS

21.1 Uses

You may come across some other names for this tense: past historic, past definite or past simple. It is used to describe a single, completed action in the past or an action which took place over a defined period of time, however long.

> *Ayer **compré** un abrigo nuevo.*
> Yesterday **I bought** a new coat.

> ***Pasé** dos años trabajando en Málaga.*
> **I spent** two years working in Malaga.

Don't be tempted simply to use the preterite whenever you want to say 'I went', 'he was' and so on. The English past simple form is often used where you'll actually need the imperfect in Spanish (see Chapter 22 on the preterite and imperfect together).

> *Todos los días **iba** al colegio en el autobús.*
> **I went** to school every day by bus.

21.2 Formation

a) The stem for most verbs is as for the present tense, i.e. the infinitive minus the *-ar*, *-er* and *-ir*. You will notice that *-er* and *-ir* verbs share the same set of endings; these endings are, in any case, very similar to those for *-ar* verbs. The **nosotros** form of *-ar* and *-ir* verbs is the same as for the present tense; the context usually prevents any possible confusion.

-ar	-er	-ir
comprar	beber	subir
compré	bebí	subí
compraste	bebiste	subiste
compró	bebió	subió
compramos	bebimos	subimos
comprasteis	bebisteis	subisteis
compraron	bebieron	subieron

➡ **Exercise 1**

b) The stress always falls on the ending; note that only the first and third persons singular need a written accent to show this. This means that most radical-changing verbs are no problem in the preterite; the exceptions are the *-ir* verbs in this group, which have spelling changes in the third person singular and plural forms only:

e → i	e → i	o → u
(**ie** *in present*)	(**i** *in present*)	(**ue** *in present*)
preferí	pedí	dormí
preferiste	pediste	dormiste
prefirió	pidió	durmió
preferimos	pedimos	dormimos
preferisteis	pedisteis	dormisteis
prefirieron	pidieron	durmieron

(See also Chapter 15 on radical-changing verbs.)

c) Those radical-changing verbs which are irregular (e.g. **tener**, **venir**, **querer**) are in the *pretérito grave* family (see Chapter 15 and Chapter 21, section 21.3).

d) A few verbs have minor spelling changes.

• verbs with *-y-* in the third person forms:

creer: creí, creíste, creyó, creímos, creísteis, creyeron
and also **caer**, **leer**, **oír** and verbs ending in *-uir*.

• *-er/-ir* verbs whose stem ends with an *-ñ* or *-ll* drop the *-i-* from the ending:

gruñir: gruñó, gruñeron and also **bullir**, **reñir**

• Verbs with a stem ending in *-c* need a spelling change to the *yo* form: *c* changes to *qu* because otherwise the following *e* would alter the pronunciation of the *c*:

*buscar: bus**qu**é, buscaste, buscó*, etc.
and also **acercarse**, **atacar**, **chocar**, **explicar**, **marcar**, **pescar**, **sacar**, **tocar** and all other verbs ending in *-car*.

• Verbs with a stem ending in *-g* need a spelling change to the *yo* form: *g* changes to *gu* because otherwise the following *e* would alter the pronunciation of the *g*:

*pagar: pa**gu**é, pagaste, pagó*, etc.
and also **apagar**, **cargar**, **entregar**, **llegar** and all other verbs ending in *-gar*.

• Verbs with a stem ending in *-z* also need a change to the *yo* form:

*cruzar: cru**c**é, cruzaste, cruzó*, etc., and all other verbs ending in *-zar*.

e) Note the following irregular verbs:

dar: di, diste, dio, dimos, disteis, dieron
ver: vi, viste, vio, vimos, visteis, vieron

f) Ser and **ir** share the same forms in the preterite tense:

fui, fuiste, fue, fuimos, fuisteis, fueron

21.3 The *pretérito grave*

This group of a dozen or so verbs has its own set of endings, added in each case to an irregular stem. The endings are largely familiar ones, four of them being the same as for **-er** and **-ir** verbs. Note also that the endings of the first and third person singular are like those for **-ar** verbs but are **unstressed** and have no accent.

a) *estar: estuve, estuviste, estuvo, estuvimos, estuvisteis, estuvieron*

Others in this group are:

andar: anduve ...
caber: cupe ...
hacer: hice ...
poder: pude ...
poner: puse ... (and compounds: *imponer, proponer, suponer,* etc.)
querer: quise ...
saber: supe ...
tener: tuve ... (and compounds: *mantener, obtener, sostener,* etc.)
venir: vine ...

b) Those with the stem ending in **-j** take **-eron** as the third person plural ending:

decir: dije ... dijeron
traer: traje ... trajeron (and compounds: *atraer, contraer, distraer*)
conducir: conduje ... condujeron (also *producir* and all compounds ending in **-ducir**)

➡ **Exercise 2**

21.4 *Saber* and *conocer*

✎ Note the use of the preterite of **saber** and **conocer**:

*Al leer la carta, **supe** que había ganado el Gordo.*
On reading the letter, I **realised** that I had won the jackpot.

*La **conocí** en Marbella.*
I **met** her/**got to know** her in Marbella.

➡ **Exercise 3**

¡PONTE A PUNTO!

1 El noventa y dos

Pon el verbo en la forma correcta del pretérito en cada caso.

Para España, el año 1992 (resultar) el más significativo de la nueva democracia, porque en un mismo año (celebrarse) un aniversario muy importante y también (suceder) allí varios acontecimientos de gran importancia internacional. Ya sabemos todos que en 1492, precisamente 500 años antes, el gran navegador genovés, Cristóbal Colón, (descubrir) el continente de América. Con motivo del descubrimiento del Nuevo Mundo (organizarse) varias fiestas y actividades culturales en España e Hispanoamérica. Además, en 1988, 400 jóvenes españoles e iberoamericanos (emprender) el viaje de 'Aventura 92' en el que (recorrer) los más importantes lugares colombinos. Y en 1992, España (recibir) a millones de extranjeros que (asistir) a los Juegos Olímpicos en Barcelona, (acudir) a la Expo 92 en Sevilla, y (visitar) los museos de Madrid, capital cultural de Europa del 92. Total, en el 92, España (llamar) la atención del mundo entero.

2 La vuelta al cole

Ahora, vuelve a escribir este párrafo usando el pretérito.

En el mes de setiembre, muchas familias españolas se preparan para el ritual de todos los años, o sea la vuelta al cole. Este año unos nueve millones de jóvenes volverán a su colegio. Como todos los años, cuando los padres compran los libros necesarios, pagarán precios caros, y se enfadarán al tener que enfrentarse con los atascos provocados por los autobuses escolares que empezarán a circular otra vez. Además, continuarán en el sistema educativo los cambios educativos que se introducen todos los años.

¡... Y EN MARCHA!

3 ¡Los enamorados!

a) Tu novio/a no llegó ayer a la cita que tenía contigo. Tú estás muy enfadado/a, porque te han dicho que tu novio/a salió con otro/a. Tú tienes que acusarle a tu novio/a (un(a) compañero/a de clase) de una serie de cosas, usando el pretérito.

Ejemplo:

Anoche no llegaste a mi casa a las ocho, como me prometiste.
Saliste con Maribel, ¿verdad? La llevaste a la discoteca, ¿no? ¡Canalla!

Tu compañero/a tiene que defenderse como mejor pueda, diciéndote por ejemplo:

¡Que no! Es que nos visitaron a mis abuelos. Traté de llamarte por teléfono, pero …

b) Ahora tenéis que cambiar de papeles. Tu compañero/a será el/la novio/a enfadado/a, y tú tendrás que defenderte.

c) Por fin, tienes que escribir una carta a tu novio/a acusándole o defendiéndote, ¡y explicando por qué no quieres verle/la más!

4 La abuelita

a) Le cuentas a la abuela de un(a) amigo/a cómo pasaste las vacaciones, pero no te oye muy bien. Así tu amigo/a tiene que repetir lo que dices.

Ejemplo:

Tú: *Pasé las vacaciones en Mallorca.*
Abuela: *¿Qué dices?*
Tu amigo/a: *Dice que pasó las vacaciones en Mallorca.*

b) Por fin, os cansáis de gritar. Tú escribes un resumen de tus vacaciones, y tu compañero/a escribe un resumen de lo que acabas de decir.

5 ¡El periodista sin límites!

a) Imagina que eres periodista y que acompañaste a una persona famosa en sus aventuras, por ejemplo: Cristóbal Colón, Julio César, El Cid. Primero tienes que llamar a tu redactor, contándole todo lo que ocurrió.

b) Luego tienes que escribir tú mismo/a tu reportaje para faxearselo.

6 ¡El problema de las generaciones!

a) Tu madre/padre se queja de ti. Anoche no hiciste tus deberes, esta mañana no te lavaste la cara … Le contestas, explicando que los hiciste el sábado pasado, te lavaste la cara ayer, etcétera …

b) Estás harto/a de tus padres. Escribes una carta a tu primo/a explicando por qué. Basa lo que escribes en lo que pasó en la primera parte de este ejercicio.

7 Mi currículum vitae

Imagina que vas a solicitar un empleo. Tienes que escribir una carta en la que contarás todo lo que haya sido de interés en tu vida hasta ahora. Claro, tendrás que utilizar el pretérito más que nada.

22 Preterite and imperfect tenses together

MECANISMOS

a) A reminder:

- The preterite is used for single, completed actions in the past, either one-off actions or those taking place over a defined period of time.
- The imperfect tense is used for actions in the past for which no period or moment is defined: repeated or habitual actions, descriptions, and actions which could be described as ongoing. It is often used as a setting or background to another action (which may be expressed in the preterite).

> José **andaba** por la calle cuando **se cayó** en un agujero enorme.
> José **was walking** along the road when **he fell** into a huge hole.

> Cuando **entré** en la habitación, mi padre **escuchaba** la radio.
> When **I went** into the room, my father **was listening** to the radio.

b) To sum up, it might be useful to think of the preterite being used for actions occurring at a particular time or occupying a defined slice of time. The imperfect is used for actions, situations or descriptions occupying an undefined period of progressing time whose beginning and ending is unknown and irrelevant. If in any doubt, look back at Chapters 19 and 21 before doing the following exercises.

c) This diagram may help you to understand the different uses.

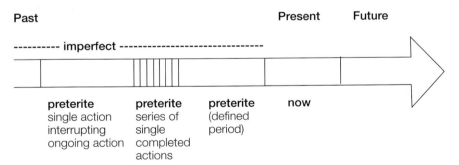

Past   Present   Future

---------- imperfect -----------------------------

preterite	preterite	preterite	now
single action	series of	(defined	
interrupting	single	period)	
ongoing action	completed		
	actions		

➤ **Exercises 1–5**

¡PONTE A PUNTO!

1 Frases rellenas

Pon los verbos cuyo infinitivo se da al final de la frase en la forma correcta del imperfecto o del pretérito.

1	Juan … el autobús todos los días.	*(coger)*
2	María … el autobús ayer.	*(coger)*
3	Don Fernando, lo siento, pero … mis deberes en casa.	*(dejar)*
4	De niño, José siempre … los libros en casa.	*(dejar)*
5	Cuando llegamos a San Salvador … sol.	*(hacer)*
6	Ayer, después del desayuno, doña Alicia … las camas.	*(hacer)*
7	Los lunes mi madre y yo siempre … en casa.	*(comer)*
8	El lunes pasado, mi novia y yo … en un restaurante.	*(comer)*
9	La nueva casa … detrás de la biblioteca.	*(estar)*
10	Mi tío … diez días en el hospital.	*(estar)*

2 ¡Gazpacho de verbos!

He aquí diez frases más en las cuales tienes que poner dos verbos, algunos en el pretérito, otros en el imperfecto.

1	Como … pobres, … pan y nada más.	*(ser, comer)*
2	Mientras su mujer … la televisión, Rafael … en la cocina.	*(ver, trabajar)*
3	Cuando … la bomba, yo … el diario.	*(caer, leer)*
4	Marcelino … a por vino, pero al cruzar la calle …	*(ir, caerse)*
5	Los moros … el mar y … España en poco tiempo.	*(cruzar, conquistar)*
6	No lo … tú, pero … la cartera en casa.	*(saber, dejar)*
7	La casa de don Miguel … en una colina, y … muy cómoda.	*(estar, ser)*
8	Yo no … mucho dinero, pues … un disco y nada más.	*(tener, comprar)*
9	Cuando … (vosotros) jóvenes, … más que ahora.	*(ser, estudiar)*
10	Don Justo … todos los días por aquella calle, pero aquel día … delante de un autobús.	*(ir, caerse)*

3 Situaciones

Escribe frases completas usando las siguientes sugerencias.

Ejemplo:

leer un libro – entrar mi hermano

Mientras mi madre leía un libro, entró mi hermano.

1 ver un vídeo – entrar mi tío
2 hacer los deberes – salir mi hermana
3 escuchar un CD – alguien llamar por teléfono
4 lavar los platos – romper un vaso
5 ir por la calle – ver un accidente
6 coger manzanas – caerse del árbol
7 jugar al fútbol – hacerse daño en el pie
8 subir la colina – ver un pájaro muy raro
9 tomar el sol en la playa – coger una insolación
10 estar en el jardín – oír el primer cuclillo.

4 ¡Ya es historia!

Vuelve a escribir la siguiente historia, poniendo los verbos en el imperfecto o el pretérito.

El otro día (ir) a un partido de fútbol con mi hermano. (Hacer) mucho frío, y nos (poner) el jersey. (Haber) mucha gente en el estadio cuando (llegar) pero pronto (encontrar) asientos. Mientras tanto, mi hermana (decidir) ir al parque con sus amigas. (Dar) de comer a los patos, pero Maribel, que es muy estúpida, (caerse) al agua, y las demás (tener) que ayudarla a salir. Maribel siempre (decir) que (saber) nadar muy bien, pero casi (ahogarse). (Quedarse) en casa de domingo a martes y (volver) al instituto el miércoles por la mañana. Mi hermana (pasar) todo el día tomándole el pelo, (estar) muy contenta, porque no le (gustar) nada Maribel que le (criticar) todos los días. ¡La pobre Maribel (quedarse) muy callada!

 ¡... Y EN MARCHA!

5 La inquisición

Un(a) amigo/a quiere saber los detalles de tu vida familiar y personal. Cuéntale lo que hiciste ayer, y lo que hacían tus amigos y los miembros de tu familia cuando los viste.

Ejemplo:

Por la mañana vi la televisión, y cuando llegó mi novia veía una película muy buena.

6 Correspondencia histórica

Escribe una carta en la que cuentas a un(a) amigo/a cómo pasaste las vacaciones o el fin de semana. Tendrás que usar el imperfecto y el pretérito.

23 Perfect tense

 ## MECANISMOS

23.1 Uses

a) The perfect tense is used in most cases as in English to say what has happened, what someone has done in the recent past.

*¿Qué **has hecho** hoy?*
What **have you done** today?

*¿**Has ido** al fútbol?*
Have you been to the football?

b) The perfect tense is not used in the sense of 'How long have you been doing something?'; the present tense is used (see Chapters 14 and 43).

23.2 Formation

a) The perfect tense in Spanish is formed by the present tense of **haber** + the past participle (see also Chapter 28).

comprar *to buy*	comer *to eat*	subir *to go up*
he comprado	**he** comido	**he** subido
has comprado	**has** comido	**has** subido
ha comprado	**ha** comido	**ha** subido
hemos comprado	**hemos** comido	**hemos** subido
habéis comprado	**habéis** comido	**habéis** subido
han comprado	**han** comido	**han** subido

b) There are only a few irregular past participles:

abrir – abierto	open(ed)	*describir – descrito*	describe(d)
cubrir – cubierto	cover(ed)	*freir – frito*	fry (fried)
descubrir – descubierto	discover(ed)	*hacer – hecho*	do/make (done/made)
decir – dicho	say/tell (said/told)	*satisfacer – satisfecho*	satisfy (satisfied)
volver – vuelto	return(ed)	*morir – muerto*	die (died/dead)
devolver – devuelto	give(n) back	*poner – puesto*	put (put)
disolver – disuelto	dissolve(d)	*romper – roto*	break (broken)
resolver – resuelto	resolve(d)	*ver – visto*	see(n)
escribir – escrito	write (written)		

and the compounds of the verbs listed above.

c) There is only ever one auxiliary verb: *haber*. The auxiliary verb and the past participle cannot be separated by pronouns to form questions: *Vd lo ha hecho* becomes *¿Lo ha hecho Vd?*, or simply remains as *¿Vd lo ha hecho?*, with the question indicated by question marks in written form and intonation in spoken form.

d) Used in this way, the past participle never changes. (For other uses of the past participle, see Chapter 28.)

¡PONTE A PUNTO!

1 Preparativos para las vacaciones

Contesta con una frase completa a las preguntas siguientes. Si no estás cierto/a cómo usar los pronombres, repásalos primero en el Capítulo 12 (12.2).

Ejemplo:

– *¿Has puesto tus zapatos en la maleta?*
– *Sí, claro que los he puesto.*

1   ¿Has preparado la máquina fotográfica?
2   ¿Has encontrado los pasaportes?
3   ¿Has reservado un hotel?
4   ¿Has conseguido billetes para el ferry?
5   ¿Has visto el pronóstico del tiempo?
6   ¿Has dejado nuestra dirección a los vecinos?
7   ¿Has hecho una lista de compras?
8   ¿Has comprobado el aceite del coche?
9   ¿Has cerrado todas las ventanas?

2 30 años de cambios

Convierte los infinitivos en tiempo perfecto.

En las tres décadas desde la muerte de Franco en 1975, España (ver) muchísimos cambios. Por ejemplo, (crearse) las Autonomías, y éstas (fomentar) sus idiomas regionales. De esta manera mucho poder (devolverse) a las regiones. También la izquierda política (ganar) cuatro elecciones generales. Los partidos (alternarse) democráticamente y más recientemente los socialistas (volver) al poder. España (pedir) y (conseguir) acceso a la Unión Europea. Esto (causar) algunos problemas pero también (traer) muchas ventajas. Barcelona (seleccionarse) para ser ciudad anfitriona de los Juegos Olímpicos del 1992, y Sevilla (celebrar) su momento de gloria con la Expo del mismo año. Las autoridades (construir) nuevos ferrocarriles de alta velocidad, y (proyectar) extender esta red a varias otras ciudades de la península. Durante todo este tiempo, la Familia Real española (lograr) mantener una gran popularidad y se dice que el Rey (hacer) mucho por España. El príncipe Felipe, heredero del trono, (cumplir) más de treinta años y (completar) gran parte de su formación para suceder a su padre, (elegir) una novia y (casarse). Aunque España (tener) ciertas dificultades económicas y sociales durante esta época, es cierto que (decir) adiós para siempre a la dictadura.

¡... Y EN MARCHA!

3 Turistas

Trabaja en parejas. Estás sentado/a en un banco en la calle en tu propia ciudad o región, hablando con un(a) turista que pasa unos días por allí. Tienes que preguntarle lo que ha hecho durante su estancia, y él/ella tiene que contestar a cada pregunta.

Ejemplo:

– ¿Ha visto usted el castillo?
– Sí, lo he visto/No, no lo he visto.

> **Verbos útiles:** ver, visitar, oír, tomar, comer, probar, ir, comprar, viajar, fotografiar

4 Confesiones

Todos hemos hecho cosas que no debíamos haber hecho y no hemos hecho cosas que debíamos haber hecho. Discute con tus compañeros/as vuestros 'pecados' – verdaderos o imaginarios – y confiésalos, empleando el tiempo perfecto, claro. ¡Cinco confesiones, cada uno!

Ejemplo:

He puesto arsénico en el café del profesor. No he comprado un regalo para el cumpleaños de mi novio/a.

5 El progreso científico

Discute con tus compañeros/as los avances que han hecho los científicos en los últimos años. ¿Qué otros avances se han hecho en la medicina, la ingeniería, la química, la electrónica u otras ciencias? Escribe una lista de los más importantes.

Ejemplo:

Los médicos han descubierto cómo escoger el sexo de un bebé.

> **Verbos útiles:** descubrir, inventar, encontrar, hallar, mejorar, construir, componer, desarrollar, producir, reproducir, elaborar

6 Promesas quebrantadas

Imagina que vives en un pueblo en España y que tienes que ir al colegio en la ciudad diariamente en el tren, pero el servicio es muy malo. Escribiste una carta a la dirección de los ferrocarriles, que te respondieron con la carta siguiente, prometiendo varias mejoras.

Muy señor(a) nuestro/a

Lamentamos los varios problemas que ha tenido Vd con el servicio de trenes y otras facilidades y le prometemos que estamos haciendo todo lo posible para mejorar la situación cuanto antes. En contestación a los problemas que Vd ha mencionado:

- *Vamos a restaurar el tren de las 0715 que suprimimos hace tres meses, en vista de las quejas de gran número de usuarios de dicho servicio.*
- *Estamos a punto de comprar unos nuevos vagones con mayor capacidad sentada.*
- *En el próximo mes cambiaremos de empresa de limpieza, lo que asegurará un servicio más eficaz.*
- *Las obras que ha habido en la vía se completarán dentro de pocos días, lo que asegurará mayor puntualidad de nuestros trenes.*
- *Las reparaciones de los aseos de la estación se terminarán antes del fin del mes, fecha en la que se volverán a abrir.*
- *Estamos conscientes de las deficiencias higiénicas de la fonda de la estación y estamos tratando de rectificarlas.*
- *En breve le garantizamos que dentro de pocas semanas nuestro servicio llegará a ser de los mejores que hay.*

Le/la saluda atentamente

Tres meses más tarde es evidente que no ha cambiado nada. Tú escribes otra carta a la dirección ferroviaria, empleando varios ejemplos del perfecto y subrayando lo que prometieron hacer y que **todavía no han hecho**.

24 Pluperfect and other compound tenses with *haber*

MECANISMOS

Like the perfect, the pluperfect and the other compound tenses in Spanish are formed with a tense of **haber** and the past participle. The participle remains unchanged throughout.

24.1 The pluperfect tense

This tense means 'had bought/eaten' and it is called the pluperfect (= more than perfect) because it tells you what had happened before the other events expressed in the perfect, or, more likely, the preterite:

*Cuando llegamos, ya **habían terminado**.*
When we arrived, they **had** already **finished**.

(i.e. the finishing had happened before the arriving).

The pluperfect consists of the imperfect of **haber** + the past participle:

comprar *to buy*	comer *to eat*	subir *to go up*
había comprado	**había** comido	**había** subido
habías comprado	**habías** comido	**habías** subido
había comprado	**había** comido	**había** subido
habíamos comprado	**habíamos** comido	**habíamos** subido
habíais comprado	**habíais** comido	**habíais** subido
había comprado	**habían** comido	**habían** subido

➡ **Exercise 1**

129

24.2 The future perfect tense

The future perfect tells you what will have happened:

Habrán terminado antes de que lleguemos.
They will have finished before we arrive.

It consists of the future of *haber* + the past participle:

habré habrás habrá habremos habréis habrán	comprado / comido / subido

24.3 The conditional perfect tense

The conditional perfect tells you what would have happened:

Habrían terminado antes de que llegásemos.
They would have finished before we arrived.

Hubieran llegado.
They would have arrived.

It consists of the conditional of *haber* + the past participle:

habría habrías habría habríamos habríais habrían	comprado / comido / subido

Note: The *-ra* form (but not the *-se* form) of the imperfect subjunctive of *haber* (*hubiera*, etc.) is often used instead of the true conditional in this tense.

Note that both the future perfect and conditional perfect can be used to express supposition:

Ya *habrán llegado*.
They **must have arrived**. (by now, i.e. in the present)

Ya *habrían llegado*.
They **must have arrived**. (by then, i.e. in the past)

➡ **Exercises 2, 3**

24.4 The past anterior

The past anterior means 'had bought/eaten' and is now a mainly literary tense,
used after time expressions such as **cuando** (when), **así que/en cuanto** (as soon as),
no bien (no sooner), **apenas** (hardly).

> *Apenas **hubimos llegado** cuando terminaron.*
> Hardly **had we arrived** when they finished.

In modern speech, however, the preterite would be used:

> *Apenas **llegamos** cuando terminaron.*

It consists of the preterite of **haber** + the past participle:

hube	
hubiste	
hubo	comprado / comido / subido
hubimos	
hubisteis	
hubieron	

 ¡PONTE A PUNTO!

1 Por qué Darren no aprobó sus exámenes

He aquí la triste historia de Darren, que tuvo grandes problemas con sus estudios y que
dejó el colegio sin aprobar sus exámenes. Empareja las dos partes de las frases siguientes
para hacer el mejor sentido: en cada frase la segunda parte contiene un verbo en
pluscuamperfecto que describe lo que ya había pasado para explicar la circunstancia de la
primera.

1	A Darren le faltaba autodisciplina	a	todos los otros la habían terminado ya.
2	Darren no venía mucho a clase	b	porque había estado ausente cuando la discutían en clase.
3	Darren hablaba y escribía mal el español	c	Darren ya había decidido no proseguir con sus estudios.
4	Cuando Darren empezó a leer *Bodas de sangre*	d	porque había decidido que era más divertido quedarse en la cama.
5	Cuando Darren decidió por fin asistir a clase con regularidad	e	porque se había negado a estudiar la gramática.
6	Darren no entendía bien la obra *Bodas de sangre*	f	porque sus padres le habían mimado demasiado de niño.
7	Básicamente Darren suspendió	g	su profesora ya se había hartado de él.
8	Cuando casi todos sus compañeros de clase fueron a la universidad	h	porque no había estudiado lo suficiente.

2 La capital más céntrica del mundo

Pon cada infinitivo en el tiempo compuesto que le corresponda.

Antes del reinado de Felipe II en el siglo XVI, Madrid (ser) un pueblo de poca importancia. Antes de su reinado los reyes de España (tener) sus cortes en varias ciudades del país. Cristóbal Colón, por ejemplo, (ir) a Barcelona para consultarse con la reina Isabel. Es de suponer que a Colón esto no le (gustar) nada, puesto que (tener) que dejar todo su equipo en el suroeste de España. Pero (ser) necesario cumplir con la voluntad real.

Ya durante los siglos siguientes, Madrid (aumentar) bastante su tamaño, y se (hacer) una ciudad importante. Pero ¿cómo (poder) decidir Felipe II construir una ciudad capital en un terreno tan inclemente? Claro que la mayoría de las capitales del mundo se (construir) en un río importante, pero Madrid no. Efectivamente, el río Manzanares hasta tiempos muy recientes no (ser) más que un cauce seco durante lo más del año y nunca (pasar) por el centro como en otras capitales.

3 Mamá se preocupa

Johnny va a visitar a su tía en Méjico. Traduce las preocupaciones de su madre al español, empleando tiempos compuestos.

1 *I wonder if he has arrived yet?*
2 *I wonder if the plane was on time?*
3 *I wonder if he packed his socks?*
4 *Will he have been airsick?*
5 *Will the plane have been diverted if it's foggy?*
6 *I wonder if my sister was there to meet him?*
7 *Will he have remembered to give her the present?*
8 *I wonder if he has taken enough money?*
9 *Would it have been better to have taken traveller's cheques?*
10 *I wonder what he will have said to his aunt?*

¡… Y EN MARCHA!

4 ¿Te acuerdas … ?

Estás ayudando a un víctima de un accidente a acordarse de lo que había hecho antes del accidente. Trabajando en parejas, uno/a hace las preguntas, el/la otro/a contesta.

Ejemplo:

– *¿A qué hora habías salido de casa?*
– *Había salido sobre las seis.*

Sigue haciendo preguntas sobre lo que había hecho: *¿Qué? ¿Quién? ¿Con quién? ¿Cómo? ¿Por qué? ¿Cuándo? ¿Dónde? ¿De dónde?*

5 ¿Qué había pasado?

Recientemente hiciste un día de senderismo con tus amigos en las montañas de la costa norte española. Durante vuestro paseo, confrontasteis varias eventualidades: cada uno tiene que sugerir en pluscuamperfecto lo que había pasado para causarlas o por qué no hubo problema:

- teníais que pagar para aparcar vuestro microbús
- la telecabina no funcionaba
- los arroyos de montaña corrían muy rápidamente
- uno de los refugios de montaña estaba cerrado con llave
- un sendero que atravesaba los acantilados a orillas del mar estaba bloqueado
- encontrasteis unas ovejas muertas
- cayó una niebla espesa durante una hora pero no estabais en peligro
- al volver al microbús, éste no arrancaba

Ejemplo:

No visteis ciertos pájaros: ya habían emigrado hacia África; seguro los había, pero habíamos dejado los gemelos en casa; como hacía calor no habían salido para buscar comida; etc.

¡Seguid inventando más circunstancias y más explicaciones!

6 Conjeturas

Tu mejor amigo/a y su familia se han ido de vacaciones a dar la vuelta al mundo. Tú y tus compañeros estáis celosos. Estáis conjeturando lo que habrán hecho hasta ahora.

Ejemplo:

Habrán visitado la Gran Barrera Coralina en Australia.

¿Qué otras cosas habrán hecho?

7 Más conjeturas

¿Qué habrías hecho tú si tú hubieras dado la vuelta al mundo?

25 Modal auxiliaries: 'must', 'ought', 'should', 'can', 'could'

 **MECANISMOS**

25.1 'Must'

The idea of 'having to' or 'must' can be conveyed by a number of expressions in Spanish:

a) ***Tener que*** + infinitive:

> ***Tenemos que comer*** *para vivir.*
> **We have to/must eat** in order to live.

b) ***Deber*** + infinitive:

> ***Debes ir*** *en seguida.*
> **You have to/must/should go** immediately.

Tener que and ***deber*** are often interchangeable, although ***tener que*** tends to imply that circumstances oblige you to do something, whereas ***deber*** can imply some sort of moral obligation (remember that as a noun ***el deber*** means 'duty'). This difference becomes more evident in the negative:

- ***no debes hacerlo*** you mustn't do it (i.e. it's not allowed or it would be wrong)
- ***no tienes que hacerlo*** can also mean 'you mustn't do it', but is as likely to mean 'you don't have to do it' (i.e. no obligation).

c) ***Haber de*** expresses 'have to' in the sense of 'to be to':

> *¿Qué* ***hemos de*** *hacer?*
> What **are we to** do?

> ***Has de venir*** *a las doce.*
> **You must come/You are to come** at twelve o'clock.

This verb is more commonly used in Latin America than in Spain.

d) ***Hay que*** is impersonal, i.e. it is always third person singular, and is used where the emphasis is more on the action than the doer, or where the doer is obvious from the context:

> ***Hay que*** *terminar antes de las cinco.*
> **We/You/They must** finish before five.

The negative can mean both 'mustn't' and 'no need to':

No hay que *cruzar esta línea.*
You/We/One mustn't cross this line.

No hay que *terminar hoy.*
You don't have to/needn't finish today.

e) *Hace falta* is another 'impersonal' way of expressing obligation, and works very similarly to **hay que**:

Hace falta *terminar a las cinco.*
We/You must finish at five.

A personal obligation can be introduced by using an indirect object:

Me *hace falta terminar hoy.*
I have to finish today.

*¿***Te** *hace falta terminar hoy?*
Do **you** have to finish today?

A Martín le *hace falta terminar hoy.*
Martin has to finish today.

In the negative it tends to be used more in the sense of 'no need to':

No (te) hace falta *terminar hoy.*
You don't have to finish today.

You will find further information on how these indirect object ('back-to-front') verbs work in Chapter 26.

f) 'Must' with the idea of probability is expressed by **deber de** + infinitive.

Deben de *ser las once y media.*
It must be half past eleven.

Debe de *haber ido con José.*
She must have gone with José.

✎ Note that the **de** is often omitted.

➥ **Exercise 1**

25.2 'Ought', 'should'

Be careful with 'should': it can mean the same as 'would', but here we are concerned with it when it means the same as 'ought'.

Use the conditional of **deber**:

Deberías *ir a ver a un médico.*
You should go and see a doctor./**You ought to** go and see a doctor.

25.3 'Ought to have', 'should have'

a) The simplest way to say what you ought to have or should have done, referring to a circumstance some time in the past, is to use the imperfect of **deber** + the infinitive of **haber** + the past participle:

> **Debías haber venido** antes.
> **You ought to have/should have come** earlier. (But you didn't, so there's nothing that can be done about it now.)

b) If the circumstance is still applicable in the present, use the conditional or the **-ra** imperfect subjunctive of **deber** + the infinitive of **haber** + past participle:

> **Deberías/Debieras haber contestado** a la carta.
> **You ought to have answered** the letter. (i.e. you have not yet done it, but still could)

c) An alternative way of expressing these examples is to use **habrías/hubieras debido** + infinitive:

> **Habrías/Hubieras debido venir** antes.
> **You ought to have come** earlier.

> **Habrías/Hubieras debido contestar** a la carta.
> **You ought to have answered** the letter.

➤ **Exercise 2**

25.4 'Can'

'Can' or 'to be able to' is usually **poder**, and indicates the physical or circumstantial ability to do something:

> **No puedo** abrir esta botella. ¿**Puedes** ayudarme?
> **I can't** open this bottle. **Can you** help me?

Two points to watch, however:

- When an acquired skill or 'know-how' is involved, you use **saber**:

> **Sé** conducir, pero **no puedo** practicar porque no tengo coche.
> **I can** (= know how to) drive, but **I can't** practise because I don't have a car. (i.e. circumstances don't allow it)

- With verbs of perception, especially **ver** and **oír**, **poder** is often not used:

> ¿**Oyes** truenos? No, **no oigo** nada. ¡Tampoco **veo** relámpagos!/¡**No veo** relámpagos tampoco!
> **Can you hear** thunder? No, **I can't hear** anything. Neither **can I see** any lightning!/ **I can't see** any lightning either!

25.5 'Could'

'Could' may be the conditional or the past tense of 'can'. To find out, convert it into terms of 'to be able to', and then use the appropriate Spanish tense:

a) 'You couldn't do that (even) if you tried' (= 'You wouldn't be able to do that [even] if you tried' i.e. conditional):

> **No podrías hacerlo** aunque trataras.

b) 'I tried to do it but I couldn't' (= 'I tried to do it but I wasn't able to', i.e. past tense, imperfect or preterite according to sense):

> Traté de hacerlo pero **no pude/podía**.

25.6 'Could have'

a) Use the imperfect of **poder** + the infinitive of **haber** + past participle to express what could have happened but didn't happen:

> **Podía haber venido** a vernos.
> **He could have (was able to) come** to see us (but didn't).

b) Use the conditional of **poder** or **-ra** imperfect subjunctive + the infinitive of **haber** + past participle to express the possibility of what could/might have happened:

> **Podrían/Pudieran haber visto** lo que hacíamos.
> **They could have seen (would have been able to see)** what we were doing. (This just states the possibility, without comment or implication.)

c) *Habrían/Hubieran podido ver* is also possible for 'They could have seen/would have been able to see'.

➡ **Exercises 3, 4, 5**

 **¡PONTE A PUNTO!**

1 Una compradora prudente

Expresa las frases siguientes en todas las maneras posibles según las explicaciones que acabas de leer, pero ¡cuidado! porque quizás no sea posible emplear todas las maneras en todos los casos.

Ejemplo:

Debo volver a casa.

Tengo que volver a casa; he de volver a casa; hay que volver a casa; me hace falta volver a casa.

1 Esta mañana, Carmen *tuvo que* ir de compras.
2 *Debía* comprar carne
3 pero *no le hacía falta* gastar demasiado dinero.
4 – Cuando vas de compras, – se decía – siempre *hay que* buscar los precios más bajos.
5 – También *debo* comprar cerveza – dijo para sí,
6 – pero *no tengo que* comprar demasiada porque mi marido la beberá toda.
7 Como no quedaba pescado en su pescadería preferida, Carmen pensó: – Pues, ¿qué *he de* hacer?
8 En efecto, no hubo remedio. Como sólo hay dos pescaderías *le hizo falta* ir a la otra.
9 Cuando volvió a casa, su marido le dijo: – Cariño, *no te hacía falta* comprar pescado, acabo de volver de la pesca ¡y cogí dos truchas grandes!
10 – ¡Estupendo! – respondió Carmen. – Entonces *habrá que* guardar el que compré yo en el congelador.

2 Deberes

Algunos de tus amigos tienen o han tenido problemas. Empareja una frase de la primera serie con otra de la segunda para indicar lo que deberían hacer o deberían haber hecho.

1 A Ana le duele la garganta desde hace varios días.
2 A Roberto le robaron el teléfono hace tres días.
3 Clara perdió el tren otra vez.
4 Alfonso se siente cansado después de jugar al fútbol.
5 La novia de Santi está enfadada y no quiere verle más.

a Entonces debía haber informado en seguida a la policía.
b Pues debería entrenarse con más frecuencia.
c Debería ir a ver al médico.
d Entonces no hubiera debido olvidar su cumpleaños.
e Pues debía haberse levantado más temprano.

3 Posibilidades e imposibilidades

Tus amigos siguen teniendo sus problemas. Descubre por qué, emparejando las dos series de frases.

1 Javier quiere comprar una nueva cámara digital.
2 Montse tenía miedo porque tuvo que volver sola a casa andando.
3 Después de salir con sus compañeras, Olga ya no tiene dinero.
4 Luis decidió no comprarle a su hermano un nuevo MP3 para su cumpleaños.
5 Cristina no fue a Barcelona en tren.

a Como tenía suficiente dinero podía haber ido en taxi.
b No pudo conseguir un billete.
c No hubiera podido ahorrar bastante dinero.
d Podía haber ahorrado unos euros para otro día.
e Podría buscarla en e-bay.

4 Obligaciones y probabilidades

Traduce las frases siguientes al español con la expresión más adecuada.

1 *He must have left by now.*
2 *We have to leave before ten o'clock.*
3 *You will have to be quick to catch that train.*
4 *That must have been quite a problem for you.*
5 *The Spanish no longer have to do military service.*
6 *The England team must have had a bad day.*
7 *It must be raining. I can see people with umbrellas.*
8 *You will have to take your raincoat.*
9 *One really must learn to respect the law.*
10 *It must have been quite a difficult exercise!*

5 Oportunidades perdidas

Una madre inglesa se queja de su hijo a una madre española. Tienes que explicarle a la madre española lo que dice la inglesa.

1 *He could have studied more.*
2 *He shouldn't have worked so much at the supermarket.*
3 *He could have worked on Saturdays only.*
4 *He could have got up earlier.*
5 *He shouldn't have spent so much time with that girl.*
6 *He ought to realise that he needs to pass his exams.*
7 *He could take the exams again next year, of course.*
8 *He could pass in Spanish if he tried.*
9 *He tried to study French but he couldn't do it.*
10 *I should have been more sympathetic, but I tried and couldn't.*

¡... Y EN MARCHA!

6 ¡Fuego!

> **Incendio en un piso sevillano**
> Ayer una familia sevillana por poco muere carbonizada. Se escaparon todos de su piso al momento mismo que éste se convirtió en una bola de llamas. Parece que un vecino había visto pocos minutos antes cables eléctricos con el metal expuesto, ropa secándose junto a la estufa eléctrica, una sartén de aceite hirviendo sobre la cocina, un montón de papeles encima del televisor, una colilla de cigarrillo humeando en la alfombra, y ni un solo detector de humo. ¡Todo un incendio esperando su momento para estallar!

Discute con tus compañeros/as cómo los dueños del piso sevillano podían haber evitado el incendio. ¿Qué podían haber hecho?

¿Cuáles son las medidas que se deberían tomar para evitar la posibilidad de incendio?

7 En el cole

No estás contento/a de la organización en tu colegio. ¿Qué deberían hacer las autoridades para que sea un sitio más agradable? Y los estudiantes, ¿cómo podríais vosotros ayudar en este propósito?

¿Estás contento/a de la manera en que se organiza la enseñanza en general en tu país? A tu modo de ver, ¿qué cambios debería hacer el gobierno? ¿Hay cambios que debía haber hecho hace mucho tiempo?

8 Medio ambiente

Toma un aspecto del medio ambiente que te interese y considera las medidas que se podrían o se deberían tomar para su conservación. Por ejemplo, si te preocupa el tema de la capa del ozono, considera lo que ha ocasionado la situación actual y explica lo que no debíamos haber hecho para causarla. Luego sugiere lo que podríamos o deberíamos hacer para mejorar la situación.

Ejemplo:

No debíamos haber usado tantos aerosoles. Deberíamos limitar el uso de los coches.

26 *Gustar* and other 'back-to-front' verbs

 MECANISMOS

A number of verbs, such as ***gustar***, work 'back to front' when compared with their English equivalents:

> ***Me gusta*** *mucho el chocolate.*
> **I like** chocolate a lot.

26.1 *Gustar*

a) In practice, the English object is the Spanish subject, and therefore if you like something plural, the verb is plural in Spanish.

> *Me gusta**n** **los** chocolate**s**.*
> I like chocolates. (Chocolates please me.)

As this concept seems to cause problems for English speakers, study the following table carefully.

(A mí) ***me*** *gusta* ***el cine****.*	I like the cinema.
(A mí) ***me*** *gusta**n*** ***las películas****.*	I like films.
(A ti) ***te*** *gusta el cine.*	You like ...
(A ti) ***te*** *gustan las películas.*	
(A él) ***le*** *gusta el cine.*	He likes ...
(A él) ***le*** *gustan las películas.*	
(A ella) ***le*** *gusta el cine.*	She likes ...
(A ella) ***le*** *gustan las películas.*	
A mi novio/a ***le*** *gusta el cine.*	My boy/girlfriend likes ...
A mi novio/a ***le*** *gustan las películas.*	
(A usted) ***le*** *gusta el cine.*	You like ...
(A usted) ***le*** *gustan las películas.*	
(A nosotros) ***nos*** *gusta el cine.*	We like ...
(A nosotros) ***nos*** *gustan las películas.*	
(A vosotros) ***os*** *gusta el cine.*	You like ...
(A vosotros) ***os*** *gustan las películas.*	
(A ellos/ellas) ***les*** *gusta el cine.*	They like ...
(A ellos/ellas) ***les*** *gustan las películas.*	
A mis amigos ***les*** *gusta el cine.*	My friends like ...
A mis amigos ***les*** *gustan las películas.*	
(A ustedes) ***les*** *gusta el cine.*	You like ...
(A ustedes) ***les*** *gustan las películas.*	

b) The *a mí, a ti* … in brackets is often put in for emphasis. Remember that the English subject is the indirect object in Spanish, and this is why there is no differentiation between masculine and feminine:

Le gusta = He/She likes

So where there is a noun subject in English (My friends like …), this is expressed as the indirect object in Spanish, preceded by *a*:

A mis amigos les gusta …

c) When you want to say you like doing something, use the infinitive:

> *¿Te gusta **bailar**?*
> Do you like **dancing**?

Don't forget that this verb is almost always used only in the third person, in all tenses:

> *¿**No te gustó** la película, verdad?*
> **You didn't like** the film, did you?

> *¿Qué **te gustaría** hacer ahora?*
> What **would you like** to do now?

➡️ **Exercise 1**

26.2 Other similar verbs

The following are other Spanish verbs which work in a similar way.

Use:

encantar to express what you love or adore:

> ***Me encanta** la música.*
> **I love** music.

interesar to say what you're interested in:

> ***No nos interesa** el teatro.*
> **We're not interested** in the theatre.

emocionar to say what you're thrilled by:

> *A mi hermana **le emocionan** las películas de miedo.*
> **My sister is thrilled** by horror films.

entusiasmar to say what you're keen on:

> *A nuestra profesora **le entusiasman** los viejos coches.*
> **Our teacher is very keen** on old cars.

apetecer to say what you fancy:

> ¿*Te apetece* tomar algo?
> **Do you fancy** a drink?

quedar to say what's left:

> *A Enrique le quedaba* muy poco dinero.
> **Henry had** very little money **left**.

faltar to say what's missing or lacking:

> *A la casa le faltaban* todos los cristales.
> **The house was missing/lacked** all its window panes.

sobrar to say what's too much or over:

> *Nos sobra* tiempo.
> **We've got plenty** of time. (more than enough time)

doler to say what hurts or aches:

> *Me duelen* las muelas.
> **I've got** tooth**ache**.

hacer falta to say what you need:

> *A Miguel le hacía falta* más tiempo.
> **Michael needed** more time.

 Note: don't confuse this with *faltar*, above, and see also Chapter 25 for the use of *hacer falta* meaning 'must/have to'.

➡ **Exercises 2, 3**

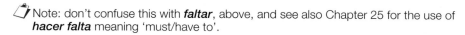 **¡PONTE A PUNTO!**

1 Gustos

Rellena los espacios en blanco en las frases siguientes con una palabra o frase de las que aparecen en la caja.

gustan	a usted	a mis padres	nosotros	le	vivir	les
gustaría	os	a ti				

1   A ... nos gusta mucho el cine español.
2   Y a tus compañeros, ¿qué tipo de película ... gusta más?
3   A tu hermana, ¿qué ... gusta hacer en sus ratos libres?
4   Y ..., ¿te gusta también hacer eso?
5   A mí no me ... las clases de historia.
6   A Chus le ... jugar al baloncesto esta tarde si puede.
7   Estoy seguro que a vosotros ... gustaría jugar con él.
8   Señora Smith, ¿... le gusta enseñar el español?
9   ... les gusta mucho la comida española, sobre todo la paella.
10 En efecto, ¡les gustaría mucho ... en España!

2 El pasado y el futuro de mi educación

Rellena los espacios en blanco con un verbo de los siguientes.

me apetecería	me dolería	me interesa	me sobran	me faltan
me gustaría	me encantan	me interesan	me gustaban	me queda

Cuando tenía 14 años, no . . **1** . . nada las matemáticas. A los 16 años tuve que decidir qué asignaturas . . **2** . . seguir estudiando. Escogí el español entre otras porque . . **3** . . las lenguas. Ahora . . **4** . . entrar en la universidad. El problema es que todavía . . **5** . . los títulos necesarios. El otro problema es que . . **6** . . poco tiempo para conseguirlas. . . **7** . . los consejos de mis amigos y familiares, pero no . . **8** . . algunos de los cursos que ofrecen las universidades. No . . **9** . . seguir un curso que encontrara aburrido, pues . . **10** . . la cabeza.

3 ¡Estas expresiones idiomáticas!

Explica a un(a) amigo/a español(a) cómo se dicen las expresiones siguientes en español.

1   *Mike doesn't like Coca-Cola.*
2   *Peter didn't like the film.*
3   *Sandra loves playing tennis.*
4   *Andrew isn't interested in working here.*
5   *Our children fancy going to Spain this year.*
6   *My father isn't keen on gardening.*
7   *Barbara was thrilled by that book.*
8   *There are no more copies left.*
9   *Grandma has more than enough money.*
10 *That car had two wheels missing.*
11 *Maria's legs hurt.*
12 *Dad needed a new suit.*

 # ¡... Y EN MARCHA!

4 La comida

Con tus compañeros/as piensa en varios platos británicos, españoles y de otras nacionalidades, y di hasta qué punto te gustan, empleando:
no me gusta(n) (nada); no me gusta(n) mucho; me gusta(n) mucho/muchísimo/bastante/ un poco; me encanta(n)

Ejemplo:

Me gustan muchísimo las alubias en salsa de tomate.

Haz una encuesta de los gustos de tus compañeros/as seguida por un reportaje oral o escrito.

Ejemplo:

A Daniel le gustan las zanahorias pero las patatas no.
A Linda le encantan las ensaladas pero no le apetece comer carne.

5 Actividades preferidas

Otra encuesta. Pregunta a cada uno/a de tus compañeros/as y a tu profesor(a) cuáles son las tres actividades de ocio que más les gustan. Luego haz un reportaje sobre lo que te han dicho.

Ejemplo:

En sus ratos libres a mi profesor(a) de español le gusta ir a la piscina, hacer bricolaje y viajar por España.

6 El fin de semana

Es viernes por la tarde. Usando varios verbos impersonales, haz preguntas a tus compañeros/as de clase sobre sus proyectos para el fin de semana.

Ejemplo:

–¿Te apetece ir a la discoteca esta noche?
– Sí, me apetece./No, no me apetece.
– ¿Te interesa ver el fútbol mañana por la tarde? ...

7 Hacen falta explicaciones

Un(a) estudiante debe hacer una observación cualquiera, y los otros tienen que ofrecer comentarios utilizando los verbos que se han explicado en este capítulo. Trata de usarlos en una variedad de tiempos.

Ejemplos:

– Marisa no compró nada en las tiendas ...
        ... porque le faltaba/no le quedaba dinero/tiempo.
        ... porque no vio nada que le gustara/interesara/apeteciera.
        ... porque le dolían los pies y volvió temprano a casa.

– Javi fue al cine anoche ...
        ... porque le apetecía ver la nueva película de Almodóvar.
        ... porque le emocionan/entusiasman/gustan/encantan las películas de
        aventuras.
        ... porque le hacía falta/apetecía salir a algún sitio con su novia.

27 Prepositions and the infinitive

 MECANISMOS

27.1 Infinitives

A large number of verbs can be followed by another verb in the infinitive form. In some cases the verb links directly to a following infinitive, and others take **a** or **de**, or more unusually, other prepositions.

The lists which follow give the most common verbs. For a fuller list, consult a more detailed grammar book*.

a) The following verbs are followed directly by an infinitive with no intervening preposition:

aconsejar	to advise
acordar	to agree to
amenazar	to threaten to
anhelar	to long to
confesar	to confess to
conseguir	to succeed in
creer	to believe
deber	to have to/must/ought
decidir	to decide to
dejar	to let/allow
desear	to want/wish to
esperar	to hope/expect/wait
evitar	to avoid ...-ing
fingir	to pretend to
hacer	to make
imaginar	to imagine ...-ing
intentar	to try to
jurar	to swear to
lograr	to manage to/succeed in
mandar	to order to
necesitar	to need to
negar	to deny
ofrecer	to offer to
oír	to hear ...-ing
olvidar	to forget to
ordenar	to order to
parecer	to seem to

---

*For example: *A new reference grammar of modern Spanish* 4th edition by John Butt and Carmen Benjamin (Hodder & Stoughton)

pedir	to ask to
pensar	to plan to/intend to
permitir	to allow to
poder	to be able to
preferir	to prefer to
pretender	to try to
procurar	to try hard to
prohibir	to forbid ... to
prometer	to promise to
querer	to want to
recordar	to remember to
rehusar	to refuse to
resolver	to resolve to
saber	to know how to
sentir	to be sorry to
soler	to be accustomed to
temer	to fear to
ver	to see ... -ing

*Deseo **hablar** con mi novia.*
I wish **to speak** to my girlfriend.

*Queremos **aprender** a volar.*
We want **to learn** to fly.

*No sé **nadar**.*
I can't (don't know how to) **swim**.

b) The following verbs are followed by **a** + an infinitive:

acertar a	to manage to
acostumbrar a	to be accustomed to
alcanzar a	to manage to
animar a	to encourage to
aprender a	to learn to
atreverse a	to dare to
ayudar a	to help to
comenzar a	to begin to
comprometerse a	to undertake to
conducir a	to lead to
contribuir a	to contribute to
convidar a	to invite to
decidirse a	to decide to/make up one's mind to
dedicarse a	to devote oneself to
desafiar a	to challenge to
disponerse a	to get ready to
echarse a } *empezar a*	to begin to
enseñar a	to teach to

147

forzar a	to force to
impulsar a	to urge to
incitar a	to incite to
inclinar a	to incline to
invitar a	to invite to
ir a	to be going to
limitarse a	to limit oneself to
llegar a	to end up (-ing)
llevar a	to lead to
mandar a	to send to
meterse a	to begin to
negarse a	to refuse to
obligar a	to oblige to
pasar a	to go on to
persuadir a	to persuade to
ponerse a	to begin to/set about (-ing)
precipitarse a	to rush to
prepararse a	to get ready to
resignarse a	to resign oneself to
tender a	to tend to
volver a	to (do something) again

*Aprendo **a volar**.*
I'm learning **to fly**.

*Se echó **a correr**.*
He began **to run**.

*Volvemos **a estudiar**.*
We're **studying** again.

c) The following verbs are followed by ***de*** + the infinitive.

acabar de	to have just
acordarse de	to remember
acusar de	to accuse of
alegrarse de	to be pleased to
avergonzarse de	to be ashamed to
cansarse de	to tire of
cesar de	to stop (-ing)
cuidar de	to take care to
*deber de	to have to/must (supposition)
dejar de	to stop (-ing)
disuadir de	to dissuade from
encargarse de	to take charge of
guardarse de	to take care not to
*haber de	to have to
hartarse de	to be fed up with

jactarse de	to boast of
olvidarse de	to forget to
parar de	to stop (-ing)
pasar de	to be uninterested in (-ing)
pensar de	to think about
presumir de	to boast about (-ing)
terminar de	to stop (-ing)
tratar de	to try to

* see Chapter 25

*Acaba **de llegar**.*
He/She **has** just **arrived**.

*No dejan **de hablar**.*
They never stop **talking**.

*Trataba **de conducir**.*
He/She was trying **to drive**.

d) The following take other prepositions (***en**, **por**, **con***) before a following infinitive:

consentir en	to consent to
consistir en	to consist of
convenir en	to agree to
dudar en	to hesitate to
hacer bien en	to be right to
hacer mal en	to be wrong to
insistir en	to insist on
interesarse en	to be interested in
pensar en	to think of (-ing)
persistir en	to persist in
quedar en	to agree to
tardar en	to take a long time (-ing)
esforzarse por	to struggle to
estar por	to be in favour of
luchar por	to struggle for
optar por	to opt for
amenazar con	to threaten to

*Papá insiste **en quedarse** en casa.*
Dad insists on **staying** at home.

*Pienso **en vender** la casa.*
I'm thinking of **selling** the house.

*Estamos **por ir** en tren.*
We favour **going** by train.

e) Note two very commonly used verbs which take *que* + infinitive:

tener que to have to
hay que it is necessary to

> *Tengo que **estudiar** mucho.*
> I have to **study** a lot.

> *Para hacer una tortilla, ¡hay que **romper** huevos!*
> To make an omelette, you have to **break** eggs!

➡ **Exercises 1, 2**

27.2 Infinitive or finite verb?

The infinitive is also used after several subordinating prepositions: *al*, *hasta*, *para*, *por*, *sin*, *antes de*, *después de*. However, these can only be followed by an infinitive if there is no change of subject, otherwise the appropriate form of finite verb must be used.

> *Seguiré trabajando **hasta terminarlo**.*
> **I** shall work until **I** finish it.

But

> *Seguiré mirándole **hasta que termine**.*
> **I** shall watch him until **he** finishes.

> *Hice esto **para ayudarte**.*
> **I** did this to help you. (**I** did it, **I** helped)

But

> *Te llamé **para que me ayudases**.*
> **I** called **you** to help me. (so that **you** would help me)

> *Lo hizo **sin querer**.*
> **He** did it without meaning to. (**he** did it, **he** didn't mean to)

But

> *Lo hizo **sin que yo lo quisiera**.*
> **He** did it without **my** wanting him to.

> *Vamos a visitarla **antes de regresar**.*
> Let's visit her before going home. (**we** visit, **we** go home)

But

> *Vamos a visitarla **antes de que se vaya**.*
> Let**'s** visit her before **she** goes. (**we** visit, **she** goes)

Exercise 3

(See also Chapter 35 on the subjunctive of futurity.)

¡PONTE A PUNTO!

1 Las vacaciones

En las siguientes frases se usan algunos de los verbos que figuran en las listas. Tienes que poner *a, de, en, por*, etcétera – si hace falta.

1   El año pasado, mi padre decidió … pasar las vacaciones en España.
2   Empezó … informarse sobre el viaje, los hoteles y las playas.
3   Mi madre prefirió … ir en coche, y no en avión.
4   Los dos se dedicaron … finalizar los detalles.
5   Por fin nos preparamos … ponernos en camino.
6   No pudimos … coger el ferry desde Plymouth, a causa de un incendio a bordo de uno de los buques.
7   Pero al fin llegamos a Francia y tratamos … encontrar una pensión.
8   Al día siguiente logramos … viajar casi ochocientos kilómetros.
9   Al llegar a nuestro hotel en España, comenzamos … broncearnos y a pasarlo bien.
10 Después de dos semanas de divertirnos, nos dispusimos … volver a casa.

2 Los exámenes

Rellena los espacios en blanco con el verbo que mejor convenga de la lista que se da abajo; no olvides poner *a, de*, etcétera – si hace falta – entre el verbo y el infinitivo.

Hace un año ya, . . **1** . . hacer los exámenes de GCSE. Después de varios años de estudio, por fin . . **2** . . poner a prueba todo lo que sabía. Durante las últimas semanas, . . **3** . . repasar todas mis asignaturas, y sólo . . **4** . . estudiar para comer y beber. El hecho es que . . **5** . . sacar notas bastante buenas, pues . . **6** . . seguir estudiando en el Sixth Form, porque . . **7** . . hacerme médico. Había . . **8** . . evitar todos los quehaceres de casa, lo que les enfadó a mis padres, pero había . . **9** . . dedicarme totalmente a mis estudios.

Por fin llegaron los exámenes, y . . **10** . . hacer lo mejor que podía. Todos los días . . **11** . . estudiar durante dos o tres horas por la tarde, y a acostarme temprano.

Después de los exámenes, . . **12** . . esperar los resultados.

Afortunadamente, . . **13** . . sacar buenas notas. En efecto, me . . **14** . . entrar en el Sixth Form, y mis padres me . . **15** . . seguir estudiando. Mis profesores me . . **16** . . estudiar cuatro asignaturas, pero yo . . **17** . . estudiar tres solamente. Al fin . . **18** . . estudiar cuatro, pero mis padres me . . **19** . . seguir trabajando en el café donde trabajé durante el verano.

¡Otra vez . . **20** . . estudiar!

aconsejar	dejar	esforzarse	necesitar	querer	comprometerse		desear
esperar	optar	resignarse	decidir	disponerse	invitar	persuadir	
resolver	dedicarse	disuadir	lograr	prepararse	tener		

3 Sustituciones

Escribe una nueva versión de las siguientes frases, sustituyendo una de las expresiones que se explican en la sección 27.2: *al, hasta, para, por, sin, antes de, después de.*

1   Cuando llegué a casa, preparé la cena.
2   Veré el partido, pero dejaré de hacerlo cuando vea el primer gol.
3   Compré este regalo; voy a dárselo a mi novia.
4   Volví a casa inmediatamente porque perdí la cartera.
5   Llegué al cole, pero no vi a mi amigo.
6   Vamos a pararnos a tomar algo de beber; luego iremos a casa.
7   Iremos al cine, y luego iremos al restaurante.

 # ¡... Y EN MARCHA!

4 Intenciones y razones

a) Habrás notado que muchos de los verbos de las listas expresan deseos, obligaciones e intenciones, y que otros expresan razones o explicaciones. Cuéntales tus intenciones a tus amigos/as. Te preguntarán por qué vas a/quieres/tienes que hacerlo. Contesta a esta pregunta, dando una razón empleando otro de los verbos que se mencionan en este capítulo.

Ejemplo:

– Mañana espero ir a Ayacucho.
– ¿Por qué?
– Pues, prometí visitar a mi amiga.

b) Escribe una serie de frases de este tipo, expresando tus intenciones y dando las razones.

Ejemplo:

Necesito comprar un regalo para mi novia para ayudarla a olvidar lo que ocurrió ayer.

c) Escribe 100 palabras sobre tus ambiciones para el futuro, usando uno de estos verbos en cada frase. Una cosa: ¡no debes usar el mismo verbo más de una vez!

5 Huevos y tortillas

A lo mejor, habrás oído alguna vez el siguiente refrán:

'No se puede hacer una tortilla sin romper huevos.'

Trata de inventar otros refranes nuevos del mismo estilo. También podrías sugerir posibles temas a tus compañeros/as: a ver si saben inventar un nuevo refrán. Algunos serán quizá un poco controvertidos, otros podrían tener un tema ecológico.

Ejemplo:

No se puede comer carne sin matar a un animal.
No se puede hacer papel sin cortar un árbol.
No se puede construir un coche sin producir residuos tóxicos.

Si quieres, puedes escribir 50 palabras sobre este tema, empleando unas cuantas frases con la misma estructura.

6 El sabueso y el sospechoso

Un día, al llegar a casa, encuentras a un detective que te espera en el umbral de tu puerta. Al parecer, ha habido une serie de asesinatos y atracos en tu pueblo y ¡te sospechan a ti! Un(a) compañero/a de clase será el detective: te hará una serie de preguntas sobre lo que has hecho durante el día. Tienes que contestar como mejor puedas. Los dos tenéis que usar las siguientes estructuras: *antes de* + infinitivo, *después de* + infinitivo, *sin* + infinitivo.

Ejemplo:

– ¿Qué hizo usted esta mañana después de salir de casa?
– Pues, fui al colegio y llegué a las nueve.
– ¿Qué hizo al llegar?
– Fui a la clase de inglés. Después de terminar esta clase, fui al patio de recreo a buscar a mis amigos.
– ¿Qué hizo antes de comer a mediodía?
– Fui a hablar con el director. Después de salir de su despacho, fui inmediatamente al comedor. Al entrar, vi el cadáver del cocinero ...

Una vez terminada la interrogación, tienes que escribir tu declaración. ¿Eres inocente, o no?

28 Participles and gerunds

There are two types of participle: the present participle, or 'gerund', and the past participle. These two types of verb form may seem to be similar, but they differ substantially in function and should not be confused.

28.1 Past participles

a) The past participle is used to form compound tenses such as the perfect and pluperfect tenses (see Chapters 23 and 24).

> He **perdido** mi cartera.
> I've **lost** my wallet.

> Dijo que había **perdido** su cartera.
> She said she had **lost** her wallet.

b) But the past participle can also be used as an adjective, following the normal rules of agreement.

> La cartera **perdida** es de cuero marrón.
> The **lost** wallet is made of brown leather.

> Oficina de objetos **perdidos**.
> **Lost** property office.

c) The past participle is often used after **estar** to describe the result of an action, including certain physical positions such as sitting, leaning, standing and lying, which do not take the gerund as in English.

> Mis padres **estaban sentados** en el salón.
> My parents **were sitting** in the lounge.

d) You will recognise past participles in many nouns, usually in the feminine form of a past participle, though many are masculine:

entrada	entrance
salida	exit, departure
llegadas	arrivals
un billete de ida y vuelta	return ticket (= a going and coming back ticket!)

154

There are some other more unexpected ones:

un helado	ice-cream (= a frozen!)
un batido de leche	a milk-shake
un puesto	a place, a stall (put up temporarily)

Past participles are also used to form the passive (see Chapter 31).

28.2 Present participles or 'gerunds'

Most Spanish grammar books refer to *el gerundio* as 'the gerund', rather than 'the present participle'. This is probably because it cannot be used as an adjective as in other languages ('running water', *'eau courante'*), and never changes its ending to agree with any other part of speech. To be consistent with other grammars you may use, we call it 'the gerund' throughout this book.

a) The gerund has a verbal/adverbial function meaning 'while ...' or 'by ... ing':

Viajando por la Mancha, vimos muchos molinos de viento.
While travelling through la Mancha, we saw lots of windmills.

Abriendo la ventana, se ve un panorama magnífico.
By opening the window you can see a magnificent view.

b) The gerund can also be used with the verb *estar* to form the present or imperfect continuous tense (see Chapter 20).

*Manuel **está trabajando** en la biblioteca.*
Manuel **is working** in the library.

c) A gerund cannot be used as an adjective, and so has no agreement with a noun, nor can it be used as a verbal noun. This means that it cannot be used for 'I like swimming', for example, when Spanish uses the infinitive instead: *me gusta nadar*. (See also Chapter 13.) Where an adjective is needed to convey the idea of '... ing', most Spanish verbs have a version ending in *-ante/-iente*, or *-ador(a)/-edor(a)/-idor(a)* based on the infinitive.

*agua **corriente***	**running** water
*un ruido **ensordecedor***	a **deafening** noise
But:	
*agua **hirviendo***	**boiling** water

The only way to find out whether a verb has one of these forms at all, and if so which one, is to look in a dictionary. Sometimes another type of adjective entirely may be needed to translate an adjective which ends in '... ing' in English.

Remember:

- The gerund is not used in Spanish to convey ideas such as 'sitting' and 'standing'; instead the past participle is used as described in section 28.1.
- The verbal noun function in Spanish is performed by the infinitive as in the following examples (see Chapter 26):

*Me gusta **nadar** … pero mi hermano no sabe **nadar** muy bien.*
I like **swimming** … but my brother can't **swim** very well.

Exercises 1–6

 ¡PONTE A PUNTO!

1 Dicho y hecho

Añade el participio pasado y el gerundio de los siguientes verbos (puedes consultar la lista de verbos al final de este libro).

Infinitivo	Participio pasado	Gerundio	Infinitivo	Participio pasado	Gerundio
decir	**dicho**	**diciendo**	descubrir		
hacer			regresar		
saber			componer		
salir			quemar		
reparar			oír		
ver			querer		
escribir			volver		
conocer			pensar		
mantener			dormir		
romper			ir		

2 Mientras tanto …

Sustituye la frase subrayada con un gerundio apropiado como en el ejemplo.

Ejemplo:

Mientras pasábamos por Castilla la Mancha, vimos muchos molinos de viento.
Pasando por Castilla la Mancha, vimos muchos molinos de viento.

1   Mientras viajaba a España, leí una novela interesante.
2   Cuando jugaba al fútbol, me torcí el tobillo.
3   Mientras comía pescado, Luisa tragó un hueso.
4   Cuando besó a su amiguita, Pepe ruborizó.
5   Mirábamos la carrera cuando vimos un coche que chocó.
6   Mientras don Eduardo corría, tuvo un ataque cardíaco.
7   Durante la corrida, vi a un matador recibir una herida grave.
8   Mientras paseaban por el parque, los niños vieron una ardilla.
9   Al subir una cuesta, se averió el coche.
10 Mientras dormía, doña Gimena tuvo un sueño curioso.

3 Traducción

Traduce las siguientes frases al español, pero ten cuidado con las palabras que terminan con '-ing' en inglés.

Last summer, as we were feeling adventurous, my sister and I decided to go on a walking holiday in Wales. On our first day, after walking for about twenty kilometres, our legs were tired and we felt like sleeping for a week, so we set about looking for a youth hostel. Unfortunately we had forgotten to bring our youth hostel map, which I had left on the kitchen table at home! After another hour of walking we found a hostel by a river. When we went in, a young woman was booking a room, so we watched the river flowing by while waiting. After booking two rooms with running water, we went to the kitchen to prepare our supper, and then sat watching television before going to bed at ten o'clock, exhausted by our first day of walking, but convinced that we were going to enjoy the rest of our holiday exploring this part of Wales.

4 ¡Escoge bien!

Escoge el participio o gerundio para completar cada frase (ten cuidado con las concordancias necesarias).

1   La ventana está …   roto/rompiendo
2   He … a mi profesor en la calle.   viendo/visto
3   Están … en el comedor.   sentado/sentando
4   En nuestra habitación, había agua …   corriendo/corrido/corriente
5   El lago estaba …   helado/helando
6   Don Quijote quería ser un caballero …   andando/andante/andado
7   A mí me encantan los pescaditos …   frito/friendo
8   El alumno tenía varias asignaturas …   pendiendo/pendiente/pendido
9   Por favor, quiero una ida y … a Madrid.   volviendo/vuelta
10 Mamá acaba de comprar unos … de oro.   pendiendo/pendiente/pendido

5 Adán y Eva

Completa la lista con infinitivos, adjetivos o sustantivos adecuados. En algunos casos, no existe un adjetivo o sustantivo que corresponda con el infinitivo.

Infinitivo	Adjetivo	Sustantivo
	cubierto	
abrir		
freír		
		satisfacción
		vista
	cerrado	
volver		
parecer		
		permisión
	caído	
		puesta
	variado	

6 Menú del día

He aquí una lista de platos y bebidas, pero están un poco confundidos. Tienes que poner las palabras de la lista de la derecha en la posición correcta para que correspondan a las de la izquierda. Verás que se trata de participios pasados que se usan como adjetivos.

Ejemplo:	*café*		*cortado*
1	carne	a	asado
2	leche	b	tostado
3	tomate	c	fundido
4	patatas	d	desnatado
5	huevos	e	salado
6	pollo	f	picada
7	pan	g	frito
8	manzanas	h	hervida
9	filete	i	pasado por agua
10	bistec	j	fritas
11	huevo	k	escalfados
12	agua	l	empanado
13	queso	m	batida
14	nata	n	asadas
15	bacalao	o	estofado

¡... Y EN MARCHA!

7 ¿Cómo se hace?

Usando un gerundio adecuado, explica a tu compañero/a cómo se hacen las siguientes cosas. Luego inventa otros ejemplos.

Ejemplo:

ganar un partido de rugby

Se gana un partido de rugby usando mucha violencia.

1   construir una casa
2   ligar con un(a) chico/a
3   beber mucho sin emborracharte
4   hacer feliz a tu novio/a

8 ¿Qué han hecho y qué están haciendo?

Imaginando que sois agentes secretos, con tus amigos/as describid lo que han hecho y lo que están haciendo las personas que observáis.

Ejemplo:

A: *¿Qué han hecho estos científicos rusos?*
B: *Han inventado un proceso nuevo para cambiar el hierro en oro.*
A: *¿Y, qué están haciendo ahora?*
B: *Están inventando unos gemelos de rayos X.*

29 Imperatives

 **MECANISMOS**

29.1 Uses

The imperative or 'command form' of the verb is used to express direct orders. Each imperative form is based on the present tense of the verb. Because Spanish has four ways of saying 'you', there are four positive (DO!) and four negative (DON'T!) forms.

29.2 Formation

29.2.1 Positive familiar commands

a) The positive command for **tú** is almost the same as the present tense **tú** form of the verb – just take away the **-s**:

hablas —→ *habla*   *comes* —→ *come*   *subes* —→ *sube*

Irregular forms are as follows:

decir —→ *di*   *poner* —→ *pon*   *tener* —→ *ten*
hacer —→ *haz*   *salir* —→ *sal*   *venir* —→ *ven*
ir —→ *ve*   *ser* —→ *sé*

Compounds of these verbs follow the same patterns.

b) For the positive command in the **vosotros** form, take the infinitive of the verb and replace the **-r** with **-d**:

hablar —→ *hablad*   *comer* —→ *comed*   *subir* —→ *subid*

29.2.2 Positive formal commands

The positive command for **usted** and **ustedes** uses the appropriate form of the present subjunctive:

hablar —→ *hable (Vd)*   *comer* —→ *coma (Vd)*   *subir* —→ *suba (Vd)*
　　　　　 hablen (Vds)   　　　　　 *coman (Vds)*   　　　　　 *suban (Vds)*

As you can see, you just need to take the **usted** or **ustedes** form of the indicative and swap **a** for **e** or **e** for **a**.

➡ **Exercises 1, 2**

29.2.3 Negative commands

All negative commands use the present subjunctive as follows (see Chapter 32).

a) Familiar:

no hables	*no comas*	*no subas*
no habléis	*no comáis*	*no subáis*

b) Formal:

no hable (Vd)	*no coma (Vd)*	*no suba (Vd)*
no hablen (Vds)	*no coman (Vds)*	*no suban (Vds)*

As you can see, all **usted** and **ustedes** commands and all negative commands use the subjunctive; only the **tú** and **vosotros** positive commands have separate forms.

29.3 Object pronouns with imperatives

Object pronouns and reflexive pronouns are attached to the end of positive commands but precede negative commands as with other parts of the verb. Note that where they are attached to the end of positive commands, an accent is usually needed to keep the stress in the same place when it is now two syllables from the end.

Familiar sing.	*Familiar pl.*	*Formal sing.*	*Formal pl.*	
cómelo	comedlo	cómalo	cómanlo	*eat it*
háblame	habladme	hábleme	háblenme	*talk to me*
levántate	levantaos	levántese	levántense	*get up*
no lo comas	no lo comáis	no lo coma	no lo coman	*don't eat it*
no me hables	no me habléis	no me hable	no me hablen	*don't talk to me*
no te levantes	no os levantéis	no se levante	no se levanten	*don't get up*

Note:

- The **vosotros** command of a reflexive verb loses its **'d'** before the pronoun **-os**, with the one exception of **ir**: **idos** (go away).
- There is a tendency in spoken Spanish to use the infinitive instead of the **vosotros** command form, especially with **-ir** verbs, e.g. **¡Vestiros!** (Get dressed!)

29.4 Other ways of expressing commands

a) *Que* with the appropriate part of the present subjunctive can be used to express a command for any person, a kind of encouragement to do something.

> *¡Que te mejores pronto!*
> **Get well** soon.

> *¡Que saquéis todos buenas notas!*
> **Make sure you** all **get** good marks.

> *¡Que no nos vea mamá!*
> **Mum had better not see** us!

b) Infinitives are often used to express commands, especially on warnings, notices and in instructions, such as in recipes (see Chapter 13).

> *No asomarse por la ventanilla.*
> **Don't lean** out of the window.

> *Lavar y pelar las patatas.*
> **Wash** and **peel** the potatoes.

c) The command 'let's …' is expressed by using *vamos a* + the infinitive.

> *Vamos a ver lo que pasa.*
> **Let's see** what is going on.

Alternatively, you can use the 'we' form of the present subjunctive (see Chapter 37):

> *Paguemos y salgamos en seguida.*
> **Let's pay** and **leave** right now.

¡PONTE A PUNTO!

1 Tortilla española

He aquí unas instrucciones para hacer una tortilla española. Los verbos vienen en la forma del infinitivo.

Tomar medio kilo de patatas y cuatro huevos. Lavar y pelar las patatas y cortarlas en trozos. Cascar y batir los huevos en una fuente grande. Poner media taza de aceite en una sartén y calentar: añadir las patatas y freírlas un poco. Echar las patatas en la fuente y mezclarlas con los huevos; añadir un poco de sal y pimienta y mezclar bien. Poner un poco más de aceite en la sartén, y cuando esté caliente, añadir las patatas y los huevos. Freír bien y servir caliente o fría.

a) Cámbialos a la forma del imperativo de 'tú'.

b) Luego repítelo con la forma de 'usted'.

c) Ahora tienes que usar las instrucciones para explicar a unos amigos cómo se prepara una tortilla española. Tienes que cambiar los verbos a la forma plural del imperativo (*vosotros*).

2 Modo de empleo

Esta serie de frases describe lo que se tiene que hacer para utilizar varios productos – o sea el 'modo de empleo'. Cambia los verbos a la forma del imperativo para *usted*.

1   Conservar el producto en una nevera.
2   Mantener el producto bien frío.
3   No lavar esta prenda en agua caliente.
4   Servir la salsa con arroz o macarrones.
5   No dejar al sol.

3 ¿Lo hago o no?

Tu amigo, que es un poco estúpido, quiere saber qué tiene que hacer con los ingredientes del Ejercicio 1. Contesta a sus preguntas.

Ejemplos:

¿Tengo que romper las patatas?
– ¡No, no las rompas, pélalas!

¿Tengo que freír los huevos?
– Sí, fríelos, ¡pero bátelos primero!

1   ¿Tengo que lavar las patatas antes de pelarlas?
2   ¿Tengo que batir las patatas?
3   ¿Tengo que batir los huevos?
4   ¿Tengo que poner la botella de aceite en la sartén?
5   ¿Tengo que pelar los huevos?
6   ¿Tengo que cortar los huevos en trozos?
7   ¿Tengo que mezclar las patatas con los huevos batidos?
8   ¿Tengo que asar la tortilla?
9   ¿Tengo que servir la tortilla caliente o fría?

Ahora, cambia todas las formas al plural.

Ejemplos:

¿Tenemos que romper las patatas?
– ¡No, no las rompáis, peladlas!

¿Tenemos que freír los huevos?
– Sí, freídlos, ¡pero batidlos primero!

 ¡... Y EN MARCHA!

4 El atracador

Imagina que eres atracador, y que un(a) compañero/a de clase es tu primera víctima. Dile lo que quieres que haga, utilizando el imperativo. Puedes ser un atracador cortés, utilizando las formas del usted, o menos formal, utilizando las formas del tú.

Ejemplo:

¡Deme todo su dinero!/¡Dame todo tu dinero!
¡Enséñeme su reloj!/¡Enséñame tu reloj!
¡Quítese ese abrigo!/¡Quítate ese abrigo!

5 El nuevo empleado/La nueva empleada

Tú eres dueño/a de empresa, o jefe de un departamento. Tu compañero/a de clase es el/la nuevo/a empleado/a. Tienes que explicarle exactamente lo que tiene que hacer.

Ejemplo:

Camarera: Pon las mesas, prepara los menús, llena los jarros de agua fresca ...
Cartero: Pon las cartas en el orden de los números de las casas, ponlas en tu cartera, llévalas a las casas ...

Otras posibilidades: cocinero/a, labriego/a, dependiente, albañil, taxista, cobrador(a) de autobús, barrendero/a, recepcionista, azafata.

6 La visita

Tu amigo/a español(a) va a pasar las vacaciones en tu casa. Escríbele una carta, dándole una serie de instrucciones para ayudarle a organizar el viaje y a encontrar tu casa. Dile también lo que debería traer en cuanto a ropa y otras cosas que necesitará para las actividades y excursiones que vas a organizar para él/ella.

7 Gastronomía

Has inventado un plato nuevo, y acabas de servirlo por primera vez a unos amigos. Te piden la receta: explícasela usando el imperativo, especificando los ingredientes que hay que comprar, y el método de preparar la receta. He aquí unas sugerencias.

tortilla de pescado	uvas rellenas
paella londinense	sapo en el agujero
pastel de pastor	sopa de plátano
flan con rata	gazpacho inglés
bocadillos a la gitana	fabada australiana

Después, otros amigos te piden estas recetas por escrito. Escoge dos o tres de las más sabrosas para escribirlas.

8 Publicidad

Si tienes una revista o un periódico español, mira los anuncios. Verás que muchos de ellos contienen instrucciones o consejos en la forma imperativa. Imagina que trabajas para una compañía internacional de publicidad. Tienes que escribir la versión española de varios anuncios que se ven en la tele y en los periódicos ingleses. Trata de escoger los que usan la forma del imperativo.

Ejemplo:

¡Compra el nuevo detergente Dash, para tener menos trabajo y más limpieza! ¡Compra dos paquetes y te regalamos otro gratis! ¡Lava todas las prendas de la familia, por sucias que estén, con el nuevo detergente DASH!

30 *Ser* and *estar*

✖🔧 MECANISMOS

To be, or not to be? That is indeed the question! It may help you to understand why there are two verbs in Spanish for 'to be'. To understand which to use, it is useful to look back at Latin, the mother of languages such as Spanish, French and Italian.

- ***Ser*** comes from the Latin verb 'esse', which was used to refer to 'being' in the sense of existence, and gives us words like 'essence' and 'essential', describing what things are like **in essence**.
- ***Estar***, on the other hand, derives from the Latin verb 'stare', which meant 'to stand', 'being' in the sense of **position/place**, referring to temporary **states**, usually resulting from actions or events. This gives us words like 'stationary', 'static', 'station', 'state'.

There are cases where either can be used, sometimes with a difference in meaning, but in the majority of cases only one is correct. Therefore it is well worth knowing a few rules of thumb to enable you to decide which to use and where.

30.1 Uses of *ser*

Ser is used for the following purposes.

a) To describe **who** or **what** somebody or something is, such as the type of person, their job or profession and so on:

> *Alfonso **es** médico.*
> Alfonso **is** a doctor.

> *El señor de la foto **era** mi padre.*
> The man in the photo **was** my father.

> *Este libro **es** una novela francesa.*
> This book **is** a French novel.

b) To describe the natural, innate characteristics of a thing or person:

> ***Es** una chica muy feliz.*
> **She is** a very happy girl.

> *Mi anillo **es** de oro.*
> My ring **is** made of gold.

> *Estos señores **son** muy ricos.*
> These people **are** very rich.

> ***Soy** de Granada.*
> **I am** from Granada. (i.e. I am a native of …)

166

c) To tell the time:

> ***Es*** *la una.*
> **It is** one o'clock.

> ***Son*** *las cinco y media.*
> **It is** half past five.

> ***Eran*** *las diez y veinte.*
> **It was** twenty past ten.

d) To express possession:

> ***Es*** *mío.*
> **It is** mine.

> ***Son*** *de la profesora.*
> **They belong** to the teacher.

30.2 Uses of *estar*

Estar is used for all other aspects of 'to be'.

a) To refer to place or location, to say where somebody or something is:

> *Madrid* ***está*** *en el centro de España.*
> Madrid **is** in the centre of Spain.

> *El año pasado* ***estuvimos*** *un mes en España.*
> Last year **we were** in Spain for a month.

b) To refer to the (temporary) state or condition of somebody or something, usually expressed via an adjective or a past participle used as an adjective:

> ***Estaba*** *muy cansado cuando llegó.*
> **He was** very tired when he arrived.

> ***Estamos*** *tristes, después de oír las noticias.*
> **We are** sad, having heard the news.

c) To describe what is (or was) actually going on, forming the present continuous and other continuous tenses together with the gerund:

> ***Estoy*** *escribiendo.*
> **I am** writing.

> ***Estaban*** *leyendo cuando entró mi madre.*
> **They were** reading when my mother came in.

d) To describe a state resulting from an action, often by means of a past participle used as a sort of adjective.

(See also Chapter 31 for use of **estar** with a past participle.)

> *Mis amigos **estaban** sentados.*
> My friends **were** sitting down.

e) **Estar** is also used in the following expressions:

- To express prices:

> *¿A cuánto **está?***
> How much **is it**?

> ***Está** a tres euros.*
> **It's** three euros.

- To express dates:

> *¿A cuántos **estamos**?*
> What **is** the date?

> ***Estamos** a quince de octubre.*
> **It's** the fifteenth of October.

- In the expression **estar por** (to be in favour of/inclined to):

> ***Estoy por** ir al cine.*
> **I'm in favour of** going to the cinema.

- In the expression **estar para** (to be about to, in the mood for):

> ***Estaba para** salir.*
> **He was about to** go out.

30.3 Changes of meaning

a) Both *ser* and *estar* can be used in the passive voice (see Chapter 31).

b) Some adjectives have a different meaning depending on whether they are used with *ser* or *estar*.

ser aburrido/a	to be boring	*estar aburrido/a*	to be bored
ser listo/a	to be clever	*estar listo/a*	to be ready

c) In addition, when *estar* is used with an adjective normally used with *ser*, it tends to mean 'to appear' or 'to look'.

> *¡**Estás** muy guapa hoy!*
> **You look** lovely today!

> *¡Qué viejo **estás**!*
> **You do look** old!

30.4 Summary

To sum up:

- ***Ser*** is used to indicate what somebody/something is and its natural, basic, expected qualities.
- ***Estar*** is used to indicate where somebody/something is and states brought about by circumstances.
- If in doubt, ask yourself if there is a good case for ***estar***. If not, use ***ser***. This is not a foolproof rule, but it is usually helpful.

However, beware of apparent anomalies:

> ***Están** muertos.*
> **They are** dead.
> (This seems permanent but it's because they have *died*, i.e. brought about by circumstances.)

> ***Es** joven.*
> **He is** young.
> (He just **is** – it's a basic characteristic of his.)

But:

> *¡Qué joven **está**!*
> **Doesn't he look** young!/**Isn't he** young!
> (This is not an expected quality – it's a surprise that he looks so young.)

➡ **Exercises 1, 2**

¡PONTE A PUNTO!

1 Un pueblo curioso

He aquí la descripción de uno de los pueblos más viejos de Inglaterra. Tienes que rellenar los espacios en blanco con la forma más apropiada de los verbos *ser* y *estar*.

El pueblo de Totnes . . **1** . . situado en el sur del condado de Devon, que . . **2** . . una región turística muy popular en el suroeste de Inglaterra. . . **3** . . situado en la parte más alta del estuario del río Dart, y . . **4** . . por aquí por donde tienen que pasar las carreteras hacia las playas y pueblos de los South Hams, en el extremo sur de Devon. . . **5** . . un pueblo de unos doce mil habitantes y en el verano . . **6** . . lleno de turistas que llegan en tren, autocar o hasta en barco, haciendo excursión por el río Dart.

Lo que no sabe mucha gente . . **7** . . que Totnes . . **8** . . un pueblo muy histórico. . . **9** . . el segundo pueblo inglés en recibir la cédula real. En efecto, . . **10** . . su nombre también el que revela un poco de su historia: Totta's Ness, o sea la nariz de Totta; esto . . **11** . . el promontorio en el que el rey sajón de esta región, Totta, hizo construir un pequeño castillo. En el pueblo hay muchas casas y otros edificios muy antiguos. Hace varios años uno de estos monumentos, el arco de la Puerta del Este, . . **12** . . destruido por un incendio, en el que . . **13** . . quemados también varios edificios vecinos. Pero reconstruyeron este arco, y ya . . **14** . . terminado.

Totnes tiene otro aspecto muy curioso: . . **15** . . la capital de la sociedad alternativa de la región, o sea . . **16** . . lleno de hippies, y de otra gente que lleva un estilo de vida poco convencional. También hay allí muchos artistas, músicos y escritores, atraídos por el centro cultural de Dartington, que . . **17** . . situado al lado de Totnes. Aquí . . **18** . . el Colegio de Música y también el Colegio de Arte que ahora . . **19** . . cerrado.

2 El enigma de Hamlet o las Islas Británicas

Rellena el espacio en blanco en cada una de las frases siguientes con la forma correcta del verbo *ser* o del verbo *estar*.

El Reino Unido . . **1** . . un estado independiente. . . **2** . . compuesto de cuatro países: Inglaterra, Escocia, el País de Gales e Irlanda del Norte. Inglaterra . . **3** . . el más grande de estos países. Inglaterra, Escocia y Gales . . **4** . . situados en la isla de Gran Bretaña. Juntas, las islas de Gran Bretaña e Irlanda . . **5** . . las Islas Británicas. . . **6** . . invadidas por muchas razas – entre otras por los celtas, anglos, sajones, romanos, y normandos. Hace miles de años, Gran Bretaña . . **7** . . unida con Francia por un puente de tierra. Luego . . **8** . . creado el Canal de la Mancha cuando subió el nivel del mar. Ahora . . **9** . . construido el Túnel de la Mancha. Gran Bretaña ya no . . **10** . . isla.

¡... Y EN MARCHA!

3 Los desconocidos

El/La profesor(a) o un miembro de la clase tiene que preparar tarjetas con los nombres y algunos datos importantes de varios personajes famosos de hoy o de la historia. Preferiblemente estos constituirán parejas, por ejemplo Juan Carlos y Sofía, Felipe y Letizia, Antonio y Cleopatra. Se distribuye una tarjeta a cada miembro de la clase, y todos tienen que buscar su pareja dirigiendo preguntas a los demás, y usando sólo los verbos *ser* y *estar*.

Ejemplo:

¿Eres hombre o mujer?
¿Estás vivo/a o muerto/a?
¿Eres inglés/inglesa o español(a)?
¿Eres/Fuiste rey/reina/científico/a/explorador(a)?

No se permite usar la pregunta *'¿Quién eres?'* ni empezar con la pregunta *'¿Eres (+ nombre)?'*

4 Tu pueblo

Escribe o cuenta la historia de tu ciudad/pueblo/región, usando los verbos *ser* y *estar.* Si sabes bastantes detalles, podrías contrastar cómo es ahora y cómo era hace muchos años, dónde estaban ciertos edificios y dónde están ahora.

Ejemplo:

Mi pueblo es muy grande ahora, pero hace treinta años era muy pequeño. Antes era un pueblo industrial; ahora ya no lo es. Hace muchos años Correos estaba al lado de la iglesia; ahora está en el centro.

5 Tu familia

Escribe o cuenta la historia de tu familia: cómo es ahora, y cómo ha sido en el pasado. Trata de usar los verbos *ser* y *estar* cuando sea posible.

Ejemplo:

Mi familia es muy grande, pero mi abuelo era hijo único. Mi abuelo era muy alto, pero mis hermanos y yo somos muy bajos. Hasta hace cinco años la familia vivía en otro sitio, pero ahora está en ...

6 El dibujo misterioso

Cada miembro de la clase tiene que preparar – en secreto – un dibujo que contenga varios objetos predeterminados: digamos un comedor con una mesa, cuatro sillas, un aparador, etcétera. Luego, en parejas o todos juntos, tratáis de copiar el dibujo de un(a) compañero/a sin mirarlo, haciendo preguntas.

Ejemplo:

¿Dónde está la mesa? ¿Dónde están las sillas? ¿El aparador, está a la derecha o a la izquierda?

Luego podéis comparar las diferencias de los dos dibujos, haciendo como un juego de 'Antes y después'.

Ejemplo:

Antes el aparador estaba detrás de la mesa, ahora está delante, etcétera.

7 Descripciones

En voz alta describe varios objetos nombrados por tus compañeros/as. A ver si aciertas a reconocer las palabras que dicen. Igualmente, podrías escribir unas descripciones más detalladas.

Ejemplo:

Mi bolígrafo es de plástico, es rojo y es muy útil. Sirve para escribir apuntes, cartas, etcétera. Es un Parker.

8 Se busca ...

Al parecer, un amigo de tu familia es un criminal buscado por la policía. Después de varios años de llevar una vida respetable, o por lo menos así lo creían todos, la policía ha descubierto que es jefe de un grupo de gángsteres. El hombre se ha escapado, y tú tienes que dar a la policía una descripción escrita, con todos los detalles posibles, para ayudarles a coger al criminal.

MECANISMOS

31.1 The passive

a) A passive verb is one where the subject suffers or undergoes the action. In the sentence 'My friend sold the house', the verb is active because the subject (my friend) performed the action of selling the house, which is the direct object. However, we can turn the sentence round and say 'The house was sold by my friend'. The verb is now passive because the subject is now what underwent the action of selling, i.e. the house, and my friend becomes what is known as the 'agent', the person by whom the action was done.

Active	Passive
The government won the elections. *El gobierno ganó las elecciones.*	The elections **were won by** the government. *Las elecciones **fueron ganadas por** el gobierno.*
The authorities will fix the prices. *Las autoridades fijarán los precios.*	The prices **will be fixed by** the authorities. *Los precios **serán fijados por** las autoridades.*

You can see that the passive in English is made up of the relevant tense of 'to be' (is/was/will be) and the past participle of the verb denoting the action in question. You do exactly the same in Spanish, using the relevant tense of **ser** (not **estar**) plus the past participle, but remember that in Spanish you must also make the past participle agree with the subject (hence **ganadas** and **fijados** in the above examples).

b) It is not always necessary to express the agent by whom the action was done:

> *Por fin los documentos **fueron firmados**.*
> At last the documents **were signed**.

c) The passive is very common in English, but rather less so in Spanish, where alternative constructions are often used in its place (see section 31.3 below).

31.2 *Ser* and *estar* with the past participle

It is important to differentiate between **ser** and **estar** used with the past participle:

Ser indicates the action being done and **estar** the resultant state after the action has taken place.

> *Los documentos* **fueron** *firmados.* (i.e. someone signed them)
> *Los documentos* **estaban** *firmados.* (i.e. the signature was on them)
> The documents **were** signed.

> *La casa* **fue** *construida en una colina.* (i.e. someone built it there)
> *La casa* **estaba** *construida en una colina.* (i.e. that was its situation)
> The house **was** built on a hill.

➡ **Exercises 1, 2**

(See also Chapter 30 on **ser** and **estar**.)

31.3 Alternatives to the passive

The passive can be (and often is) avoided in Spanish as follows:

a) Make the sentence active:

> *La casa fue vendida por mi amigo.* ⟶ *Mi amigo vendió la casa.*
> The house was sold by my friend. ⟶ My friend sold the house.

Although the basic sense is the same, the emphasis is different (i.e. the emphasis on 'my friend' is lost).

b) Make the verb active, but keep the object first and reinforce it with an object pronoun:

> ***La casa la vendió*** *mi amigo.*

This keeps the emphasis as it would have been in the passive.

c) Make the verb reflexive:

Se vende *casa*
House **for sale**

But you cannot do this if you wish to use **por** + an agent. If you just want to say the house was sold, then the simplest way in Spanish is: **La casa se vendió.** 'The house was sold.' (you can't say who by).

La guerra **se declaró** *en 1939.*
War **was declared** in 1939.

Se servirá *la cena a las nueve.*
Supper **will be served** at nine.

If the subject is plural, the verb is also plural:

Las ventanas **se rompieron** *ayer.*
The windows **were broken** yesterday.

Note: **se** is often used in recipes:

Se ponen *el beicon y los huevos en una sartén.*
The bacon and eggs **are put** in a frying pan.

It is not usual to use this construction when the subject is a person. 'The recruit was killed' would not be **el recluta se mató**, as this would be suicide, so you use the impersonal (not the reflexive) **se**:

d) The impersonal **se** is used rather like the impersonal *'on'* in French:

Al recluta **se le mató/Se le mató** *al recluta.*
The recruit **was killed**.

A Roberto **se le vio** *en la calle.*
Robert **was seen** in the street.

Note the use of the personal **a** before **recluta** and **Roberto**.

This construction is very useful to get over phrases where the subject would have been the **indirect object** if the verb had been active.

Se nos *dijo …*
We were told …

Se me *dio …*
I was given …

A mi hermana se le *regaló un ordenador.*
My sister was given a computer.

The verb remains singular even if the English subject is plural:

A Roberto y Ana se les **vio** *en la calle.*
Robert and Anne were seen in the street.

e) The impersonal *se* can be used rather like 'one' in English:

> *No **se hace** esto.*
> **One doesn't do** that./That **isn't done**.

But if the verb is already reflexive, ***uno*** has to be used:

> *Estando de vacaciones, **uno se levanta** tarde.*
> While on holiday **one gets up** late.

f) The impersonal *se* can sometimes appear rather stilted nowadays, and yet another common way, especially in spoken Spanish, is to use the third person plural; so some of the above examples could be expressed as follows:

> *Al recluta **le mataron** con una bala.*
> The recruit **was killed** with a bullet.

> *A Roberto **le vieron** en la calle.*
> Roberto **was seen** in the street.

> *A mi hermana **le regalaron** un ordenador.*
> My sister **was given** a computer.

> ***Me lo dijeron** anoche.*
> I **was told** last night.

> ***Nos lo dijeron** anoche.*
> We **were told** last night.

 **Exercises 3, 4**

¡PONTE A PUNTO!

1 Problemas de carreteras

Pon el verbo en el tiempo de la pasiva que convenga al sentido.

Ejemplo:

Ayer la carretera (bloquear) ⟶ *Ayer la carretera fue bloqueada.*

Ayer cayó mucha nieve y la carretera Burgos–San Sebastián (cortar) en dos sitios. La carretera (despejar) por dos grandes quitanieves que (traer) desde Burgos. Mientras tanto los chóferes de los coches y camiones atascados (alojar) en el colegio de un pueblo vecino. Las comidas de emergencia (preparar) por el personal de cantina y unos padres de los colegiales. Aunque ésta es una circunstancia que (prever) por las autoridades, casi siempre (sorprender) por las dificultades que trae. Los usuarios de dicha carretera esperan que algo (hacer) antes del próximo invierno. El MOPU (Ministerio de Obras Públicas) ha asegurado que el trayecto de la carretera (mejorar) y que si va a haber problemas de nieve, unos avisos (transmitir) por la emisora de radio local.

2 La ciudad de Plasencia

Cambia los verbos de activa a pasiva.

1 Alfonso VIII, rey de Castilla, fundó Plasencia en 1180.
2 Este rey la ubicó sobre el río Jerte.
3 Las autoridades la amurallaron para protegerla.
4 El rey también inició el famoso mercado del martes.
5 El concejo restauró el ayuntamiento varias veces.
6 Pusieron nombres a las varias puertas de la ciudad, según la dirección de la carretera que salía por ellas.
7 Comenzaron la catedral vieja en el siglo XIII.
8 En la Casa de las Dos Torres, derribaron una de las torres a principios del siglo XX.
9 Recientemente han construido una Ciudad Deportiva municipal, con excelentes instalaciones.

3 Problemas de carreteras

Vuelve a hacer el Ejercicio 1 – pero empleando *se* o un verbo en activa.

4 En familia

Expresa las frases siguientes, que suenan bastante feas, en un estilo más adecuada, empleando *se*.

1 En mi casa todas las decisiones *son tomadas* con todos mis familiares juntos.
2 Cada sábado una cantidad de dinero de bolsillo *es distribuida* entre mis hermanos.
3 Este dinero *es gastado* en ropa y CDs
4 menos una parte que *es ahorrada*.
5 *Es ingresada* en la Caja de Ahorros.

Ahora continúa, pero empleando la tercera persona del plural del verbo.

6 Si me comporto mal, *se me pone* alguna sanción.
7 *Se me prohíbe* salir durante dos o tres días.
8 Pero nunca *se usa* violencia conmigo.
9 *Se dice* que soy un chico bastante normal.
10 ¡*Se me considera* muy inteligente!

5 Una señora británica visita los Picos de Europa

Una amiga británica, que acaba de visitar Cantabria en el norte de España y que ha escrito una carta sobre el tema a su amiga española en Madrid, quiere que se la traduzcas al español antes de echarla al correo. El problema es que la señora es muy aficionada al uso de la pasiva en inglés. ¿Sabes traducirla a un estilo de español que parezca natural?

Last week was spent in a hotel in the north of Spain, where we were treated very well. In the evening we were given a three-course meal and a bottle of wine. If desired, breakfast was served in our rooms. It was said in the tour operator's brochure that the hotel was two-star, but we were informed when we got there that this had been changed to three stars this year. On Tuesday we were taken to the Picos de Europa, and were provided with a picnic meal by the hotel. When the village of Fuente Dé was reached, we were told that we would be taken up to the top of the mountain in the cable car and then brought down and picked up by the coach at six o'clock. It was reckoned that a pleasant day was had by most of us.

 ¡... Y EN MARCHA!

6 Historia de nuestro colegio

Tú y tus compañeros/as de clase estáis preparando una historia de tu colegio, en la que muchos verbos estarán en pasiva. Podéis empezar:

El colegio fue planificado/fundado/construido en ...

Pero ¡cuidado!, tendréis que decir *'se le dio/puso el nombre de ...'* o *'le dieron/pusieron el nombre de ...'.*

A ver cuántas frases conseguís hacer, con pasiva donde sea admisible, y evitándola donde no lo sea.

7 Mi ciudad o pueblo

Con un plano o unas postales de tu pueblo o ciudad, describe su desarrollo a un(a) compañero/a, usando cuando sea posible, verbos en pasiva o con *se*.

Por ejemplo, hablando de un nuevo supermercado puedes decir:

El supermercado Tesco fue construido/se construyó hace tres años, y al mismo tiempo la carretera fue ensanchada/se ensanchó.

Pero ¡no te olvides de decir también lo que será hecho/se hará en el futuro! Si prefieres, puedes escribir tu descripción en forma de carta.

8 Un poco de cocina

Trae tu receta preferida a clase y explícasela a tus compañeros/as. De ser posible, prepárala en clase, mostrándoles a tus compañeros/as cómo hacerla. Claro que tienes que usar *se* con los verbos. ¡Que aproveche!

32 Tenses of the subjunctive

MECANISMOS

32.1 The subjunctive

The subjunctive itself is not a tense, but an alternative form of the verb which has to be used in certain circumstances. Grammar books usually refer to it as the subjunctive **mood**, and it is true that it does often convey a particular mood of, for example, sadness, joy, anger, doubt or uncertainty.

Exactly where and how to use the subjunctive will be explained little by little in the chapters which follow (Chapters 33–37). If you follow the explanations and do the exercises and activities which accompany the explanations, you should be well on the way to acquiring that feeling or instinct for the subjunctive, which plays a very important part in both spoken and written Spanish.

32.2 Tenses of the subjunctive

The subjunctive has several tenses.

32.2.1 Present subjunctive

a) Regular verbs

Usually the formation of the present subjunctive causes no problems, as you merely exchange the ending of the present indicative (the 'normal' present tense) as follows: *e* for *a*, or *a* for *e* or *i* (but remember that the first person [*yo*] also ends in *-e* or *-a*).

-ar: comprar *buy*	-er: beber *drink*	-ir: subir *go up*
compre	beba	suba
compres	bebas	subas
compre	beba	suba
compremos	bebamos	subamos
compréis	bebáis	subáis
compren	beban	suban

b) **Radical-changing verbs** (see Chapter 15)

- Those verbs which have only one change in the present indicative have the change in the same place in the present subjunctive (*e* ⟶ *ie*, *o* ⟶ *ue*, *u* ⟶ *ue*):

pensar (e ⟶ ie) to think	volver (e ⟶ ue) to return	jugar (u ⟶ ue) to play
piense	vuelva	juegue
pienses	vuelvas	juegues
piense	vuelva	juegue
pensemos	volvamos	juguemos
penséis	volváis	juguéis
piensen	vuelvan	jueguen

- Those verbs which have the additional *e* ⟶ *i* and *o* ⟶ *u* change (e.g. in the gerund and other parts) also have this change in the first and second persons plural:

preferir to prefer	dormir to sleep
prefiera	duerma
prefieras	duermas
prefiera	duerma
prefiramos	durmamos
prefiráis	durmáis
prefieran	duerman

- Those *-ir* verbs, such as **pedir**, which have the *e* ⟶ *i* change retain it in all six parts:

pedir to ask for
pida
pidas
pida
pidamos
pidáis
pidan

c) **Irregular verbs**

The first person singular is the stem for almost all present subjunctives, so those with an irregularity in the stem carry it through into this tense.

- Those verbs, such as **poner** (to put) whose stem in the first person singular (**yo**) form ends with **-g-**, retain the **-g-** throughout the present subjunctive.

poner (pongo): ponga, pongas, ponga, pongamos, pongáis, pongan

Similarly:

caer (caigo): caiga ...	fall
hacer (hago): haga ...	do/make
salir (salgo): salga ...	go out/leave
traer (traigo): traiga ...	bring
valer (valgo): valga ...	be worth

✎ Note: verbs of this sort which also have a radical change in the indicative (**decir** (*to say/tell*), for example) lose the radical change in the present subjunctive and retain the same consistent stem ending in **-g-** throughout:

*decir (**di**go): di**g**a, di**g**as, di**g**a, di**g**amos, di**g**áis, di**g**an*

Similarly:

*oír (oigo): oi**g**a ...*	hear
*tener (tengo): **ten**ga ...*	have
*venir (vengo): **ven**ga ...*	come

- Verbs with their infinitives ending in **-ecer**, **-ocer**, **-ucir**, whose first person singular stem ends in **-zc-**, retain the **-zc-** throughout:

*conducir (conduzco): condu**zc**a, condu**zc**as, condu**zc**a, condu**zc**amos, condu**zc**áis, condu**zc**an*	leave/drive
*conocer (conozco): cono**zc**a ...*	know
*parecer (parezco): pare**zc**a ...*	seem

- **Estar** and **dar** are predictable, but don't forget the accents:

dar *to give*	estar *to be*
d**é**	est**é**
des	est**és**
d**é**	est**é**
demos	estemos
deis	est**éis**
den	est**én**

- Spelling changes are sometimes necessary because of swapping **-a/-e** endings. Stems ending in **-c-, -z-, -g-, -gu-** are especially subject to this:

cazar (cazo, cazas ...): ca**ce**, ca**ces** ...	hunt
coger (cojo, coges ...): co**ja**, co**jas** ...	catch
sacar (saco, sacas ...): sa**que**, sa**ques** ...	take out
seguir (sigo, sigues ...): si**ga**, si**gas** ...	follow

The final letter of the stem is constant in the subjunctive.

- The following verbs have a totally irregular stem which remains constant with the usual **-a-** type endings:

ser (to be): sea, seas, sea, seamos, seáis, sean

Similarly:

caber: **quepa** ...	fit
*haber: **haya** ...	have
ir: **vaya** ...	go
saber: **sepa** ...	know

(* The present subjunctive of **haber** – **haya** – is used with the past participle to form the perfect subjunctive.)

32.2.2 Imperfect subjunctive

There are two forms of the imperfect subjunctive which, with one exception (see Chapter 18 section 18.3 and Chapter 38 section 38.4), are completely interchangeable. The stem is always the third person plural (**ellos**) of the preterite, including whatever irregularity that may contain.

a) Regular verbs

-ar: comprar → compr**aron**		-er: beber → beb**ieron**		-ir: subir → sub**ieron**	
comprara	comprase	bebiera	bebiese	subiera	subiese
compraras	comprases	bebieras	bebieses	subieras	subieses
comprara	comprase	bebiera	bebiese	subiera	subiese
compráramos	comprásemos	bebiéramos	bebiésemos	subiéramos	subiésemos
comprarais	compraseis	bebierais	bebiese	subierais	subieseis
compraran	comprasen	bebieran	bebiese	subieran	subiesen

b) Radical-changing verbs (see Chapter 15)

Verbs that change in the third person of the preterite (**e** → **i** or **o** → **u**) also have this change in the imperfect subjunctive, but the stem remains constant throughout.

dormir (durmieron): durmiera/durmiese ...	sleep
preferir (prefirieron): prefiriera/prefiriese ...	prefer
pedir (pidieron): pidiera/pidiese ...	ask (for)

c) All verbs with *'pretérito grave'* (see Chapter 21) keep the preterite stem with *-iera/-iese* endings:

estar (estuvieron): estuviera/estuviese ...	be
tener (tuvieron): tuviera/tuviese ...	have

d) Verbs with *-y-* replacing *-i-* in third person preterite retain the *-y-*:

caer (cayeron): cayera/cayese ...	fall
creer (creyeron): creyera/creyese ...	believe
leer (leyeron): leyera/leyese ...	read
oír (oyeron): oyera/oyese ...	hear

Similarly:

huir (huyeron): huyera/huyese ... and other verbs ending in *-uir*.	flee

e) Other verbs which lose the *-i-* in the third person preterite ending also lose it in this tense:

decir (dijeron): dijera/dijese ...	say/tell
reñir (riñeron): riñera/riñese ...	scold/quarrel
traer (trajeron): trajera/trajese ...	bring

Similarly:

conducir (condujeron): condujera/condujese ... and all verbs ending in *-ducir*.	lead/drive

32.2.3 Perfect subjunctive

The perfect subjunctive is formed with the present subjunctive of *haber* + the past participle:

haya comprado	**haya** bebido	**haya** subido
hayas comprado	**hayas** bebido	**hayas** subido
haya comprado	**haya** bebido	**haya** subido
hayamos comprado	**hayamos** bebido	**hayamos** subido
hayáis comprado	**hayáis** bebido	**hayáis** subido
hayan comprado	**hayan** bebido	**hayan** subido

32.2.4 Pluperfect subjunctive

The pluperfect subjunctive is formed with the imperfect subjunctive of **haber** (either form) + the past participle:

hubiera subido	**hubiese** subido
hubieras subido	**hubieses** subido
hubiera subido	**hubiese** subido
hubiéramos subido	**hubiésemos** subido
hubierais subido	**hubieseis** subido
hubieran subido	**hubiesen** subido

32.3 Sequence of tenses with the subjunctive

Usually, when the main verb of the sentence is in the present, the future, the perfect or the imperative, the subjunctive verb dependent on it will be in the present or perfect tense:

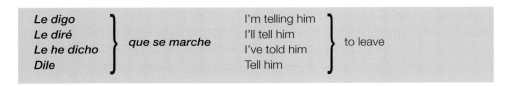

Le digo — I'm telling him
Le diré — I'll tell him
Le he dicho } *que se marche* — I've told him } to leave
Dile — Tell him

When the main verb is in the imperfect, the preterite, the pluperfect, the conditional or the conditional perfect, the subjunctive verb dependent on it will be in the imperfect or pluperfect tense:

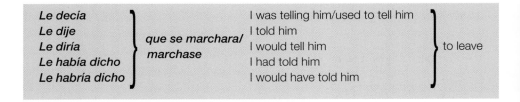

Le decía — I was telling him/used to tell him
Le dije — I told him
Le diría } *que se marchara/marchase* — I would tell him } to leave
Le había dicho — I had told him
Le habría dicho — I would have told him

Sometimes, however, if the sense demands it, these sequence rules can be broken:

Siento que estuvieras enfermo.
I'm sorry you were ill.

Activities practising the use of the subjunctive follow in the *¡Ponte a punto!* and *¡ … Y en marcha!* sections of Chapters 33–37.

33 Subjunctive: influence, emotion and judgement

MECANISMOS

📝 Note: the examples and exercises in this chapter use only the present or perfect subjunctive, which you will find set out on pages 179–182 and 183.

33.1 Influencing others

The action is expressed in the subjunctive in Spanish with verbs of wanting, liking, ordering, advising, allowing or causing someone or something to do an action, or with verbs of avoiding, preventing or prohibiting someone or something (from) doing an action.

But the subjects of the two verbs must be different. Compare:

Quiero ayudar.
I want **to help**. (i.e. I both want and help)

¿Quieres que ayude?
Do **you** want **me** to help? (i.e. **You** want … **I** help)

Dile a Miguel que venga aquí.
Tell Michael **to come** here.

Trata de impedir que se escapen.
Try to prevent **them (from) escaping**.

La ley no permite que se venda.
The law doesn't allow **it to be sold**.

No me gusta que hagas eso.
I don't like **you doing** that.

The most common verbs used with a subjunctive in this way are:

decir	mandar*	sugerir	querer	desear
permitir*	exigir	pedir	implorar*	consentir en
recomendar*	preferir	prohibir*	impedir*	aconsejar*
hacer*	conseguir	lograr		

*Verbs marked with an asterisk may also be used with an infinitive, even if the subjects are different:

No nos permiten hacerlo./No permiten que lo hagamos.
They don't allow **us to do it**.

185

33.2 Emotional reactions

The subjunctive is used after verbs and other expressions of joy, sadness, anger, sorrow, fear and other emotions:

*Mi padre está bastante enfadado **que vaya** a suspender.*
My father is quite annoyed **that I'm going** to fail.

*Nos alegra mucho **que puedas** estar aquí.*
We're very pleased **(that) you can** be here.

33.3 Value judgements

Closely related to these emotions are all 'value judgements' – reactions of indignation, incredulity, justification, approval, disapproval or concern. After such expressions the subjunctive is also used:

*Es una vergüenza que **no podamos** salir sin el miedo de atracos.*
It's a disgrace that **we can't** go out without fear of muggings.

*¿Cómo justificaremos que **se gaste** tanto dinero?*
How can we justify so much money **being spent**?

*No me gusta que **ocurra** así.*
I don't like **it happening** like that.

➡ **Exercises 1, 2, 3**

 ## ¡PONTE A PUNTO!

1 El nuevo club de jóvenes

Acaba de abrirse en un barrio de una ciudad española un nuevo club de jóvenes. He aquí algunos de los deseos y preferencias del jefe. Cambia el infinitivo al presente del subjuntivo.

El jefe:

1 desea que todos (disfrutar) de las instalaciones del club.
2 prefiere que los jóvenes (jugar) al ping-pong u otros juegos en el club.
3 no quiere que éstos (meterse) en algún lío en las calles.
4 sugiere a todos los jóvenes del barrio que (venir) a divertirse allí.
5 no permite sin embargo que (fumar).
6 recomienda que tampoco (beber) alcohol.
7 ha conseguido que un grupo de empresarios de la ciudad (ofrecer) cinco mil euros anuales al club.
8 está enfadado que el concejo municipal no (contribuir) nada.
9 cree que es una vergüenza que las cosas (ser) así.
10 se indigna de que el alcalde ni siquiera (querer) venir a hablarle.

2 Una crisis futbolística

El día 28 de diciembre, día de los Santos Inocentes, apareció el siguiente artículo en la prensa madrileña. Tienes que escribir los verbos en presente del subjuntivo.

El director del club de fútbol Real Madrid se declara tanto sorprendido como triste que su mejor jugador español *querer* irse a jugar a Inglaterra. A las preguntas de nuestros reporteros, el favorito de los forofos madrileños respondió que no quiere que su vida *seguir* siendo siempre igual. Hay gran consternación que *escoger* este momento para hacer que su carrera *cambiar* de dirección, puesto que todos quieren que *desempeñar* un papel significativo en el éxito de su equipo en el campeonato actual. Muchos encontrarán incomprensible que un jugador tan sobresaliente *decidir* irse a la patria del gamberrismo futbolístico y ¡seguro que habrá los que traten de impedir que se *marchar*! Las autoridades del club inglés de Tranmere Rovers están muy contentas que su adquisición española *firmar* el contrato, pero algo asombradas de que los madrileños lo *tomar* tan mal.

3 ¡Qué niños tan traviesos!

Una familia española con dos niños jóvenes, Jaime de tres años y Pablo de cinco, pasa algún tiempo en tu casa. Tu madre, que no habla español, empieza a exasperarse de sus actividades y quiere que le traduzcas a la madre española lo que dice. Tienes que utilizar el presente del subjuntivo en cada frase.

1 *I don't like Jaime writing on the walls!*
2 *I prefer both children to play outside!*
3 *Tell Pablo to wash his hands!*
4 *Tell Pablo to turn down the TV!*
5 *I don't want them to paint the cat!*
6 *Tell them not to put dirty shoes on the table!*
7 *Ask Pablo not to jump on the bed!*
8 *It's terrible that they go to bed so late!*
9 *It's best that you all go home tomorrow!*

¡... Y EN MARCHA!

4 ¡Qué asco!

Todos/as tus compañeros/as de clase hacen cosas que no te gustan. Tú tienes que decirles que no te gusta que hagan estas cosas y lo que prefieres que hagan.

Ejemplo:

Felipe, ¡no me gusta que pongas los pies en la mesa! ¡Prefiero que los pongas en el suelo!

5 ¡Esos concejales municipales!

Imagínate que los sucesos siguientes han ocurrido en tu ciudad o pueblo. Con tus compañeros/as de clase apuntad vuestras reacciones.

Ejemplo:

Las autoridades construyen un vertedero de basuras al lado del hospital.

– Es asqueroso que construyan eso allí.
– Encuentro incomprensible que hagan tal cosa.
– ¡Qué bueno que hayan decidido por fin construir el vertedero!

En esta región:

1 … el año que viene cierran la estación y eliminan la línea de ferrocarril.
2 … ponen un rascacielos enfrente de la iglesia parroquial.
3 … cierran la piscina cubierta.
4 … prohíben los perros en el parque municipal.
5 … el año que viene se abrirá un nuevo polígono industrial.
6 … han ensanchado la carretera de circunvalación.
7 … van a peatonalizar las calles céntricas.
8 … están renovando el alumbrado público en los barrios exteriores.
9 … habrá obras de carretera durante todo el verano.

Ahora añade tus reacciones a unos sucesos que han ocurrido, ocurren o van a ocurrir de verdad en tu propia ciudad o pueblo.

6 En los márgenes de la sociedad

Estudia el texto siguiente y luego discute con tus compañeros/as vuestras reacciones a lo que dice, usando expresiones que necesiten el subjuntivo. Quizás antes de empezar, deberíais hacer una lista de posibles frases que expresen vuestras reacciones:

Es increíble/insoportable que …/Lamentamos que … , etcétera.

Ejemplo:

– *Es increíble que los niños muy jóvenes tengan que vivir así.*
– *No es verdad que la policía los mate.*

En los márgenes de la sociedad

En varios países pobres, y a veces en los comparativamente ricos, de Latinoamérica, existen unos problemas sociales horrendos. Se oye hablar de chicos y chicas muy jóvenes que han sido abandonados por sus padres, o que han huido de casa, que viven en las calles, viviendo de la mendicidad o del robo. Se dice que por la noche los busca la policía y los mata. Eso por lo menos es lo que se lee en la prensa. Una parte de la causa es que sus padres han tenido que dejar sus pueblos en el campo, puesto que no encuentran trabajo allí, y han acudido a las ciudades, pero tampoco han podido encontrar trabajo, y no pueden soportar una familia. Cuando los jóvenes viven así, las drogas y la prostitución pueden ser otro problema, sobre todo si les parecen ser la única manera de hacerse con qué vivir. La iglesia trata de ayudar, tanto políticamente como con apoyo financiero donde éste sea posible, pero parece que la vida sigue siendo corta y brutal para estos jóvenes.

---

34 Subjunctive: doubt, disbelief and possibility

 MECANISMOS

The subjunctive is used in various situations where there is an element of doubt or uncertainty.

34.1 Expressions of doubt

The subjunctive is used after expressions implying doubt or uncertainty:

dudar que	to doubt whether
es dudoso que	it's doubtful whether
parece dudoso que	it seems doubtful that
resulta dudoso que	it turns out (to be) doubtful that
temer que	to be afraid that
esperar que	to hope that

> **Dudo que sepamos** *la solución del problema.*
> **I doubt whether we know** the answer to the problem.

> **Es dudoso** *que nos* **ayuden**.
> **It's doubtful** whether **they will help** us.

34.2 Expressions of uncertainty

Expressions of certainty in the negative become expressions of doubt (and take the subjunctive), but expressions of doubt in the negative become expressions of certainty (and therefore take the indicative). Compare the following examples:

> **Es cierto** *que* **saben** *la verdad.*
> **It's certain they know** the truth.

> **No es cierto** *que* **sepan** *la verdad.*
> **It's not certain** (i.e. it's doubtful) **they know** the truth.

> **Es de dudar** *que* **sepan** *la verdad.*
> **It's to be doubted** whether **they know** the truth.

> **No cabe duda** *de que* **saben** *la verdad.*
> **There's no (room for) doubt** that **they know** the truth. (i.e. it's certain)

34.3 Expressions of disbelief

The subjunctive is also used after verbs of knowing, saying and thinking in the negative or to ask questions with negative implications. This can be regarded as a further extension of doubt: if you don't know, can't say, or don't think that something is the case, then that is doubt!

No creemos que *sea* el caso.
We don't think that that **is** the case.

No puedo decir que *tenga razón*, aunque lo creo.
I can't say that he **is right**, although I think so.

No sabía que *pensaras* así.
I didn't know you **thought** (like) that.

¿Tú crees que todo *salga* bien?
Do you think everything **will turn out** all right?

Era difícil creer que *tuvieran* éxito.
It was **difficult to believe** they **would be successful**.
(implying that you couldn't believe it)

In this category, too, is *negar* (to deny) which takes the subjunctive:

Siempre negaba que *ocurriera*.
He always **denied** it **was happening/would happen**.

34.4 After statements of possibility and likelihood

As a logical extension of the above, possibility implies some doubt; so, too, does probability, as it is not total certainty.

The most common phrases of this kind requiring the subjunctive are:

Es posible que ...	It is possible that ...
Parece/Resulta posible que ...	It seems possible that ...
Es probable que ...	It is likely/probable that ...
Parece/Resulta probable que ...	It seems likely/probable that ...
Hay/Existe la posibilidad de que ...	There is the possibility that ...
Hay/Existe la probabilidad de que ...	There is the likelihood/probability that ...
Puede (ser) que ...	It may be that ...

*Hay que admitir la **posibilidad** de que **tengan razón**.*
One has to admit the **possibility** that **they are (may be) right**.

*Es **probable** que lo **sepan** ya.*
It's **probable/likely** they **know** already.

*Parecía **posible** que nos **ayudasen**.*
It seemed **possible** that they **would help** us.

➥ **Exercises 1, 2, 3 (Exercises 1 and 2a use only the present subjunctive)**

¡PONTE A PUNTO!

1 El pronóstico del tiempo

Añade una frase que requiera el presente del subjuntivo a las frases siguientes, cambiando el verbo debidamente.

Ejemplos:

Lloverá mañana ⟶ Es posible/Hay la posibilidad de que llueva mañana.

No lloverá mañana ⟶ Es dudoso/No creemos que llueva mañana.

1 Hará mucho calor en el sur.
2 Nevará en los Pirineos.
3 Hará viento en las costas gallegas.
4 No soplará el viento en las costas mediterráneas.
5 Se formarán brumas ligeras en el valle del Ebro.
6 Las temperaturas serán muy altas en el interior.
7 Las temperaturas no bajarán mucho al anochecer.
8 Caerán lluvias torrenciales en las montañas cantábricas.

2 Cómo ser pesimista – con la ayuda del subjuntivo

a) Anita tiene poca confianza en el futuro de sus relaciones amorosas. He aquí algunas de las observaciones recientes que ha hecho a sus amigas. Pon los verbos al presente del subjuntivo.

1 Dudo que mi novio me (querer).
2 Es posible que (tener) otras novias.
3 Temo que ellas le (gustar) más que yo.
4 No veo probable que me (casar).
5 En efecto, es muy posible que (quedarme) soltera.
6 Espero que un chico (decidir) casarse conmigo.
7 Pero dudo que mi personalidad abierta y risueña (atraer) a nadie.
8 Pero hay que ser optimista y creer en la letra de la canción, y en la posibilidad de que 'algún día (venir) mi príncipe'.

b) Ahora una de sus amigas le confía a otra lo que le ha dicho Anita. Esta vez tienes que completar las frases cambiando los subjuntivos al imperfecto correspondiente.

1 Anita dudaba que su novio la (querer).
2 Dijo que era posible que (tener) otras novias.
3 Temía que ellas le (gustar) más que ella.
4 No veía probable que se (casar).
5 En efecto, era muy posible que (quedarse) soltera.
6 Esperaba que un chico (decidir) casarse con ella.
7 Pero dudaba que su personalidad abierta y risueña (atraer) a nadie.
8 Pero había que ser optimista y creer en la letra de la canción, y en la posibilidad de que 'algún día (venir) su príncipe'.

3 La España de hoy en día

Pon los verbos en el tiempo correcto del indicativo o subjuntivo según el sentido.

Ya sabemos que España (estar) de moda tanto en Europa como en el mundo entero. Es probable que esta popularidad (seguir). No cabe duda de que se (poder) ver toda clase de producto español en las tiendas europeas. Es dudoso que (haber) una buena discoteca en Londres o París donde no se oiga algún conjunto español. Para los españoles mayores, es difícil creer que la actitud de los extranjeros hacia su país (haber) cambiado tanto. A fin de cuentas, algunos de ellos no creían que la democracia se (establecer). Lo que es cierto es que España ya (poder) contarse como uno de los países principales en la diplomacia europea. ¿Quién hubiera creído hace treinta años que Madrid se (hacer) centro diplomático europeo o que España (participar) plenamente en la UE? ¿Puede que lo (estar) soñando?

 ¡... Y EN MARCHA!

4 La semana que viene

Discute con tus compañeros/as de clase las cosas que – posiblemente – ocurrirán durante los próximos ocho días. Claro que tenéis que emplear las frases que se facilitan en la sección *Mecanismos*.

Ejemplo:

El martes es posible que tengamos examen en español.
El domingo hay la probabilidad de que vengan a visitarnos unos amigos.

Apunta una posibilidad o probabilidad para cada día de la semana.

5 ¡Escándalos!

Trabajando en parejas, uno/a hace alguna observación en forma de pregunta acerca de sus amigos/as o profesores del colegio; el/la otro/a tiene que contradecirle, expresando sus dudas o su ignorancia.

Ejemplo:

– ¿Sabes que el señor X va a comprar un coche nuevo?
– ¡Hombre! ¡Yo no sabía que tuviera bastante dinero para eso!
– ¡Caramba! ¡Dudo que sepa conducir!

6 El fantasma

Trabaja con un(a) compañero/a expresando vuestras dudas acerca de la autenticidad y la veracidad histórica de la siguiente historia – ¡usando frases que exijan el subjuntivo, claro!

Ejemplo:

No creo que un caballero de la edad media se llame así.

El castillo de Fuentenegra (siglo XI) en la provincia de Salamanca acaba de ser adquirido por un nuevo dueño. Plácido Lunes Cantante, 39 años, adquirió el castillo muy barato. La razón es que, según las tradiciones de la comarca, el castillo está habitado por un fantasma. No sólo fantasma, sino fantasma activo, por no decir hiperactivo.

Parece que durante la época romana, el castillo era uno de los muchos que se habían construido en la frontera. El dueño de entonces, don Sebastián Santos, caballero, tenía un vecino, don Julio Catedrales Tenor, que vivía en otro castillo, al otro lado de la calle. Este vecino era algo loco, pero inventor muy genial, y le gustaba experimentar con la tecnología militar de la época. Don Sebastián y su vecino se odiaban uno a otro y, de vez en cuando, si el uno veía al otro en las murallas de su castillo, le invitaba a tomar un té. El vecino de Sebastián acababa de inventar una especie de arco multiflecha, o sea, una ametralladora para disparar flechas. Una noche muy oscura, cuando nada estaba visible, parece que el vecino don Julio observó a don Sebastián en una de sus murallas. Don Julio disparó, e inmediatamente el pobre Sebastián cayó víctima de un disparo de dicha máquina, siendo alcanzado por una docena de flechas de un solo golpe. Pereció agonizando en la escalera de la sala grande.

Ahora se le oye durante toda la noche bajando y subiendo la escalera, berreando de voz en grito – ¿Quién me quita estas puñeteras flechas del cuerpo? ¡¡Aaaaayyyyyyyyyy ... !! Y el pobre vuelve a expirar ruidosamente cada madrugada.

35 Subjunctive: conjunctions of futurity, purpose and other expressions

MECANISMOS

35.1 Conjunctions of futurity

a) The present subjunctive must be used after the following conjunctions when they refer to actions which have not yet taken place but which may (or may not) take place in the future.

cuando ...	when ...
así que ...	
en cuanto ...	as soon as ...
tan pronto como ...	
no bien ...	no sooner ... (than ...)
hasta que ...	until ...
después de que ...	after ...
mientras ...	as long as ... , while ...
una vez que ...	once ...

Hasta que se cambie la ley no podremos hacer nada.
Until the law **is changed**, we shan't be able to do anything.

Mientras no se cambie la ley ...
As long as the law **isn't changed** ...

Después de que se cambie la ley ...
After the law **is changed** ...

Una vez que se cambie la ley ...
Once the law **is changed** ... (it hasn't been changed yet)

b) Similarly, the imperfect subjunctive must be used when the actions **had** not yet taken place **at the time of reference**:

*Todos **estábamos** de acuerdo de que no podríamos hacer nada ...*
We **were** all agreed that we wouldn't be able to do anything ...

... hasta que se cambiara la ley.
*... **until** the law **was changed**.*

... mientras no se cambiara la ley.
*... **as long as** the law **wasn't changed**.*

... después de que se cambiara la ley.
*... **after** the law **was changed**.*

... *una vez que se cambiara* la ley.
... **once** the law **was changed**.

(In all the above cases, the law hadn't been changed yet.)

 Note that when these expressions simply record a fact, with no reference to the future, they are followed by the indicative (see Chapter 17).

35.2 Conjunctions requiring the subjunctive

The subjunctive is used after the following expressions:

antes de que ...	before
con tal que ...	provided that
a condición de que ...	on condition that
a no ser que ...	unless
a menos que ...	unless
sin que ...	without
aunque ...	even though, even if

Con tal que dimita el ministro ...
Provided the minister **resigns** ...

A menos que dimita el ministro ...
Unless the minister **resigns** ...

Aunque dimitiera el ministro ...
Even if the minister **were to resign** ...

However, when **aunque** means 'although' and simply reports a fact, it is followed by the indicative:

Aunque dimitió el ministro, no se resolvió el problema.
Although the minister **resigned**, the problem wasn't solved.

 Note: when the subjects of the two verbs are the same, it is usual to use the infinitive after *hasta*, *después de*, *antes de*, *sin*, *para* and *a fin de* (see Chapter 27):

Hasta recibir la carta no sabremos lo que dice.
Until we receive the letter, we won't know what it says.
(we both receive and won't know)

El ladrón se escapó **sin ser visto**.
The thief escaped **without being seen**. (the thief both escaped and wasn't seen)

Trabajo mucho **para mejorar** mi español.
I work hard **to improve** my Spanish. (I both work and improve)

➤ **Exercises 1, 2, 3**

35.3 Conjunctions of purpose

The subjunctive is required after various expressions meaning 'so that, in order that' and which indicate purpose:

> *para que ...*
> *a que ...*
> *a fin de que ...*
> *con el objeto de que ...* } so that, in order that
> *de modo que ...* *
> *de manera que ...* *
> *de forma que ...* *

*Traje los planes **para que** ustedes los **vieran**.*
I brought the plans **so that** you **could see** them.

 *Note, however, that when *de modo que* ... or *de manera/de forma que* ... indicate result, not purpose, they are followed by the indicative:

*Traje los planes a la reunión, **de modo/manera/forma que** todos **pudieron** verlos.*
I brought the plans to the meeting, **so (= with the result that)** everybody **was able to** see them.

 Exercise 4

¡PONTE A PUNTO!

1 En busca de trabajo

Rellena los espacios en blanco con una de las conjunciones explicadas en este capítulo, teniendo cuidado de que convenga al sentido.

. . **1**. . compre el periódico leeré los pequeños anuncios. . . **2**. . haya notado los posibles puestos, escribiré cartas, . . **3**. . digan que telefonee. . . **4**. . haya terminado de escribir las cartas, las echaré al correo. . . **5**. . las eche, compraré sellos. . . **6**. . reciba una respuesta, llamaré por teléfono, . . **7**. . el puesto parezca bien. . . **8**. . llame, fijaré una cita para entrevistarme. . . **9**. . me ofrezcan el puesto, lo aceptaré, . . **10**. . me paguen lo suficiente para vivir. . . **11**. . reciba mi primer sueldo, me compraré algo muy caro, . . **12**. . que sea lo que quiero, claro.

2 Gibraltar

Pon los verbos que van entre paréntesis en el tiempo debido del subjuntivo.

¿De quién es Gibraltar? En la época de Franco, los gibraltareños decían que no querían ser españoles, hasta que España (ser) democrática. Los ingleses decían que no dejarían la soberanía sin que los habitantes del Peñón lo (querer). Antes de que (morir) Franco, la situación no iba a resolverse. Desde la muerte de Franco, en efecto la situación ha ido cambiando, pero para que los gibraltareños (cambiar) de parecer, todavía hace falta tiempo. Con tal que lo que pase (ser) según sus deseos, un día el problema se resolverá, pero quizás no mientras (tener) sus recuerdos de la España de la dictadura. Tampoco habrá solución hasta que España y el Reino Unido (hablar) en serio y (hacer) un verdadero acuerdo. En cuanto (ocurrir) esto, entonces todos los partidos podrán estar contentos.

3 En la fábrica

Estás trabajando en una fábrica que exporta sus productos a España. Una empresa en Barcelona ha mostrado algún interés y tu jefe te ha pedido que le ayudes con una carta de respuesta que contiene las frases siguientes. ¿Cómo vas a expresarlas en español? Claro que hay que hablar de usted/ustedes a los clientes comerciales.

1   *as soon as the process is complete*
2   *when the product is ready*
3   *as soon as we know the dimensions*
4   *as long as this situation continues*
5   *until you give us the green light*
6   *once we receive a definite order* (un pedido)
7   *provided we know what you want*
8   *unless you send us a fax*
9   *even if the order is a small one*
10 *on condition that the contract* (el contrato) *is signed soon*

4 ¡Qué profesor(a) tan entusiasta!

Tu profe te explica la ayuda y los consejos que te da. Tienes que cambiar los infinitivos al presente del indicativo o subjuntivo o dejarlos como están, según el sentido.

1   Te doy este libro de vocabulario para que (aprender) veinte nuevas palabras al día.
2   Ya has hecho esto con la lista de verbos, de modo que ya (saber) muchos.
3   También te presto este libro de cuentos mejicanos de modo que (acostumbrarte) al vocabulario latinoamericano.
4   Sé que ves con frecuencia programas españoles por satélite, de manera que ya (entender) bastante bien el español hablado.
5   Voy a ponerte bajo alguna presión, con el objeto de que (estar) listo/a para los exámenes del próximo verano.
6   Para (aprobar) como debes será mucho trabajo, lo siento, pero ¡tendrás que aguantarlo!

 ¡... Y EN MARCHA!

5 Faenas domésticas

Usando las frases facilitadas arriba, trabaja con un(a) compañero/a (que será tu madre/padre) para decidir cuando harás las faenas domésticas.

Ejemplo:

– *¿Cuándo lavarás el coche?*
– *Lavaré el coche en cuanto termine el desayuno.*

Otras faenas pueden ser, por ejemplo: fregar los platos, hacer la cama, pasar el aspirador, bajar al supermercado, preparar la cena, planchar la ropa, barrer el patio, poner la mesa, quitar la mesa, cortar el césped, salir de paseo con el perro, leer los e-mail …

6 Proyectos de vacaciones

Imagínate que eres un(a) estudiante español(a) y que estás discutiendo con tus compañeros/as vuestros proyectos para unas vacaciones de verano en Gran Bretaña. Estáis mirando varias guías para decidir adónde ir, qué hacer y cuándo, y cómo alojaros. ¡A ver cuántas frases inventáis, empleando las frases que se explican al principio de este capítulo!

Ejemplo:

– En cuanto lleguemos a Londres, buscaremos un albergue juvenil.
– No quiero parar en un albergue a menos que sea cómodo.
– Iremos a Stratford-upon-Avon con el objeto de que Elena vea una obra de Shakespeare.

7 Intrusos

Estás de vacaciones en la Costa del Sol, y mientras estabas en la playa, unos ladrones han entrado en la casa que tú y tu familia habéis alquilado. Tienes que hacer una declaración a la policía sobre el incidente, y como quieres lucir tu español, escribes cada frase con *sin* y el infinitivo o *sin que* y el subjuntivo. Ten cuidado con la diferencia y ¡a ver cuántas frases escribes así! Al terminar, compara oralmente tu descripción del robo con la de tus compañeros/as.

Ejemplo:

Los ladrones entraron sin que nadie les viese y se fueron sin que el perro del vecino ladrase. Habían entrado sin romper nada.

Ten en cuenta tu ropa, tu dinero, tus otras posesiones, los muebles, las puertas y ventanas, el estado de la casa y las imprentas digitales.

8 Planificación municipal

Trabaja con un(a) compañero/a. Uno/a quiere construir una casa en la ciudad; el/la otro/a es oficial de planificación municipal. Éste/a tiene ideas muy firmes pero muy restrictivas en cuanto a su trabajo, y tiene que expresarlas empleando el subjuntivo con las frases facilitadas en este capítulo.

Ejemplo:

– Quisiera construir una nueva casa en la ciudad.
– No se puede, a menos que se haga en el estilo antiguo.
– Quisiera enseñarle los planes.
– Sí, señor/señorita, en cuanto Vd rellene este formulario.

Seguid, hablando de la fachada, las ventanas, el acceso, el garaje, el interior, la calefacción, las alcantarillas, la fecha de empezar, la empresa de constructores …

Los obstáculos pueden ser: el permiso del Ayuntamiento, el aspecto de la fachada, el acceso a la calle, la altura de la casa, un constructor designado por el Ayuntamiento y las medidas para la protección del medio ambiente, por ejemplo.

36 Subjunctive: indefinite and negative antecedents

MECANISMOS

The subjunctive must be used after various expressions where there is an indefinite or negative element.

36.1 After an indefinite antecedent

This is a use of the subjunctive which is very typical but perhaps less easy to understand. It is, in fact, a further instance of the presence of doubt requiring a subjunctive.
The 'antecedent' is the noun or pronoun to which the clause following refers back.

For example:

If you are looking for an activity which will keep you fit …

In this sentence, the word 'activity' is the antecedent, and it is indefinite, because any activity will do, so long as it keeps you fit. Therefore, in Spanish the verb 'will keep' goes in the subjunctive:

*Si buscas una actividad que te **mantenga** en forma …*

Subjunctive clauses of this kind may be introduced by the relative pronouns *que* or *quien* and also *donde* or *como*.

*¿Hay **una tienda** por aquí **donde vendan** cerámica?*
Is there **a shop** (any shop) around here **where they sell** ceramics?

*Cuéntame **los problemas que hayas tenido** en las relaciones con tus padres.*
Tell me about **the problems you have had** in your relations with your parents.
(i.e. any problems you may have had)

*Haz **como quieras**.*
Do **as you wish**.

36.2 After a negative antecedent

The subjunctive is also used when the antecedent is negative.

***No** hay **quien** me **ayude**.*
There is **no-one who will help** me./There is **no-one to help** me.

The title of García Márquez's well-known book *El coronel no tiene quien le escriba* is usually translated as 'No-one writes to the Colonel', but a more literal translation would be 'The Colonel doesn't have anyone who writes to him/The Colonel doesn't have anyone to write to him'. *No ... quien* is used here instead of *nadie que* and is, therefore, a negative antecedent, so the verb, *escriba*, is in the subjunctive.

This kind of sentence also carries more than a hint of purpose, and is often the equivalent of the English 'someone/something to ...', 'no-one/nothing to ...'.

> *Necesito a **alguien que** me **ayude** con este problema.*
> I need **someone to help** me with this problem. (i.e. someone who may help)

> *No había **nada** que le **detuviera**.*
> There was **nothing to stop** him. (i.e. nothing that would stop him)

36.3 Other negative expressions which require the subjunctive

No es que ...	It's not that ...
No puede ser que ...	It can't be that ...
No es porque ...	It's not because ...

> ***No es que/No es porque** no te **quiera** ...*
> **It's not that/It's not because** I don't **love** you ...

➡ **Exercises 1, 2, 3**

 ¡PONTE A PUNTO!

1 El tae-kwondo

Pon el verbo entre paréntesis en indicativo o subjuntivo según haga falta.

Si buscas un deporte que te (mantener) en buena forma y que al mismo tiempo (mezclar) la destreza física con el arte, ¿por qué no (probar) el tae-kwondo? No es una actividad que (requerir) gran fuerza, pero es un deporte que se (hacer) muy popular entre los españoles. Esto no es porque (ser) un deporte con orígenes europeos, puesto que (tener) sus raíces en el Oriente. Unos dicen que los españoles (necesitar) un deporte que (canalizar) la violencia. El tae-kwondo no es un deporte que se (poder) practicar dónde y cómo se (querer). Hay que haber un local que (ofrecer) sitio suficiente y un sitio donde los practicantes se (cambiar) y se (poner) el uniforme, que (ser) de rigor.

2 El cielo

Un(a) amigo/a tuyo/a te ha pedido que le traduzcas las frases siguientes para que pueda rellenar el cupón de un concurso que ha visto en una revista española. En el concurso piden unas definiciones del cielo. Claro que una condición es que se tiene que emplear frases con antecedentes indefinidos con el presente del subjuntivo.

Empieza cada frase con *'El cielo es …'* (*Heaven is …*)

Ejemplo:

El cielo es una casa que sea antigua.

Heaven is …

a … *a house which is completely automatic.*
b … *a servant to prepare my food* (un criado que …).
c … *a companion to bring me happiness.*
d … *two beautiful children to keep me busy.*
e … *a job to give me satisfaction.*
f … *a salary to pay for it all.*
g … *having no financial problems to worry me.*
h … *a lovely garden where we can relax.*
i … *common sense to bring me back* (devolver) *to reality!*

Bien, pero tu amigo/a dice que la frase tiene que empezar 'Heaven would be …' 'El cielo sería …' así que tienes que hacer la traducción otra vez, cambiando los verbos al imperfecto del subjuntivo.

3 Unas vacaciones desastrosas

Cambia los verbos que vienen entre paréntesis al indicativo o subjuntivo según el sentido. Ten cuidado con el tiempo del subjuntivo.

Las vacaciones del año pasado fueron un desastre. Buscamos unas vacaciones que (ser) interesantes y que no (costar) un dineral. Llamamos por teléfono a cierta agencia que (anunciar) vacaciones de montar a caballo. Como no hay ningún sitio por aquí donde se (poder) aprender a montar a caballo, pedimos una escuela donde se nos (enseñar). Llegó julio y fuimos en coche a la granja en Gales que (elegir). Al llegar ¡no había nadie que nos (recibir)! ¡La granja estaba desierta! Tuvimos que buscar quien nos (indicar) algún pueblo de donde (poder) llamar a la agencia. Como ya eran las nueve de la noche no conseguimos hablar con nadie que nos (ayudar). Por fin pasó un granjero en un tractor, a quien preguntamos si conocía un hotel donde nos (alojar). Él dijo que no, en esa región, no hay quien se (dedicar) siquiera a alquilar habitaciones. Tuvimos que dormir en el coche y a la mañana siguiente volvimos a casa. Como, claro, apenas había palabras que (expresar) nuestro descontento, mis padres escribieron una carta muy fuerte a la agencia. Ahora buscamos alguna medida que les (obligar) a devolvernos nuestro dinero. No es que (ser) tacaños, pero vamos, ¡qué desastre!

¡... Y EN MARCHA!

4 No es así

Un(a) de tus compañeros/as se comporta de una manera extraña, y estáis discutiendo las razones posibles. Hay que rechazar cada observación o sugerencia que se hace.

Ejemplo:

– Estará enamorado/a.
– No, no es que/porque esté enamorado/a.

5 El/La novio/a ideal

Cada uno escribe unas frases que describan el/la novio/a ideal, empezando: *Me gustaría un(a) novio/a que ...*

¡Cuidado! Como el verbo *Me gustaría* está en condicional, tendrás que emplear el imperfecto del subjuntivo.

Ejemplo:

Me gustaría un(a) novio/a que fuera muy inteligente y que tuviera los ojos azules.

6 La casa tecnológica

Tú y tus compañeros/as de clase estáis diseñando una casa que tenga toda la tecnología moderna. Hablad de los aparatos que consideréis imprescindibles, y quizás los que no, mencionando la función de cada aparato.

Ejemplo:

Necesitaremos un aparato que cierre las cortinas.
No queremos nada que no sea automático.

7 ¡Qué ciudad!

Imagina que eres habitante de la peor ciudad de tu país (¡claro que no lo es en realidad!). Tú y tus compañeros/as estáis lamentando a un(a) amigo/a español(a) la falta de todo lo necesario para una buena ciudad. Empleando verbos negativos, seguid inventando más quejas similares a los modelos.

Ejemplo:

En las calles no hay luces que funcionen.
No tenemos concejales que se interesen por los habitantes.
No hay muchos autobuses que lleguen a la hora debida.

Hablad de las escuelas, las tiendas, las calles, el hospital, los médicos, los transportes, los habitantes y las diversiones.

37 Other uses of the subjunctive

MECANISMOS

The subjunctive is used in various situations, apart from those already covered in Chapters 32–36.

37.1 Commands and exhortations

You will already have seen in Chapter 29 how the present subjunctive is used in **a)** all polite (***usted/ustedes***) commands (or imperatives), and **b)** all negative commands. This in fact only leaves the ***tú*** and ***vosotros*** positive commands which don't use the subjunctive! Refer back to Chapter 29 to remind yourself of all the details.

Quite often you can also use the present subjunctive to express a desire that someone should do something, or to encourage or exhort them to do it (or not to do it). It is the equivalent of the English 'may …' or '(don't) let …'. You simply use ***que*** + present subjunctive, usually the second or third person:

*¡Que **os divirtáis**!*
May you enjoy yourselves! (i.e. have a good time!)

*¡**Que descanse** en paz!*
May he rest in peace!

*¡**Que sea** pronto!*
Let/May it be soon!

*¡**Que no me vean** así!*
Don't let them see me like this!

It can sometimes be used to add force to a command, rather like 'mind or make sure you do/don't' in English:

*¡**Que no se lo digas** a tu madre!*
Don't tell your mother about it!

*¡Y **que no te olvides**!*
And **don't forget!/Mind you don't forget**!

*¡**Que lo tengas terminado** para mañana!*
Make sure you have it finished by tomorrow!

*¡**Que le regalemos** un MP3 para su cumpleaños!*
Let's give him an MP3 player for his birthday!

➡ **Exercise 1**

37.2 ¡Ojalá ... !

¡Ojalá ...! is used to introduce a very strong wish or desire. It originates from Arabic and means 'O Allah!'.

When it is used with the present subjunctive, this phrase suggests an open possibility, whereas with the imperfect subjunctive, the likelihood of the wish being fulfilled is more remote.

>*¡Ojalá ganen!*
>**I hope they win**!

>*¡Ojalá supiera* más español!
>**I wish I knew** more Spanish!

¡Ojalá! can also stand by itself, expressing a fervent wish that something previously mentioned will or will not happen:

>¿*Ganar el premio? ¡Ojalá!*
>Win the prize? **I wish I could**! (implying 'that'll be the day!')

➡ **Exercise 2**

37.3 Expressions with 'whatever' and 'however'

The following common expressions and variations on them use the subjunctive to express the idea of 'whatever':

Pase lo que pase ...	Whatever happens ...
Hagamos lo que hagamos ...	Whatever we do/do as we may ...
Digan lo que digan ...	Whatever they (may) say ...
Sea lo que sea ...	Whatever it is ...
Sea como sea ...	Be that as it may ...

To get over the idea of 'however' + an adjective or adverb, use ***por ... que*** followed by the subjunctive.

>***Por mucho/más que te quejes*** ...
>**However much you complain** ...

>***Por inteligentes que fuesen*** ...
>**However intelligent they were** ...

➡ **Exercise 3**

37.4 Expressions ending in *-quiera*

The equivalent ending in Spanish of English pronouns or adverbs ending in '-ever' is *-quiera*:

quienquiera	whoever
cuandoquiera	whenever
dondequiera	wherever
comoquiera	however, in whatever way
cualquiera/cualesquiera	whichever

These expressions ending in *-quiera* take the subjunctive.

> ***Quienquiera que** lo **reciba** …*
> **Whoever receives** it …

> *A **dondequiera que vayas** …*
> **Wherever you go** …

✍ Note that *cualquiera* and *cualesquiera* drop the final *a* before a noun:

> ***Cualquier** regalo que **escojas** …*
> **Whichever gift you choose** …

✍ Note: if 'whenever' simply records repeated fact, use *siempre que* with the indicative:

> ***Siempre que voy** a Caracas, me alojo en el hotel Orinoco.*
> **Whenever/Always when/Every time I go** to Caracas, I stay at the Orinoco Hotel.

37.5 After words meaning 'perhaps'

Quizá(s), *tal vez* and *acaso* all mean 'perhaps', and are often followed by the subjunctive, again where there is an element of doubt.

> ***Quizás no vengan** mañana.*
> **Perhaps they won't come** tomorrow.

> ***Tal vez** ya lo **sepan***.
> **Maybe they know already**.

➡ **Exercise 4**

¡PONTE A PUNTO!

1 Acoso maternal

Tu madre siempre os acosa a ti y a tu hermano/a, dándoos órdenes para que hagáis ciertas cosas en la casa y el jardín. Ya no les hacéis caso a sus sencillos imperativos y tiene que exhortaros con unos subjuntivos más enfáticos. Transforma sus órdenes en frases que utilicen *que* con el subjuntivo. Que tengas cuidado con la persona del verbo, porque algunas de las órdenes se dirigen solamente a ti, otras a ambos. Y hay otras que exigirán la tercera persona, puesto que otra persona tiene que hacer la acción.

1   ¡Pon tus zapatos en el armario!
2   ¡Pasa el aspirador por tu cuarto!
3   ¡Termina tu redacción sobre la literatura española!
4   ¡Pero no ocupes el ordenador toda la noche!
5   ¡Quitad la mesa en seguida, los dos!
6   ¡Y lavad los platos!
7   ¡Id al supermercado a por patatas!
8   ¡Y tiene que ser ahora mismo!
9   ¡Tu padre debe bajar la tele!
10 ¡Esos condenados perros tienen que largarse de nuestro jardín!

2 Tu madre se exaspera ...

Mira otra vez el Ejercicio 1 y las cosas que tu madre quiere que hagáis todos. Esta vez se exaspera y emplea *ojalá* con cada frase. Primero usa el presente del subjuntivo y luego, con más exasperación todavía, el imperfecto.

Tomemos el número 1 como ejemplo:

¡Pon tus zapatos en el armario!

¡Ojalá pongas tus zapatos en el armario! ⟶ *¡Ojalá pusieras/pusieses tus zapatos en el armario!*

3 Elecciones generales

Escoge un adjetivo o adverbio y también un verbo en subjuntivo de los facilitados abajo para reconstruir las frases siguientes.

1 Por ... que ... ese diputado, no conseguirá persuadirnos.
2 Por ... que ... el gobierno, no iba a hacer eso.
3 Por ... que ... al Presidente, no volveremos a elegirle.
4 Por ... escaños que ... los comunistas, no podrán formar un gobierno.
5 Por ... que ... con el resultado, la vida seguirá como siempre.
6 Por ... que ... los políticos, parece que no saben resolver nuestros problemas.
7 Por ... que ... el gobierno de ganar, siempre habría la posibilidad contraria.
8 Por ... que ... el resultado, faltarán seis semanas para el nuevo gobierno.

Adjetivos/adverbios: listos   muchos   seguro   rápidamente   tonto   más
fuerte   contentos

Verbos: estemos   sean   grite   se declare   estuviera   fuese   amemos
ganen

---

4 Más observaciones electorales

Completa las frases con una de las frases explicadas en este capítulo.

1 ... la derecha gane las elecciones.
2 ¡ ... no las ganen los comunistas!
3 ... que diga eso tiene que ser muy optimista.
4 ... que hable el presidente, siempre tiene éxito.
5 ... lo que ... , pasado mañana tendremos un nuevo gobierno.
6 ... que sea el gobierno, me es igual.
7 ... el próximo sea mejor.

 ¡... Y EN MARCHA!

5 Consejos para aceptar un animal en casa

a) Que discutáis entre vosotros lo que hay que hacer cuando se recibe a un nuevo animal, sea gato, perro, hámster, caballo u otro, en tu casa o tu jardín. Y ¡que utilicéis una buena cantidad de subjuntivos exhortativos!

Ejemplos:

Que le compremos una cesta para cama.
Que no duerma en nuestras camas.
Que le lleves al veterinario para sus vacunaciones.

b) Ahora, que cada uno prepare un decálogo, es decir, una lista de diez cosas que se deberían o no se deberían hacer para o con el animal. ¡Y que cada frase contenga un subjuntivo!

Ejemplo:

Que se le dé de comer con regularidad.

6 El último recurso

Estáis tú y tus compañeros/as con unos compañeros españoles en lo alto de una montaña. Estáis inmovilizados allí porque ha bajado una niebla muy densa, y todos empezáis a tener miedo. Haced algunas observaciones un poco nerviosas, ¡empleando expresiones que acabáis de aprender, claro!

Ejemplo:

– Pase lo que pase, por lo menos tenemos algo de comer.
– Quienquiera que nos halle, con esta niebla no vendrá hasta mañana.

7 Desaparecido/a

Uno/a de tus compañeros/as ha desaparecido. Todos tenéis que hacer sugerencias acerca de lo que le ha pasado, usando *quizás* o *tal vez*.

Ejemplo:

– Quizás haya ido al fútbol.
– Tal vez esté enfermo/a.

8 Deseos

Todos tenéis que expresar tres deseos algo remotos pero asequibles, empleando *¡ojalá!* con el presente del subjuntivo.

Ejemplo:

¡Ojalá me regalen un perro para mi cumpleaños!

Ahora, otros tres deseos más improbables, con el imperfecto del subjuntivo.

Ejemplo:

¡Ojalá tuviera millones de euros!

38 'If …' clauses

MECANISMOS

The use of *si* meaning 'if' is less complicated in Spanish than it looks, provided the following guidelines are borne in mind.

38.1 Open possibility

With a totally open possibility, use the present tense in the *si* clause, as in English. This is usually in combination with the present, future or imperative in the main clause of the sentence.

> *Si veo a Carlos, le daré tu recado.*
> **If I see** Carlos, I'll give him your message.

> *Si ves a Carlos, dale mi recado.*
> **If you see** Carlos, give him my message.

38.2 Plain fact in the past

With a statement of plain fact about circumstances in the past, use the indicative of the relevant tense in the *si* clause.

> *Si veíamos a Carlos, le saludábamos y nos parábamos a charlar si él quería.*
> **If we saw** Carlos, **we said hello** and **stopped** to chat if he wished.

38.3 Remote or hypothetical possibilities

If the possibility is remote or hypothetical, use the imperfect subjunctive after *si*, in combination with the conditional in the main clause of the sentence.

> *Si vieras a Carlos, le darías mi recado, ¿no?*
> **If you saw/were to see** Carlos, you **would give** him my message, wouldn't you?

38.4 The opposite of what actually happened

If the statement is contrary to what actually happened, use the pluperfect subjunctive in combination with the conditional perfect.

> *Si hubiera/hubiese visto a Carlos, le habría/hubiera dado tu recado.*
> **If I had seen** Carlos (but I didn't), **I would have given** him your message. (but I couldn't)

✏️ Note that after *si*, you can use either the *hubiese* or *hubiera* form of the pluperfect subjunctive, and in the main clause, either the conditional *habría* or the subjunctive form *hubiera* but **not** *hubiese*. You will meet all these variations, but you may find it easier yourself, at least until you become confident with this construction, to use the *hubiera* form (with the correct ending) in both parts of the sentence.

*Si **hubiéramos visto** a Carlos, le **hubiéramos dado** tu recado.*
If we had seen Carlos, we **would have given** him your message.

➡️ **Exercises 1, 2**

38.5 'What if ...?'

'What if ...?' is expressed by *¿Si ...?* and the present indicative or imperfect or pluperfect subjunctive, depending on the meaning:

*¿**Si Carlos viene** a vernos?*
What if Carlos comes to see us?

*¿**Si Carlos viniera/viniese** a vernos?*
What if Carlos came to see us?

*¿**Si Carlos hubiera/hubiese venido** a vernos?*
What if Carlos had come to see us?

➡️ **Exercise 3**

38.6 'As if ...'

'As if ...' is expressed by *como si ...* + the imperfect or pluperfect subjunctive:

*Era **como si no le viera**.*
It was **as if I couldn't see him**.

*Era **como si no le hubiera visto**.*
It was **as if I hadn't seen him**.

38.7 'Whether'

When *si* means 'whether' after verbs such as *saber*, it can be followed by any indicative tense that makes sense.

*No sabemos si Carlos **viene/vendrá/vendría/venía/ha venido/vino** ... a vernos.*
We don't know if/whether Carlos **is coming/will come/would come/was coming/has come/came** ... to see us.

 **¡PONTE A PUNTO!**

1 Diario de las vacaciones

Una señora muy rubia está de vacaciones con su marido en una isla española y apunta unos pensamientos sobre cada día. Pon el verbo que aparece entre paréntesis en el tiempo del indicativo o del subjuntivo que le corresponda. ¡Mira el verbo principal y ten ciudado con la concordancia de los tiempos!

---

domingo – día de llegada:

Si no (haber) mucha gente en el bar, tomaremos una cerveza.
Si (hacer) mucho calor esta tarde, la pasaremos en la playa.

lunes:

Mi marido dice que si (pasar) tanto tiempo bajo este sol, vamos a parecernos a un par de langostas.
Me pregunto qué pasaría si (coger) los dos una insolación.

martes:

Si mi marido (seguir) bebiendo y comiendo así, se va a poner enfermo.
¡Qué nubes tan amenazadoras! Si (llover) esta tarde, nos quedaremos al lado de la piscina.

miércoles:

Si nos (poner) crema de sol antes, no hubiéramos tenido la piel quemada.
Si (tener) la piel morena como los españoles, no tendríamos estos problemas.

jueves:

Si (llegar) a persuadir a mi marido, iremos de compras en la ciudad.
Si (encontrar) una muñeca típica, la compraría para mi nieta.

viernes:

Si aquella muñeca no (ser) tan cara, la hubiera comprado.
Si (saber) qué otro regalo le gustaría, se lo compraría.

sábado – día de salida:

Si el avión (llevar) retraso, tendremos que esperar en el aeropuerto.
Si (quedar) más tiempo, nos hubiera gustado visitar el interior de la isla.

---

2 Gibraltar – ¡otra vez!

Cambia el infinitivo del verbo al tiempo del indicativo o del subjuntivo que convenga al sentido.

En 1969, el General Franco dijo que si los ingleses no (entrar) en negociaciones sobre la soberanía del Peñón, cerraría la verja. Si los gibraltareños (querer) unirse a España, los británicos hubieran empezado a negociar, pero entonces aquéllos querían quedarse bajo la soberanía británica. Es de conjeturarse lo que habría pasado si los habitantes de la Roca (votar) por unirse a la dictadura. Ahora que España es una democracia y miembro de la UE, si los gibraltareños (querer) unirse a España, quizás habrá menos problemas. Pero si los ingleses (ser) verdaderamente sinceros hacia España al asunto de la soberanía, no habría tantas procrastinaciones. Pero, ¿si los gibraltareños no (tener) ganas de hacerse españoles? ¿Qué se debería hacer entonces? O ¡¿si Gran Bretaña (hacerse) dictadura?!

3 Una señora recelosa

Habiendo leído demasiado la prensa británica, la señora del Ejercicio 1 comienza a inquietarse por todos los desastres que pudieran acaecerles durante su estancia en la isla. Tienes que emplear *si* con el imperfecto del subjuntivo.

Ejemplo:

Si mi marido (caer) enfermo ⟶ *Si mi marido cayera/cayese enfermo.*

1 Si mi marido (estar) enfermo.
2 Si le (llevar) al hospital.
3 Si yo (tener) que tomar un taxi para ir a verle.
4 Si se nos (agotar) el dinero.
5 Si nos (atracar) en la calle.
6 Si alguien nos (robar) todo el dinero.
7 Si (encontrar) ratones o cucarachas en la habitación del hotel.
8 Si la comida (ser) mala.
9 Si (llegar) tarde al aeropuerto y (perder) el avión para volver a Inglaterra.
10 Y – respondió su marido, siempre paciente – ¡si todo (salir) perfectamente!

 ¡... Y EN MARCHA!

4 ¿Amigos?

Tu amigo/a quiere que le/la ayudes el sábado que viene, pero tú tienes pocas ganas de hacerlo y le pones muchas condiciones.

Ejemplo:

Bueno, te ayudaré si tengo bastante tiempo.

¡A ver cuántas más condiciones puedes imponer – por ejemplo, el tiempo que hace, tu novio/a, otros amigos, compras, ayudar en casa, tener ganas, descansar – antes de consentir en ayudarle/la!

5 Un(a) presidente prudente

Ya conocerás la situación en que se te pregunta '¿qué harías si fueras presidente?' Supongamos que ya eres presidente del gobierno. Quieres hacer muchas cosas, pero las circunstancias todavía no están lo suficientemente estables para permitirte hacerlas. Quieres bajar los impuestos, pero todavía no puedes. En una entrevista, tienes que decir en qué circunstancias los bajarías, según este modelo:

Bajaría los impuestos si la productividad industrial fuera más alta.

No olvides hablar de: los tipos de interés, el valor del euro, las próximas elecciones, los servicios sociales, las pensiones, la enseñanza, las importaciones, las exportaciones, la balanza de pagos, el paro.

6 La historia de un criminal

Pablo García, 23 años, parado, sin dirección fija, fue ayer condenado a tres años de cárcel por haber atracado y robado a una turista inglesa en Torremolinos. Parece ser que ésta no es la primera vez que comparece ante el juez, puesto que tiene una historia de criminalidad desde los catorce años.

Con tus compañeros/as, trata de analizar el caso de Pablo para descubrir cómo se desvió del buen camino. A ver cuántas razones puedes expresar, usando *si*.

Ejemplo:

Si su padre no le hubiera echado de casa a los 16 años, no se hubiera vuelto al crimen.

(No hace falta cambiar la segunda parte de la frase cada vez.)

Considera también problemas en el colegio, malas influencias, follones en casa, robo de coches, otros atracos, drogas, vivir con squatters, la falta de trabajo y otros problemas en que tú puedas pensar.

39 Negatives

39.1 Making the verb negative

In Spanish, the verb is made negative by putting **no** before it:

Vamos   We're going
No vamos   We're not going

39.2 Other negative expressions

Other negative expressions are:

nada	nothing
nadie	nobody, no-one
nunca *jamás* }	never
ninguno	no, not any, none
ni … ni …	neither … nor …
tampoco	not either, neither (negative of **también** = also)
en mi vida	never in my life
a/en { *ninguna parte* *ningún sitio* }	nowhere
ya no	no longer, not any more (always precedes the verb)

a) When these expressions follow the verb, the verb is preceded by **no**:

No vamos **nunca** al cine.
We **never** go to the cinema.

No me conoce **nadie** aquí.
No-one knows me here.

b) When the negative precedes the verb, or there is no verb, **no** is not used:

Nunca vamos al cine.
We **never** go to the cinema.

Nadie me conoce aquí.
No-one knows me here.

¿Vas mucho al cine? **Nunca**.
Do you go to the cinema much? **Never**.

215

c) *Ninguno* is the negative of *alguno*, and agrees with the noun it refers to. Like *algún*, it drops the *-o* and takes an accent on the *-u-* with a masculine singular noun.

> *No* tengo *ningún* interés.
> I have **no** interest(s).

- *Ninguno* is not usually used in the plural:

> *Ninguno* de estos objetos vale.
> **None** of these objects is/are any good.

- Note also that *alguno* used after the noun can give an even stronger negative meaning.

> *No* tengo interés *alguno*.
> I have **no** interest **at all/whatsoever**.

d) *Tampoco* is the negative of *también* (also, too):

> *Manolo quiere ver Madrid y yo quiero verla* **también**. *Yo también.*
> Manolo wants to see Madrid and I want to see it **as well**. I do **too**.

> *Manolo* **no** *quiere ver Madrid* **ni** *yo quiero verla* **tampoco**. *Ni yo* **tampoco**.
> Manolo **doesn't** want to see Madrid, and I **don't** want to see it **either**. **Neither** do I.

 **Exercises 1, 2, 3**

¡PONTE A PUNTO!

1 Depresión

Rellena los espacios en blanco con la más apta de las frases negativas siguientes.

nunca	ni … ni …	tampoco	en su vida	en ninguna parte	nada
nadie	ninguno	alguno			

Últimamente me parece que . . **1** . . me quiere y yo no tengo interés en . . **2** . . . No salgo . . **3** . . y . . **4** . . de mis amigos viene a verme. . . **5** . . me he sentido tan deprimida. No encuentro simpatía . . **6** . . . Parece que . . **7** . . mis padres . . **8** . . mis amigos quieren ayudarme. Siento que no sirvo para . . **9** . . . Mi novio me invita al cine pero no siento interés . . **10** . . en salir, y luego si le digo que no quiero ir, contesta que, bueno, pues, él no quiere ir . . **11** . . . ¡Dice que . . **12** . . ha encontrado a una persona tan difícil como yo!

2 ¡Qué distintos son!

Miguel es un chico muy bueno, ¡pero no conoces a su hermano Mateo! Cambia las frases siguientes al negativo, contrastando el comportamiento de Mateo con el de Miguel.

Ejemplo:

Miguel <u>siempre</u> prepara el desayuno en casa.

Mateo <u>nunca</u> prepara (<u>no</u> prepara <u>nunca</u>) el desayuno.

1 Miguel *siempre* ayuda a su madre.
2 A Miguel le gusta invitar *a la gente* a casa.
3 Miguel invita *tanto* a sus compañeros *como* a sus compañeras.
4 Miguel invita *también* a su novia.
5 A Miguel le interesan *muchas cosas*.
6 Miguel juega *al fútbol*.
7 Y viaja *a todas partes* con el equipo.
8 Miguel *sigue teniendo* éxito con sus estudios.

3 ¿Con 'no' o sin 'no'?

¿Te acuerdas de la regla que dice que si el negativo viene después del verbo, tienes que usar *no* antes? Para un poco de práctica, cambia las frases siguientes de modo que se pueda quitar el 'no' … ¡Cuidado! No será práctico cambiarlas todas y tienes que identificar las frases donde no sea posible.

Ejemplo:

No voy nunca al cine./Nunca voy al cine.

1 No ha llegado nadie.
2 No lo sabe ni Pedro ni Ana.
3 No lo sé yo tampoco.
4 No hemos visto a nadie.
5 No me conoce nadie.
6 No hemos oído nada.
7 No ocurre nada.
8 No he hecho tal cosa en mi vida.
9 Esto no ocurre nunca.
10 No lo encuentro en ninguna parte.
11 No conozco a ninguna de estas personas.

¡... Y EN MARCHA!

4 Los jactanciosos

Usando frases negativas, cada miembro de la clase tiene que hacer tres jactancias (¡verdaderas o ficticias!).

Ejemplo:

Yo no tengo ningún problema con la gramática española.
No hay nada que yo no entienda.
Yo nunca digo mentiras.

5 Libro de reclamaciones

A todos nos gusta quejarnos, y la mayoría de nuestras quejas son negativas. Aquí tienes la oportunidad de quejarte acerca de tu colegio. Haz una lista de tus reclamaciones y cuéntalas a tu profesor(a) o a un(a) compañero/a de clase que tiene que responder, justificándose.

Ejemplo:

Ninguno de los profesores me quiere.
Nuestras cosas no están seguras en ninguna parte.
Nunca ponen papel higiénico en los servicios.

6 ¡Qué gobierno!

¡Más quejas! Esta vez, todavía usando frases negativas, te quejas del gobierno – el británico, o el español.

Opción A: Tú haces las reclamaciones y tu compañero/a, que es diputado/a, trata de responder a tus quejas.

Opción B: Trabaja con tus compañeros/as para reunir una lista de reclamaciones contra el gobierno, que vais a presentar a vuestro/a diputado/a, que podría ser tu profesor(a).

Ejemplo:

Ningún ministro tiene ni idea de cómo vivimos nosotros.
El gobierno nunca tiene en cuenta nuestras opiniones.
No tiene ninguna solución al problema del tráfico.

40 Prepositions

MECANISMOS

A preposition tells you where a thing or a person stands in relation to another in time, place or manner. This chapter deals with prepositions other than those which have special chapters devoted to them (Chapters 41, 42 and 43).

40.1 Common prepositions

a) *A* and *en*

• *A* basically means 'to'.

    *Escribo **a** mi hermana.*
    I'm writing **to** my sister.

It sometimes means 'at' or 'in', especially after a verb of motion:

    *Llegaron **a** Salamanca.*
    They arrived **at/in** Salamanca.

• *En* basically means 'in', 'on', and often 'at'.

    *La tienda está **en** Toledo.*
    The shop is **in** Toledo.

    *Te veré **en** la estación.*
    I'll see you **at/in** the station.

Note that *en* is used for 'in (a town)': 'in Paris' is **en París** in Spanish (unlike the French *à Paris*).

• *A* usually indicates motion to a place but *en* indicates position in or on a place. Note the difference between:

    ***Estamos en** casa.*
    We're at home. (position)

    ***Vamos a** casa.*
    We're going (to) home. (motion)

Be careful with phrases such as 'We're going to eat in the restaurant', which is expressed as ***Vamos a comer al restaurante***, the idea being that in fact you are going **to** the restaurant **to** eat.

- *A* also means 'from' when used with verbs of 'separation' such as ***robar, confiscar, quitar, comprar***.

    Compré *mi casa **a** un español.*
    I bought my house **from** a Spaniard.

    Le quitaron *el pasaporte **al** inmigrante.*
    They took the immigrant's passport. (They took the passport **from** the immigrant.)

    Note: the 'personal *a*' is explained in Chapter 41.

b) *Con* means 'with' and is used much as in English; but remember the special forms:

conmigo, contigo, consigo   with me, with you, with himself/herself/oneself/yourself/
                                  yourselves (Vd(s))/themselves

c) *De*

- Besides the various usages mentioned elsewhere in this book, remember that ***de*** can mean 'from':

    *Somos/Venimos **de** León.*
    We're/We come **from** León.

- Watch out for verbs which are followed by ***de***, such as:

llenar de (to fill with), ***cubrir de*** (to cover with)

- ***Una taza de té*** can mean both a cup of tea or a teacup, just as ***una botella de cerveza*** means either a beer bottle or a bottle of beer. If a clear distinction really needs to be made, say ***una botella con cerveza*** for a bottle(ful) of beer, and ***una botella para cerveza*** for a beer bottle!

d) *Entre* means 'between' or 'among'.

entre *amigos*   **between/among** friends

Note also:
decir entre sí to say to oneself

e) *Hacia* means 'towards', or the suffix '-wards'.

hacia *el cielo*   **towards** the sky/sky**wards**

f) *Hasta* means 'until', 'up to', 'as far as'.

hasta *ahora*   **up to** now, **until** now
hasta *luego*   **till** then, 'see you'
hasta *la plaza*   **as far as** the square

g) *Según* means 'according to', or, if used with a verb, 'according to what ...'.

Según dicen ...   **According to what** they say ...

It can also stand by itself, meaning 'it depends':

– *¿De acuerdo?*   All right?
– *Según.*   It depends.

h) *Sin* means 'without'. It usually comes before a noun without the indefinite article.

sin camisa   **without** a shirt
sin dinero   **without** any money

It can also be followed by the infinitive, when it has a 'negating' effect:

sin ver nada   **without seeing** anything

i) *Sobre, en, encima de*

• *Sobre* and *en* both mean 'on (a vertical or horizontal surface)'.

en la mesa   **on** the table
en la pared   **on** the wall

• *Sobre* and *encima de* both mean 'on top of (a horizontal surface)'.

encima de/sobre la mesa   **on (top of)** the table

• *Encima de* also means 'above'.

encima de la puerta   **above** the door

• *Por encima de*, 'over', implies motion.

   *Los globos volaban **por encima de** nosotros.*
   The balloons were flying **over (the top of)** us.

j) *Detrás de* and *tras* both mean 'behind', though *tras* can also mean the same as *después de* – 'after', 'as a result of'.

tras los sucesos de hoy   **after** today's events
correr *tras* algo/alguien   to run **after** something/somebody

k) *Delante de* and *ante* both mean 'in front of', 'before' in that sense. *Ante* often suggests 'in the presence of', 'faced with':

comparecer *ante* el juez   to appear **before** the magistrate
ante este problema   **faced with** this problem

40.2 Other useful prepositions

a causa de	because of
a razón de	because of, owing to
acerca de *al asunto de* }	about, on the subject of
al lado de	beside, next to
al otro lado de	on the other side of
alrededor de	around
bajo	under
contra	against
debajo de	under, beneath
debido a	due to, owing to, because of
dentro de	inside, within
dentro de cinco minutos	in five minutes' time
desde	from, since (see also Chapter 43)
desde ... hasta ...	from ... to/until ...
después de	after
enfrente de	opposite (*not* in front of)
frente a	faced with/confronted with, in consideration of, opposite
junto a	next to
mediante *por medio de* }	by means of
a partir de	from (a time or event)
a pesar de *pese a* }	in spite of
en torno a	around

Note: ***estar en contra de***   to be against

40.3 Converting prepositions to adverbs

Finally, note that many of the prepositions which are followed by *de* can be used as adverbs by omitting the *de*.

*Los que van **delante** ...*	Those who go **in front** ...
*Viven **enfrente**.*	They live **opposite**.
*Lo que ves **debajo** ...*	What you can see **below** ...

Exercise 1

¡PONTE A PUNTO!

1 La casa de mis sueños

Rellena los espacios en blanco con una preposición que convenga al sentido.

. . **1** . . la casa . . **2** . . mis sueños habría muchas habitaciones. . . **3** . . la sala de estar, . . **4** . . el suelo, habría una alfombra persiana. . . **5** . . la chimenea habría unas butacas muy cómodas, y . . **6** . . éstas unos cojines de lujo. . . **7** . . las ventanas habría unas cortinas lujosas y . . **8** . . el marco de la ventana unas persianas para protegernos del sol. . . **9** . . la chimenea tendría una pintura de Picasso. . . **10** . . el primer piso habría varios dormitorios, cada uno . . **11** . . cuarto de baño. . . **12** . . las paredes de éstos habría azulejos. . . **13** . . el sur de España hay mucha sequía. . . **14** . . este problema instalaría . . **15** . . el techo de la casa un gran depósito para coger agua. . . **16** . . la casa tendría un jardín, donde trataría de cultivar flores . . **17** . . lo seco del clima. . . **18** . . todo este sueño me vais a preguntar ¿. . **19** . . dónde voy a sacar el dinero? Pues en efecto . . **20** . . un éxito . . **21** . . la lotería, no habrá problema, excepto que tengo que esperar . . **22** . . el año que viene el permiso de construir. . . **23** . . el régimen actual hay muchas reglas, pero no estoy . . **24** . . ellas. ¡Quiero tener buenas relaciones . . **25** . . los que viven . . **26** . . !

 ¡… Y EN MARCHA!

2 ¡Cuántas preposiciones hay!

Ejercicio de reconocimiento. Toma un artículo que te interese en cualquier periódico o revista española, y marca todas las preposiciones que encuentras. ¿Cuántas hay? ¿Cuántas palabras de cada cien son preposiciones?

3 ¡A ver si te puedes imaginar mi ciudad o mi pueblo!

Mandas una foto digital con un e-mail a tu compañero/a en Méjico, describiéndole el centro de tu ciudad o tu pueblo. Usando cuantas preposiciones puedas, tienes que explicarle dónde están situados los edificios y servicios principales en relación unos con otros.

Ejemplo:

Delante de la iglesia se encuentra una gran plaza, y a cada lado de la plaza hay tiendas. Una carretera de circunvalación pasa alrededor de la ciudad …

4 ¡Adiós y suerte a todos!

Se acerca el fin de vuestro último curso en el colegio, y para celebrarlo, tú y tu clase habéis decidido que en vez de emborracharos en la ciudad, os prepararéis una cena formal, todos vestidos como se debe, y sentados a la mesa. Tenéis que decidir dónde os sentaréis cada uno. Hablad entre vosotros, decidiendo quién (¡y quién no!) debe sentarse *entre/al lado/a la derecha/a la izquierda/enfrente de* quién (y quizás por qué …).

41 The personal *a*

a) This is one of the quirks of Spanish. The preposition **a** comes before a direct object when the object is a definite, particularised person or persons.

*Ayer vi **a Pedro**.*
I saw **Peter** yesterday.

*Llevaré **a los niños** al cole.*
I'll take **the children** to school.

It is also often used when an animal is the direct object, when the animal is 'personalised'.

*Cada noche tenemos que pasear **al perro**.*
Every night we have to walk **the dog**.

b) The personal **a** is not used, however, if the direct object is not definite. Compare these two examples:

*¿Conoces **al profesor** que vive cerca del colegio?*
Do you know **the teacher** who lives near the school?

*Buscamos **un profesor** que viva cerca del colegio.*
We're looking for **a teacher** who lives near the school.

In the second example, the direct object is not a definite teacher but any teacher so long as he/she lives near the school. (See also Chapter 36 on the subjunctive.)

c) The following pronouns are also preceded by **a** when they are the direct object:
alguien, alguno, uno, ambos, cualquiera, nadie, otro, ninguno, quien, ¿quién?, todos.

*No veo **a nadie**.*
I can**'t** see **anyone**.

*¿Conoces **a alguien** aquí?*
Do you know **anyone** here?

*¿**A quién** escogiste?*
Who(m) did you choose?

d) **A** is also used before *el que/el cual/la que/la cual*, etc. in a relative clause (see Chapter 44).

*Fue la mujer **a la que** habíamos visto antes aquel día.*
It was the woman **(whom)** we had seen before that day.

e) Note that *querer* without the *a* usually means 'to want', but with *a*, *querer* usually means 'to love'!

> *Quiero **una hija**.*
> I want **a daughter**.

> *Quiero **a una hija**.*
> I love **one daughter**. (but not the others)

➡ **Exercise 1**

 ¡PONTE A PUNTO!

1 En la fábrica de yogur

Rellena los espacios en blanco con la preposición *a* cuando sea necesario.

Recientemente fuimos a España mis compañeros de clase y yo con nuestra profesora. El primer día visitamos . . **1** . . una fábrica de yogur y conocimos . . **2** . . el director. ¡Éste preguntó . . **3** . . nuestra profe si entendíamos bien el español! Mientras estábamos allí visitamos . . **4** . . la sección donde mezclan el producto y fuimos a ver . . **5** . . la encargada. Ella nos enseñó . . **6** . . el proceso de producción y dijo que la fábrica emplea . . **7** . . cincuenta personas. Al terminar la visita fuimos a buscar . . **8** . . un autobús que nos llevara al centro de la ciudad. Preguntamos . . **9** . . un hombre que paseaba . . **10** . . su perro delante de la fábrica. Parecía que él no quería ayudar . .**11** . . nadie, pero poco después encontramos . . **12** . . alguien que podía ayudarnos. Vimos . . **13** . . un taxista que comía . . **14** . . un bocadillo en su taxi. Su taxi era demasiado pequeño para llevar . . **15** . . un grupo como el nuestro, pero llamó por radio . . **16** . . sus colegas que acudieron en otros dos taxis. Durante los otros días de la estancia encontramos . . **17** . . muchas personas interesantes y aprendimos . . **18** . . muchos datos nuevos sobre España.

 ¡... Y EN MARCHA!

2 ¿A quién?

Utilizando verbos tales como *ayudar, querer, observar, mirar, escuchar, admirar, considerar, odiar, detestar, aborrecer, aprobar, desaprobar,* haz preguntas a tus compañeros/as.

Ejemplo:

– *¿A quién ayudas más en casa?*
– *Ayudo más a mi madre./No ayudo a nadie.*
– *¿A qué deportista admiras?*
– *Admiro a Rafael Nadal.*
– *¿A cuál consideras el mejor conjunto de tu país?*
– *A ...*

42 *Para* and *por*

The two prepositions *para* and *por* are often confused but basically *para* usually means 'for', and *por* usually means 'by', 'through' or 'because of' and, only in certain contexts, 'for'.

42.1 Uses of *para*

a) to indicate destination, objective, purpose or intention:

*Este regalo es **para ti**.*
This present is **for you**. (i.e. its destination)

*Café **para todos**.*
Coffee **for everyone**.

*Estudio **para abogado**.*
I'm studying **to be a lawyer**.

*Salimos **para la costa**.*
We set out **for the coast**.

***Para mí** una ensalada.*
A salad **for me**.

*¿**Para qué?*** means 'What for?'/'For what purpose?' and presupposes the answer *para* + infinitive or *para que* + subjunctive ('in order to'/'in order that') (see Chapter 36).

*¿**Para qué** haces footing? Hago footing **para** mantenerme en forma.*
Why do you jog? **(What for?)** I jog **(in order) to** keep fit.

b) to express 'in view of', 'considering':

*El supermercado es muy feo **para** su situación.*
The supermarket is very ugly **for** its position.

c) with *estar* to convey the sense of 'to be on the point of':

*Estaba **para** decirlo.*
I was **about to** say so.

d) in expressions of time:

- to convey 'by a certain time':

*Estará listo **para** las ocho.*
It will be ready **by** eight o'clock.

- to convey 'for a particular time':

*Estamos citados **para** las tres.*
We have an appointment **for** three o'clock.

*Nos queda dinero **para** dos días.*
We have enough money left **for** two days.

- to express 'around', 'towards':

*Te veo **para** las cinco.*
I'll see you **around/towards** five o'clock.

42.2 Uses of *por*

Por occurs more frequently than *para* and has a wider range of uses.

a) meaning 'through' in the physical sense:

*Pasamos **por** Córdoba.*
We passed **through** Cordoba.

b) meaning 'because of', 'on account of':

*No podíamos ver **por** la gente que había.*
We couldn't see **for/because of** the people.

*Le quiero **por** su bondad.*
I love him **for** his kindness.

*Me intereso **por** su carácter.*
I'm interested **in** her character.

*Tiene curiosidad **por** las casas antiguas.*
He has an interest **in** old houses.

c) with an infinitive, meaning 'through … -ing', 'because of … -ing':

*Eso fue **por** no saber lo que hacía.*
That was **through** not knowing what I was doing (i.e. **because** I didn't know what I was doing)

d) to express the agent ('by') with a passive verb (see Chapter 31):

*La fábrica fue construida **por** una empresa del pueblo.*
The factory was built **by** a village firm.

e) to express 'by means of':

*Funciona **por** presión atmosférica.*
It works **by (means of)** atmospheric pressure.

*Conseguí los billetes **por** tu ayuda.*
I got the tickets **through/by means of** your help.

*Mando la respuesta **por** fax.*
I'm sending the answer **by** fax.

f) to convey 'on behalf of', 'in support of', 'for the sake of':

*Lo hice **por** ti.*
I did it **for/in support of/on behalf of** you.

*No estoy **por** la caza.*
I'm not **for/in favour of** hunting.

*¡**Por** Dios!*
For God's sake!

g) to express 'in exchange for':

*Gracias **por** tu ayuda.*
Thanks **for (in exchange for)** your help.

*Pagué demasiado **por** estos zapatos.*
I paid too much **for (in exchange for)** these shoes.

h) with units of measure to convey 'per':

*A doscientos kilómetros **por** hora.*
At 200 kilometres **per** hour.

*Tres veces **por** día.*
Three times **per/a** day.

(*Al día* is probably more usual.)

i) in the sense of 'to get':

*Voy al supermercado **por (a por)** leche.*
I'm going to the supermarket **for/to get** some milk.

*Le mandaron **por** los bomberos.*
They sent him **for** the fire brigade.

j) in a place context, 'through', 'over', 'around':

*un viaje **por** Europa*	a trip **around/all over** Europe
***por** la calle*	**in** the street/**outdoors**
***por** aquí/allí*	this/that **way**, **around** here/there

k) in a time context:

- with parts of the day, 'in', 'at':

por la mañana/tarde/noche   in the morning/afternoon, **at** night

- *sólo por* … just for … (time):

    Préstamelo sólo por un día.
    Lend it to me **just for** a day.

l) With projected future time, either *para* or *por* may be used, meaning 'for':

    Voy a Inglaterra para/por un mes.
    I'm going to England **for** a month.

42.3 Summary

To decide whether to use *por* or *para* in the translation of 'for', think first of the meaning of 'for' in English.

- If it means 'intended for/destined for/for a purpose', use *para*.
- If it means 'in exchange for/because of/on behalf of/in support of/through', use *por*.

Note: *por ahora* (for now), but *para siempre* (for ever)!

Exercises 1, 2

¡PONTE A PUNTO!

1 Los niños de la calle

Rellena los espacios en blanco con *para* o *por*.

Si viajas . . **1** . . muchas de las ciudades de Sudamérica . . **2** . . la tarde o . . **3** . . la noche, verás a niños y niñas muy jóvenes . . **4** . . las calles. . . **5** . . ellos resulta una vida muy peligrosa puesto que la policía tiene mucho interés . . **6** . . el aspecto de la ciudad, y queda poco simpatía . . **7** . . estos pequeños mendigos. Hay ciertos individuos y organizaciones que tratan de hacer algo . . **8** . . ellos, pero . . **9** . . esas partes del mundo son una minoría. . . **10** . . los gobiernos es un problema, puesto que queda muy poco dinero . . **11** . . ayudarles. . . **12** . . mí, yo creo que . . **13** . . conseguir cualquier éxito, las organizaciones caritativas internacionales y los gobiernos tendrán que hacer más . . **14** . . resolver este problema. . . **15** . . ahora parece que se puede hacer muy poco.

2 Concursos televisados

Rellena los espacios en blanco en el diálogo siguiente con *para* o *por*, según convenga.

– . . **1** . . mucha gente los concursos televisados son un sueño.
– Pero . . **2** . . tomar parte hay que someterse a unas pruebas de selección.
– Si te escogen quizás cobres miles de euros . . **3** . . sólo contestar a unas preguntas.
– . . **4** . . tener éxito no tienes que ser inteligente.
– . . **5** . . mí esto no importa. . . **6** . . no tener problemas de dinero yo haría cualquier cosa.
. . **7** . . tener una familia que gasta tanto, yo no tengo dinero . . **8** . . nada.
– Bueno, me voy. Tengo que ir al supermercado . . **9** . . provisiones. Sólo pagué 2,50 euros . . **10** . . carne ayer. Luego quiero estar en casa . . **11** . . las cinco . . **12** . . ver *El precio justo* en la tele.

¡... Y EN MARCHA!

3 Visitantes intergalácticos

Recientemente, en un caso muy extraño, han venido a tu región unos visitantes del espacio cuyo único idioma terrestre es el español. Hacen una visita a tu clase, donde todos tenéis que responder a sus preguntas acerca del uso de varios objetos corrientes en la clase. Una mitad de la clase hace el papel de los extraterrestres, la otra mitad sois vosotros mismos.

Ejemplo:

– *¿Para qué sirve esto?*
– *Es un bolígrafo. Sirve para escribir.*

4 ¡Estos niños inquisitivos!

Ya sabes lo inquisitivos que son los niños de unos tres o cuatro años. Tú estás trabajando de *au pair* en una familia española y te han encargado de llevar a su hijo Pablito o su hija Conchita a la ciudad. El/La niño/a (tu compañero/a de clase) te hace un sinfín de preguntas sobre lo que hacéis y veis. Todas las preguntas, claro, empiezan con *¿Para qué?* o *¿Por qué?*, y tú tienes que contestar.

Ejemplo:

– *¿Por qué vamos en autobús y por qué no vamos andando?*
– *Porque es muy lejos para ir andando.*
– *¿Para qué sirve este botón?* (señalando el botón del timbre en el autobús)
– *Para parar el autobús.*

5 ¿Para qué estamos aquí?

Estás teniendo una discusión filosófica con un(a) amigo/a español(a) (tu compañero/a de clase). Para empezar, todos tenéis que pensar en cinco preguntas por lo menos acerca de nuestra existencia que empiecen con *¿Para qué?* o *¿Por qué?* y tu compañero/a tiene que contestar a las preguntas.

Ejemplo:

– *¿Para qué existen las religiones?*
– *Para dar sentido a la vida.*
– *¿Por qué todavía hay tantas guerras?*
– *Porque los humanos todavía no han aprendido a respetar las creencias de otros.*

43 How long for?

MECANISMOS

When you want to say in Spanish how long you have been doing something, you have to take a number of factors into consideration. Here is some guidance.

43.1 How long you have been doing something

a) If you have been doing something for a period of time and **are still doing it**, you need to use the present tense in one of the following constructions (1, 2 or 3):

> *1)* **Vivimos** aquí **desde hace** cuatro años.
> *2)* **Hace** cuatro años **que vivimos** aquí.
> *3)* **Llevamos** cuatro años **viviendo** aquí.
> **We've been living** here for four years.

> *1)* **Estudio** español **desde hace** seis meses.
> *2)* **Hace** seis meses **que estudio** español.
> *3)* **Llevo** seis meses **estudiando** español.
> **I've been learning** Spanish for six months.

To sum up:

---

1) Action in present tense + **desde hace** + time

    or

2) **Hace** + time + **que** + action in present tense

    or

3) **Llevar** in present tense + time + action in gerund

The construction with **llevar** is very common and a useful idiom to know.

Note: you can use **llevar** without the gerund to indicate that you have **been** somewhere for a certain time:

> **Llevamos media hora** aquí.
> **We've been** here **(for) half an hour**.

b) To ask how long someone has been doing something you would say:

¿Cuánto tiempo hace que …/Desde cuándo … (+ present tense)**?**
¿Cuánto tiempo llevas/lleva Vd … (+ gerund)**?**

232

43.2 How long you **had been** doing something

a) If you **had** been doing something, and **were still doing it** at the point of reference, you use the same construction, but put the verbs, including **hace**, in the imperfect, **hacía**.

1) **Vivíamos** *allí* **desde hacía** *cuatro años, cuando nació Jaime.*
2) **Hacía** *cuatro años* **que vivíamos** *allí, cuando nació Jaime.*
3) **Llevábamos** *cuatro años* **viviendo** *allí, cuando nació Jaime.*
We had been living there for four years when James was born.

1) **Estudiaba** *español* **desde hacía** *seis meses cuando fui a España por primera vez.*
2) **Hacía** *seis meses* **que estudiaba** *español cuando fui a España por primera vez.*
3) **Llevaba** *seis meses* **estudiando** *español cuando fui a España por primera vez.*
I had been learning Spanish for six months when I went to Spain for the first time.

b) The question 'How long had you been …ing?' would be:

¿Cuánto tiempo hacía que …/Desde cuándo … (+ imperfect tense)**?**
¿Cuánto tiempo llevaba(s) … (+ gerund)**?**

43.3 Since when?

You also use **desde** + a particular occasion or date or **desde que** + a clause with the present or imperfect if the action is or was still going on.

Desde *su casamiento* **viven** *en Barcelona.*
Since their marriage **they have been living** in Barcelona.

Desde que *se casaron* **viven** *en Barcelona.*
Since they got married **they have been living** in Barcelona.

Desde *diciembre el Real Madrid* **estaban** *a la cabeza de la liga.*
Since December Real Madrid **had been** at the top of the league.

Desde que *ganó el partido contra el Sevilla en diciembre, el Real Madrid* **estaba** *a la cabeza de la liga.*
Since they won the match against Seville in December, Real Madrid **had been** at the top of the league.

43.4 'Ago'

Hace + a period of time means 'ago'.

Hace *tres años.*
Three years **ago**.

43.5 Completed periods of time

a) When you wish to talk about something which happened for a period of time in the past and is now completed, use **durante** (although Latin-American speakers tend to use **por** instead of **durante**).

> *Habló **durante** tres horas.*
> He spoke **for** three hours.

> **Durante** *dos años no sabíamos dónde estaba.*
> **For** two years we didn't know where he was.

b) A number of verbs closely associated with time are just followed by the period of time without a word for 'for', as often happens in English.

> ***Vivimos tres años*** *allí.*
> **We lived** there (for) **three years**.

> ***Estuve dos días*** *en Granada.*
> **I was** in Granada (for) **two days**.

c) When referring to time in the future, use either **para** or **por** for 'for':

> *Vamos a Madrid **para/por** una semana.*
> We're going to Madrid **for** a week.

Again, with verbs such as **estar** and **vivir**, the preposition may be omitted, with the timespan immediately after the verb:

> ***Estaremos tres días*** *en Barcelona.*
> **We'll be** in Barcelona **for three days**.

d) The question 'How long for?' in these examples of completed or projected actions is simply **¿(Durante/Por) cuánto tiempo?** + verb in the relevant tense:

> *¿**(Durante) cuánto tiempo** vivisteis allí?*
> **(For) how long** did you live there?

> **(Por) cuánto** *tiempo vas a Madrid?*
> **(For) how long** are you going to Madrid?

➡ **Exercises 1, 2**

¡PONTE A PUNTO!

1 Detalles personales

Cambia las frases siguientes usando *llevar* con el gerundio.

Ejemplo:

Aprendo francés desde hace seis años.

Llevo seis años aprendiendo francés.

1 Sé nadar desde hace diez años.
2 Viajo al extranjero desde hace once años.
3 Vivimos en esta ciudad desde hace siete meses.
4 Salgo con mi novio/a desde hace año y medio.
5 Hago mis *A levels* desde hace nueve meses.
6 Hace mucho tiempo que hablo español.
7 Hace casi un año que estamos en esta clase.
8 Hace varios años que admiramos a nuestro/a profesor(a) de español.

2 ¿Cómo preguntarlo?

Tu ciudad o pueblo acaba de hermanarse con un pueblo/una ciudad – digamos que se llama Torrenueva – en España. Una familia, amigos tuyos, está a punto de recibir a un(a) invitado/a español(a) en su casa, pero no hablan muy bien el español. Entonces quieren saber cómo hacer las siguientes frases en español.

1 *How long have you (tú) lived in Torrenueva?*
2 *How long have you been learning English?*
3 *How long were you on the plane from Alicante?*
4 *Had you been waiting long at the airport when we arrived?*
5 *I have been learning Spanish for three months.*
6 *I have been learning it since January.*
7 *We have been living here since my dad changed his job.*
8 *He had been working for his company for five years when we moved house.*
9 *Before that we lived in America for five years.*
10 *We came here four years ago.*

¡... Y EN MARCHA!

3 Entrevista

Estás buscando un empleo, y para prepararte para la entrevista, pides a tu compañero/a de clase que te haga las preguntas que pudieran hacerte. Todas las preguntas tienen que empezar con ¿*Desde cuándo ... ?* o ¿*Cuánto tiempo llevas ... (-ando/-iendo) ... ?*

Ejemplo:

– ¿Cuánto tiempo llevas en tu colegio actual?
– Llevo seis años allí.
– ¿Desde cuándo estudias idiomas?
– Estudio francés desde hace seis años y español desde hace cuatro.

4 Currículum vitae

Ya has practicado para la entrevista, pero te han pedido que escribas un 'C.V.', detallando los aspectos más importantes de tu vida, tus estudios y tu personalidad. Escribe una pequeña 'autobiografía' indicando el tiempo que has pasado en cada etapa o aspecto de tu vida. Incluye por lo menos diez expresiones que indiquen el tiempo que pasaste en cada actividad o etapa.

Ejemplo:

Nací en Birmingham y viví allí tres años ...
Llevaba dos años yendo al colegio en Worcester, cuando mi padre cambió de trabajo ...

44 Relative pronouns and adjectives

 MECANISMOS

- A relative pronoun or adjective is one which joins two clauses in order to give more information about a noun or pronoun, for example: the house in **which** (where) I was born, the woman **who** left her gloves on the bus, the person **whose** photo was in the paper, the one **that** got away, etc. – in other words, 'who', 'whom', 'which', 'that', 'whose', 'where', 'when'.
- It is important to differentiate between **relative** pronouns or adjectives, which are link words, and **interrogative** pronouns or adjectives which ask questions. In English, words such as 'who', 'what' and 'which' have both a relative and interrogative function, and the same is true in Spanish. Interrogative (question) words are dealt with in Chapter 45.
- Remember: relative pronouns do **not** ask questions and do **not** have accents.

What follows below should give you guidance through an area of Spanish where only some rules are hard and fast. Here are the main rules, with some variations you are sure to meet.

44.1 'Restrictive' and 'non-restrictive' clauses

It is helpful to remember that:

- a 'restrictive' relative clause is one which, quite literally, restricts the scope of the antecedent, and there is no comma or pause between the antecedent and the relative pronoun. For example:

The girl who works in the tourist office is our neighbour.

(i.e. Which girl? – The one who works in the tourist office. The relative clause restricts the reference to this one particular girl.)

- a 'non-restrictive clause' does not restrict the scope of the antecedent; it simply provides more information, and the antecedent and relative pronoun are separated by a comma. For example:

The girl, who works in the tourist office, is our neighbour.

In this case, 'who works in the tourist office' simply adds some extra information about the girl.

44.2 Relative pronouns 'who', 'whom', 'which' and 'that' as subject or direct object

The relative pronoun can never be omitted in Spanish as it often is in English.

44.2.1 As subject

a) The relative pronoun *que* is usually used, referring to a person or persons or a thing or things, as the subject of a 'restrictive clause'.

> *El problema **que** se plantea es éste.*
> The problem **which** presents itself is this.

> *La chica **que** trabaja en la oficina de turismo.*
> The girl **who** works in the tourist office.

b) If the clause is 'non-restrictive' (i.e. simply gives more information about the antecedent), you can also use *que* or else *quien* or *el cual (/la cual/los cuales/las cuales).*

> *La **chica, que/quien/la cual** trabaja en la oficina de turismo, fue víctima del accidente.*
> The **girl, who** works in the tourist office, was a victim of the accident.

Note the comma (or a pause in speech) in this case.

44.2.2 As object

Use *que* as the direct object of the clause, referring either to a person or a thing.

> *El problema **que** prevemos es éste.*
> The problem **(which/that)** we foresee is this.

> *La chica **que** vimos en la oficina de turismo …*
> The girl **(whom)** we saw in the tourist office …

When a person is the object, as in the above example, the tendency is to use the personal *a* with *el que* or *quien* in non-restrictive clauses:

> *La chica **a la que/a quien** vimos en la oficina de turismo …*
> The girl, who(m) we saw in the tourist office …

> *La chica, **a la que** habíamos visto en la oficina de turismo, fue víctima del accidente.*
> The girl, **(whom)** we had seen in the tourist office, was a victim of the accident.

44.2.3 After prepositions

a) After prepositions use *el que/la que/los que/las que* when referring to people or things, or *quien/quienes* when referring to people only, though there is a tendency for *a, de, con* and *en* to be followed by *que* without the article *el/la/los/las*.

> *La oficina **en (la) que** vimos a esa mujer …*
> The office **in which** we saw that woman …

La mujer **con la que/con quien** *hablamos en la oficina …*
The woman we spoke **with*** (**with whom** we spoke) in the office …

✒ * Note that the preposition ('with' in this case) cannot come at the end of the clause as in English, and must always precede the relative pronoun.

b)   There is yet another form which may be used with a preposition: *el cual/la cual/ los cuales/las cuales*, and which tends to be used after the longer compound prepositions, such as *delante de, detrás de*, in non-restrictive clauses. In spoken Spanish, however, this tends to sound rather stilted.

Los árboles, **debajo de los cuales** *estaban sentados …*
The trees **under which** they were sitting/The trees they were sitting under …

Both *el que* and *el cual* take their gender and number from the noun they refer to – *los cuales* refers to *los árboles* in this example.

44.2.4 'Which' for ideas

When 'which' refers to an idea, not to a noun with a specific gender, *lo que* or *lo cual* is used.

Llegaron tarde, **lo que** *me dio más tiempo para preparar algo de comer.*
They arrived late, **which** gave me more time to prepare something to eat.

44.3 *Cuyo*

The relative adjective *cuyo/a/os/as* means 'whose' and agrees with the **thing possessed**.

Es un director **cuyas películas** *son muy divertidas.*
He's a director **whose films** are very amusing.

44.4 'The one(s) which', 'that which'

a) *El que/La que* mean 'he/she who', 'the one which'; *los que/las que* mean 'those who', 'the ones who/which'.

Hablando de películas, **la que** *me gusta más es …*
Talking of films, **the one (which)** I like best is …

b) *Lo que* means 'what' in the sense of 'that which'.

Eso no es **lo que** *quiero.*
That isn't **what** I want.

➠ **Exercises 1, 2**

¡PONTE A PUNTO!

1 La familia real española

Rellena los espacios en blanco con una palabra relativa que convenga al sentido.

El papel . . **1** . . tiene el rey de España no es ejecutivo. Juan Carlos es un rey . . **2** . . papel se describe en la constitución como 'parlamentario'. Sin embargo en 1981 fue el rey . . **3** . . impidió el golpe de estado . . **4** . . hubiera aniquilado la joven democracia española. Don Juan Carlos fue traído desde Portugal a España cuando tenía muy pocos años por el General Franco, . . **5** . . quería educarle en su molde. Cuando don Juan Carlos sucedió a Franco, los españoles, . . **6** . . pensaban que sería como el viejo general, bajo . . **7** . . habían vivido tantos años, tuvieron una sorpresa muy grande. El líder comunista, . . **8** . . le apodó al rey don Juan Carlos el Breve, admitió más tarde que se había equivocado.

El rey y la reina Sofía, . . **9** . . familia consiste en dos hijas y un hijo, . . **10** . . es el príncipe de Asturias y heredero del trono, llevan una vida bastante modesta para la realeza en el palacio de la Zarzuela, . . **11** . . se encuentra en las afueras de Madrid. Una cosa . . **12** . . le irrita al rey es cuando los presidentes visitantes, con . . **13** . . tiene que encontrarse, se atildan con medallas y otros adornos. Él dice que prefiere llevar un traje de negocios, . . **14** . . por lo menos es más cómodo. A veces en invierno una cosa . . **15** . . le gusta hacer es escaparse a las pistas de esquí, . . **16** . . se mezcla con la gente. Las condiciones bajo . . **17** . . vive la familia real española parecen algo más normales que . . **18** . . llevan sus equivalentes en el Reino Unido, . . **19** . . son mucho más ricos.

2 Guía turística

El director de turismo de tu región tiene una cinta muy vieja de un comentario sobre la región y quiere que tú lo transcribas para volver a hacer una mejor grabación. Has transcrito todo lo que puedes, pero por desgracia no se oyen bien ciertas palabras y ahora tienes que adivinar las palabras que faltan. ¡Qué coincidencia que todas sean expresiones relativas! Rellena entonces los espacios en blanco.

Aquí se encuentra la abadía, . . **1** . . es una gran iglesia del siglo XV, y al lado . . **2** . . ustedes verán lo . . **3** . . se llama la Pump Room, . . **4** . . fue construida en el siglo XVIII. Es un edificio . . **5** . . exterior es muy típico de esa época, y debajo . . **6** . . se descubrieron en el siglo XIX los famosos Baños Romanos. Continuamos por esta calle, . . **7** . . hasta hace unos pocos años llevaba mucho tráfico, pero . . **8** . . ahora está peatonalizada, . . **9** . . les ha gustado a la mayoría de los habitantes. Ésta es una ciudad . . **10** . . centro es muy compacto, pero . . **11** . . ha sido parcialmente estropeado por estos edificios modernos, delante de . . **12** . . ustedes se encuentran ahora. Más abajo, los arcos del ferrocarril son obra del famoso ingeniero Brunel, de . . **13** . . ya les hemos hablado y . . **14** . . fama es internacional.

¡... Y EN MARCHA!

3 Careo de sospechosos

Tus compañeros/as de clase tienen que adivinar a quién estás describiendo. Decidid primero entre vosotros a qué tipo de persona vas a describir – a vuestros amigos/as, profesores, estrellas de televisión o cine, personajes deportivos, etc. Se pueden escoger también ciudades o países. Tenéis que emplear por lo menos dos cláusulas relativas en cada descripción.

Ejemplo:

Es el futbolista que juega en el Real Madrid y que está casado con una chica 'Spice'. (David Beckham)
Es una profesora con quien estudiamos francés y cuya hija está en cuarto curso de este colegio. (la sra X)

4 Definiciones

Trabaja con una pareja. Uno/a de vosotros es un(a) estudiante de español que tiene problemas de vocabulario, y te pide explicaciones de palabras que no conoce. Claro que las explicaciones tienen que contener palabras relativas.

Ejemplo:

– ¿Quieres explicarme qué es una panadería?/el ozono?
– Es una tienda en que se vende pan.
– Es un gas que es un compuesto del oxígeno, que es muy importante para la protección contra la radiación y cuya capa en ciertos sitios se hace peligrosamente tenue.

5 Los padres españoles

Dos miembros de la clase son el padre y la madre de un(a) nuevo/a alumno/a español(a), y los/las otros/as les enseñan el colegio. Los padres hablan poco inglés, y hay que explicarles todo acerca del colegio, empleando un plano, a ser posible. Claro que las respuestas tienen que contener expresiones relativas.

Ejemplo:

– Qué es esta aula?
– Es el aula en que estudiamos geografía.
– ¿Quién es aquel hombre?
– Se llama 'caretaker': es el hombre que mantiene la limpieza del colegio.

45 Interrogatives and exclamations

 MECANISMOS

45.1 Interrogatives

a) Interrogatives are words which are used to ask questions. Not all questions contain one, of course: a question in Spanish can be the same as a statement, with the question marks indicating the question in written form, and the appropriate intonation pattern identifying it as a question in spoken form.

In some cases, especially with 'yes/no' questions, there is a word-order pattern similar to that found in English questions – where the subject and verb are inverted – but this is not essential due to the flexibility of Spanish word order generally, and in particular because in Spanish subject pronouns are not usually needed; this is precisely why the inverted ¿ is used in written Spanish to indicate that a question follows.

> *¿Vas al bar conmigo?*
> Are you going to the bar with me?
> (same as statement)

> *¿Pepe sabe que vamos?/¿Sabe Pepe que vamos?*
> Does Pepe know we are going?
> (with or without inversion)

> *¿Va a la discoteca, o no?*
> Is he/she going to the disco, or not?
> (no separate subject word, no inversion possible)

b) Interrogative words all ask for a specific piece of information in the answer, rather than simply for a 'yes' or 'no' response. They all have a written accent on the stressed vowel, which affects the emphasis of the question word. They can all be used in both direct and indirect questions (see Chapter 46) and always carry the accent, whether in direct or indirect questions. Most are pronouns or adverbs, and two (*¿cuánto/a/os/as?* and *¿qué?*) can be used either in an adjectival way or as a pronoun. *¿Cuál(es)?* is a pronoun, and has to match in number the noun to which it refers.

¿Cómo?	How?
¿Cuál? ¿Cuáles?	Which one? Which ones?
¿Cuándo?	When?
¿Cuánto/a/os/as?	How much?/How many?
¿Dónde?	Where?
¿Adónde?	Where to?
¿De dónde?	Where from?
¿Qué?	What? Which?
¿Para qué?	What for?
¿Por qué?	Why?
¿Quién(es)?	Who?
¿De quién?	Whose?

242

c) Most are straightforward in meaning and use, but the following need some explanation.

- **¿Quién?** always means 'Who(m)?', and can be used with various prepositions. **¿Quiénes?** is used when a plural answer is expected.

  ¿Quién es este chico?
  Who is this boy?

  ¿Quiénes eran?
  Who were they?

  *¿**A** quién diste la carta?*
  To whom did you give the letter?

  *¿**Con** quién fuiste?*
  Who did you go **with**?/**With** whom did you go?

  *¿**De** quiénes son estos coches?*
  Whose are these cars?

- **¿Qué?** usually means 'What?' and it, too, can be used with various prepositions.

  ¿Qué es?
  What is it?

  ¿Qué vas a hacer?
  What are you going to do?

  ¿Qué libros prefieres?
  What/Which books do you prefer?

  *¿**De** qué es?*
  What is it made **of**?

  *¿**En** qué quedamos?*
  What shall we agree **to**?

  *¿**Para** qué estudias?*
  What are you studying **for**?

  📝 Note that the preposition must come at the beginning of the sentence, with or before the interrogative, not at the end as in English.

- **¿Qué?** also means 'Which?', but only when used with a noun.

  ¿Qué película prefieres?
  Which film do you prefer?

- **¿Cuál?** means 'Which one?' and **¿Cuáles?** means 'Which ones?', implying a choice.

  Tengo dos manzanas. ¿Cuál quieres?
  I have two apples. Which (one) do you want?

  ¿Cuáles de estos sellos te gustan más?
  Which (ones) of these stamps do you like most?

- *¿Cuánto?* can be used either as an adjective or a pronoun, in which case it agrees with the noun referred to, or as an adverb, when it is invariable.

  ¿Cuántas naranjas quieres?
  How many oranges do you want?

  ¿Cuánto dinero tienes?
  How much money have you got?

  ¿Cuánto vale?
  How much does it cost?

- *¿Cómo?* usually means 'How?', but can sometimes mean 'Why?'.

  ¿Cómo lograste hacerlo?
  How did you manage to do it?

  ¿Cómo no?
  Why not?

✐ Note also its use in *¿Cómo te llamas?* 'What are you called?'

➡ **Exercise 1a**

45.2 Exclamations

Several of the interrogatives can also be used in exclamations. Note that they still carry the written accent:

¡Qué (+ noun) + *más/tan* (+ adjective)*!'* *¡Qué* (+ adjective + noun)*!'*	What a (+ adjective + noun)!
¡Cuánto/a (+ noun)*!*	What a lot of (+ noun)!

¡Qué pena!
What a shame!

¡Qué niña más guapa!
What an attractive girl!

¡Cuánta comida!
What a lot of food!

✐ Note also exclamations based on a verb: *¡Cómo* (+ verb)*!*

¡Cómo has crecido!
How you've grown!

➡ **Exercises 1b and 2**

¡PONTE A PUNTO!

1 El relleno

He aquí una serie de frases interrogativas o exclamaciones. Tienes que poner en el espacio una interrogación o una exclamación.

a)
1 ¿... llama a la puerta?
2 ¿... gente viene a la fiesta?
3 ¿... necesitas tanto dinero?
4 ¿... vas a la exposición?
5 ¿... se llaman estos animales?
6 ¿... de estos cuadros prefieres?
7 ¿... pintor los pintó?
8 ¿... vas a ir al aeropuerto?
9 ¿... encontraste mis gafas? ¿En la silla?
10 ¿... van estos niños tan de prisa?
11 ¿... llegará el autobús?

b)
12 ¡... me gusta la sopa cuando la gallina es gorda!
13 ¡... lástima!
14 ¡... chico más imbécil!
15 ¡... gente en una plaza tan pequeña!
16 ¡... CDs tienes!
17 ¡... has cambiado!
18 ¡... idiota eres!

2 Interrogatorio

He aquí un artículo que contiene muchas interrogaciones y exclamaciones: ¡por desgracia, éstas se han borrado, y tienes que rellenar los espacios en blanco!

¿Hasta . . **1** . . van a llegar los extremos, en lo que se refiere a los excesos de los jóvenes? ¡ . . **2** . . desastre la juventud de hoy! ¿ . . **3** . . se rebelan, y . . **4** . . van a terminar las manifestaciones de falta de control y disciplina? ¿ . . **5** . . gente tiene que morir y . . **6** . . coches tienen que estrellarse o incendiarse antes de que se ponga fin a lo que se llama 'joyriding'? ¿ . . **7** . . disturbios tenemos que sufrir y en . . **8** . . ciudades? ¿ . . **9** . . podrá la policía conseguir lo que necesita para poder controlarlos? ¡ . . **10** . . gente quiere ver a muchos de estos jóvenes en la cárcel! ¡ . . **11** . . valientes son algunos y . . **12** . . valientes también los bomberos que tienen que sufrir tantas injurias y ataques mientras tratan de salvar los edificios incendiados! ¡ . . **13** . . imbéciles e irresponsables son los que cometen estos delitos! ¿ . . **14** . . es la culpa de todo esto? ¿ . . **15** . . va a encargarse de una vez de esta situación? ¡ . . **16** . . nos gustaría encontrar una solución a estos problemas!

 **¡… Y EN MARCHA!**

3 El/La curioso/a impertinente

Haces el papel de un(a) niño/a muy joven, que habla con sus padres o con sus hermanos mayores. Tienes que hacerles una serie de preguntas, generales o específicas, según lo que están haciendo o diciendo. Tienen que contestarte como mejor puedan.

Ejemplo:

Tú: *¿Papá, por qué estás arreglando el coche? ¿Cuánto tiempo vas a tardar?*

Papá: *Porque está averiado y quiero continuar hasta terminarlo … ¡si me dejas en paz!*

4 ¡Qué bien!

Ahora haces el papel del padre/de la madre. Tu hijo/a te muestra algo, o te explica algo que ha hecho. Tú tienes que reaccionar como buen padre/buena madre.

Ejemplo:

Niño: *Mira, mamá, ¡mira este pajarito de papel que acabo de hacer! Qué bonito es, ¿verdad?*

Mamá: *¡Qué bonito es, en efecto! ¡Cuántos ojos tiene! Y tú, ¡qué listo eres!*

5 La carta

Imagina que vas a pasar las vacaciones viajando por Chile con un(a) amigo/a chileno/a. Escríbele, haciéndole una serie de preguntas, sobre las cosas que quieres saber, y exclamaciones, para las cosas que quieres hacer.

Ejemplo:

¿Cómo vamos a viajar, y adónde vamos primero? ¡Cuánto me gustaría visitar Valparaíso! – ¡qué ciudad más bonita!

46 Direct and indirect speech

 MECANISMOS

46.1 Direct speech

Direct speech in Spanish is essentially as in English, apart from the fact that different methods of punctuation and layout are used, as seen in the examples below.

– Hola, Juan, dijo Pablo.
'Hello, Juan,' said Pablo.

– Hola. ¿Qué vamos a hacer hoy? preguntó Juan.
'Hello. What are we going to do today?' asked Juan.

«Buenos días», dijo el cura.
'Good day,' said the priest.

46.2 Indirect speech

46.2.1 Indirect statements

The following points should be observed about indirect statements. (Note that in each example, the direct speech version is given first, so that you can see how it compares with the indirect version.)

a) In Spanish, the word ***que*** is always needed when introducing the quoted part of indirect speech, even though in English the word 'that' is usually omitted.

– Iré mañana, dijo.
'I'll go tomorrow,' she said.

Dijo que iría mañana.
She said (that) she would go tomorrow.

– No me gusta nada, contestó.
'I don't like it at all,' he answered.

Contestó que no le gustaba nada.
He answered that he didn't like it at all.

b) The sequence of tenses in indirect speech in Spanish reflects English usage fairly faithfully except in circumstances in which the subjunctive is needed (see Chapter 35).

– No puedes salir, dice mi madre.
'You can't go out,' says my mother.

Dice mi madre que no puedo salir.
My mother says I can't go out.

– No sé nada, decía.
'I know nothing,' he used to say.

Decía que no sabía nada.
He used to say that he knew nothing.

– Te quiero, dijiste.
'I love you,' you said.

Dijiste que me querías.
You told me you loved me.

46.2.2 Indirect questions

Indirect questions, similarly, should prove straightforward except that the following points need to be remembered.

a) Interrogative words still need to bear the written accent as usual, even though there are no question marks around the sentence. Thus:

Me preguntaron, '¿Dónde lo compraste?'
They asked me, 'Where did you buy it?'

becomes in indirect speech:

*Me preguntaron **dónde** lo había comprado.*
They asked me where I had bought it.

Voy a preguntarle, '¿Cómo se hace?'
I'm going to ask him, 'How is it done?'

becomes in indirect speech:

*Le voy a preguntar **cómo** se hace.*
I'll ask him how to do it/how it's done.

b) Many indirect questions may not appear obviously to be questions at all. You can identify them by asking yourself whether at the moment of speaking, the person involved would probably have asked a question. If so, use an interrogative. Note also that **qué** may often be replaced by the relative **lo que**, except before an infinitive, when **qué** must be used.

Mi amigo quería saber a qué hora íbamos a llegar.
My friend wanted to know what time we were going to arrive.

Dime cuánto tengo que pagar.
Tell me how much I have to pay.

Quiere saber qué/lo que vas a hacer.
He wants to know what you are going to do.

No sé qué hacer.
I don't know what to do.

c) Once again, the sequence of tenses is largely as in English, except where Spanish requires a subjunctive (see Chapters 32 and 35). When changing direct speech into indirect speech, verbs in the present tense change into the imperfect, and perfect or preterite into the pluperfect.

–Te he comprado un regalo porque te quiero. ⟶ *Dijo que le había comprado un regalo porque la quería.*
'I've bought you a present because I love you.' ⟶ He said that he had bought her a present because he loved her.

➥ **Exercise 1**

 **¡PONTE A PUNTO!**

1 ¿Quién dijo qué?

Cambia estos trozos de conversación de forma directa a forma indirecta como en el ejemplo.

Ejemplo:

Juana dijo – Me gusta tu camisa.

Juana dijo que le gustaba su camisa.

1 Paco dijo – Hace buen tiempo.
2 Manuela contestó – Está lloviendo.
3 El cartero confesó – Perdí muchas cartas.
4 Le dijimos – Tenemos un problema.
5 La señora Ruiz me preguntó – ¿Cómo se escribe tu nombre?
6 Vamos a Alicante, – nos dijo Malení.
7 ¿Por qué eres tan estúpido? – me preguntó Alicia.
8 No sé nada, – le respondió Alejandro.
9 ¿Qué te parece esta blusa? – preguntó Juana.
10 Me gusta, – contestó Pablo.
11 Iré cuando termine mi trabajo, – dijo.
12 Estaré dos días en Madrid antes de que llegue mi hermana, – explicó.

2 Reportaje

Cambia la siguiente conversación en discurso indirecto.

Julio: Bueno, vamos a ir a la fiesta esta tarde. ¿Qué te parece?
Marisa: De acuerdo. ¿A qué hora vamos a salir?
Julio: Sobre las ocho. Pero primero iremos a cenar a la cafetería.
Marisa: ¿Qué me pongo, el vestido rojo, o el azul? ¿Cuál prefieres?
Julio: El azul, creo. Yo me voy a poner unos tejanos y la camiseta verde.
Marisa: ¿Tenemos que llevar alguna botella a la fiesta?
Julio: No, Manuel dijo que no hacía falta. ¿Dónde nos vemos?
Marisa: Delante de mi casa, ¿no? Hasta luego.

Ejemplo:

Julio dijo que él y Marisa iban a ir ...
Marisa contestó que ...

¡... Y EN MARCHA!

3 Los sordos

Estás hablando con dos amigos/as, uno/a de los/las cuales no oye muy bien a causa de su resfriado. Por eso, tú y tu otro/a amigo/a tenéis que repetir cada uno/a lo que dice el/la otro/a.

Ejemplo:

A: *Ganamos el partido por dos a cero. ¿Qué hiciste tú esta tarde?*
B: *¿Cómo? ¿Qué dice?*
C: *Dice que ganaron el partido, y quiere saber qué hiciste esta tarde.*

4 Ayer

¿Qué tal tu memoria? ¿Recuerdas todo lo que ocurrió ayer? A ver si lo recuerdan tus compañeros/as de clase. Pide a uno/a de ellos/as que te cuente todo lo que hizo él/ella. Escúchale bien, luego escribe un resumen de lo que hizo.

En cada frase tendrás que usar una de las siguientes expresiones:

Dijo que ... Continuó que ... Añadió que ... Me aseguró que ... Preguntó si ...

Ejemplo:

John dice: Ayer me levanté a las ocho. Llamé a mi novia y la pregunté, '¿Quieres ir a la playa?'

John dijo que ayer se levantó a las ocho. Dijo que llamó a su novia, y que la preguntó si quería ir a la playa.

47 Some special suffixes

MECANISMOS

A suffix is added to the end of a word to modify its meaning. The suffixes dealt with here are:

a) diminutive, making the person or object smaller, rather like pig–piglet in English;
b) augmentative, making the object larger;
c) pejorative, bringing out, for example, the ugliness, coarseness or stupidity of the person or object;
d) *-azo*, in the sense of 'a blow with'.

All these suffixes give Spanish its own peculiar expressiveness, often adding an emotional tone to the word in question from the point of view of the speaker. They are, therefore, rather tricky ground for the non-native speaker to venture into.

47.1 Diminutives

The most usual diminutive suffix is *-ito/-ita*, but you will also come across *-illo/-illa*, *-ico/-ica*, *-ino/-ina*, *-uelo/-uela*, *-ín/-ina*, *-ete/eta*. There are also variants with the forms *-cito/-cita*, *ecito/-ecita*, *-ececito/-ececita*, depending on the word.

a) Diminutives make things smaller.

una mesita	a **small table**
un chiquito	a **little boy**

✐ Note the spelling change in ***chiquito***.

b) But sometimes they are used to denote endearment.

abuelita	**granny**
Pedrito	**little** Peter, **Pete**

c) Sometimes, though, they tone down the basic word.

¡Tontita!	(Don't be a) silly girl! (diminutive of ***tonta***, 'foolish/silly')
una mentirilla	a fib, a white lie (diminutive of ***una mentira***, 'a lie')

d) The suffix *-illo/-illa* often suggests insignificance, as other variations (e.g. *-ico/-ica*) sometimes do.

aquel hombrecillo	that little squirt
¡Mierdica!	you little turd! (M. Delibes *El Camino*)

251

47.2 Augmentatives

Augmentatives often imply clumsiness, awkwardness or excess. Common ones are *-ón/-ona*, *-azo/-aza*, *-ote/-ota*, *-udo/-uda*.

*mand**ón**/mand**ona***	bossy
*la palab**rota***	swearword
*orej**udo/a***	big-eared

The suffix *-udo* can be added to most parts of the body in this sense: *cabezudo* (with a large head), *barrigudo* (pot-bellied), etc. *Narigudo* means 'having a large nose'.

47.3 Pejoratives

The common endings are *-aco/-aca*, *-acho/-acha*, *-ajo/-aja*, *-uco/-uca*, *-ucho/-ucha*, *-ejo/-eja*. These denote ugliness, squalor, dinginess, and so on.

*un pobl**acho***	a 'crummy' village
*un hotel**ucho***	a 'grotty' hotel

47.4 *-azo*

The suffix *-azo* is also frequently used to mean 'a blow with':

*un bal**azo***	a bullet **wound**
*un puñet**azo***	**punch**, i.e. a blow with the fist
*el tejer**azo***	name given to the failed *coup d'état* (= ***golpe de estado***) by el Coronel Tejero in 1981

➡ **Exercises 1, 2**

¡PONTE A PUNTO!

1 Unos sufijitos, nada más

Añadiendo un sufijo a la palabra básica, explica estas definiciones en una palabra.

1 Un golpe con una silla
2 Una persona que tiene mucho pelo
3 Una niña muy pequeña
4 Un chico muy pequeño que se llama Miguel
5 Una mujer insignificante pero no fea
6 Un cuarto muy pequeño, oscuro y feo
7 Un libro grande, quizás difícil de manejar, algo feo de aspecto
8 Tiras un limón a alguien y le pegas
9 Alguien que tiene los ojos muy grandes
10 Una calle estrecha pero atractiva

¡... Y EN MARCHA!

2 ¡Busca el sufijo!

Toma una revista popular española y busca ejemplos de estos sufijos en algunos de los artículos. Haz una lista de ellas en su contexto y luego discute con tus compañeros/as cómo los traducirías al inglés.

48 Spanish spelling and pronunciation

 **MECANISMOS**

48.1 The Spanish alphabet

48.1.1 Vowels: *a, e, i, o, u*

These are always given their full value in speech and never omitted or reduced in value as in English and many other languages: compare the English and Spanish pronunciation of Austria/***Austria***, cafeteria/***cafetería***, union/***unión***, chocolate/***chocolate.***

48.1.2 Combinations of vowels

Vowels are either strong (*a, e, o*) or weak (*i, u*).

a) Two strong vowels occurring together are always pronounced separately and make two syllables:

*l**eo*** (le-o)   *c**ae*** (ca-e)   *r**oer*** (ro-er)   *f**eo*** (fe-o)   *f**ea*** (fe-a)

And the normal stress rules apply (see section 48.2).

b) When a strong and weak vowel occur together, they combine to form a 'diphthong', i.e. two vowels sounded together in one syllable. The stress (see section 48.2) falls on the strong vowel; and if an accent is needed it goes on the strong vowel: ***a***, ***e***, or ***o***.

*a**i**re, ace**i**te, o**i**go, A**u**stria, E**u**ropa, agr**i**a, D**i**os, habl**ái**s, com**éi**s*

This combination counts as one syllable, but if the weak vowel ***i*** or ***u*** needs to be stressed, it carries an accent and becomes a separate syllable.

*com**í**a* (and all that set of imperfect and conditional endings)

*panader**í**a* (and most shops except ***farmacia***)

*d**í**a, env**í**an, act**ú**a, ca**í**do, le**í**do*

Compare ***D<u>ios</u>*** (one syllable) and ***d<u>ía</u>s*** (two syllables).

c) When the two weak vowels occur together (***iu*** or ***ui***), they form one syllable with the stress on the second vowel.

*v**iu**do, f**ui**, r**ui**do, destr**ui**do*

Note:

- **_ciudad_** (city, town) and **_cuidado_** (care). Take care not to confuse them!
- in combination with any vowel, **_y_** is used instead of **_i_** at the end of a word: **_hay_**, **_ley_**, **_voy_**, **_muy_**.

➡ Exercise 1

48.1.3 Consonants

All other letters are consonants. The most striking point about Spanish consonants is that very few of them are ever doubled: in fact, the only double ones you will find are **_cc_**, **_ll_**, **_nn_** and **_rr_**. Pay special attention to these as indicated in this list.

_B_ and **_V_** (**_bé_**, **_uve_**) are pronounced identically, but have two different sounds depending where they occur: at the beginning of a word, rather like the English 'b' but without emitting so much air (**_buey_**, **_vocal_**); and between vowels, where you just let your lips come together lightly – a bit like an English 'w' without moving your lips outwards (**_haba_**, **_uva_**).

_C_ (**_cé_**) is pronounced 'hard' like 'k' before **_a_**, **_o_**, **_u_** and any consonant except **_h_**: **_capa_**, **_copa_**, **_cupón_**, **_cristal_**; it is pronounced 'soft' like 'th' in 'thin' before **_e_** and **_i_**: **_cero_**, **_cinco_**.

 Note:

- in southern Spain and much of Latin America, 'soft' **_c_** is pronounced as **_s_**.
- the double **_cc_** can occur, but the first is always hard and the second soft: **_acción_**, **_lección_**.
- **_qu_** provides the 'k' sound before **_e_** and **_i_**: **_que_**, **_quien_**.
- 'kw' is achieved in the combinations **_cua-_**, **_cue-_**, **_cui-_**, **_cuo-_**: **_cuatro_**, **_cuento_**, **_cuidado_**, **_cuota_**.
- **_Z_** (**_ceda_** or **_ceta_**) provides the 'th' sound before **_a_**, **_o_** and **_u_**, and on the end of a word: **_zapato_**, **_zorro_**, **_zumo_**, **_arroz_**.

This table will help you to decide whether to use **_c_**, **_z_**, or **_qu_** in combination with the following vowel:

Sound	'k'	'th' ('s' in L. America)	'kw'
before *a*	casa	zapato	cuanto
" *e*	que	cero	cuento
" *i*	quito	cita	cuidado
" *o*	como	zona	cuota
" *u*	cubo	zumo	–
at end of word	coñac	vez	–

Note: for the 'th' sound you must use **_c_** where possible (**_ce_**, **_ci_**) and that is why you write **_empecé_** and not **_empezé_**.

_CH_ (**_ché_**) is like 'ch' in 'church' – but avoid sounding a 't' before it as in 'catch': **_muchacho_**, **_chico_**, **_ocho_**. It was treated as a separate letter until 1994.

D (*dé*) is pronounced with your tongue behind your top teeth in most places: *dar*, *de*, *andando*; but like 'th' in 'then' between vowels and at the end of a word: *hablado*, *ida*, *ciudad*, *virtud*.

F (*efe*) is pronounced as in English. Note, however, that words spelt with 'ph' in English always use *f* in Spanish: *filosofía*, *fósforo*, *Felipe*.

G (*gé*) is pronounced 'hard' as in English before *a*, *o*, *u* or a consonant, though further down the throat: *gama*, *gorra*, *agua*, *grande*. Before *e* and *i* it is pronounced like the 'ch' in Scottish 'loch': *gemir*, *gigante*.

J (*jota*) also has this guttural pronunciation: *garaje*, *jota*; *j* is also used in some words that originally had an *x*: *ejemplo*, *don Quijote*, *Méjico*.

This table will help you to decide whether to use *g*, *j*, *gu* or *gü* in combination with the following vowel:

Sound	'g'	'kh' like Scottish 'loch'	'gw'
before *a*	*gama*	*jarro*	*guapa*
" *e*	*guerra*	*gesto/paisaje*	*vergüenza*
" *i*	*guitarra*	*gitano/jinete*	*argüir*
" *o*	*golpe*	*jota*	*antiguo*
" *u*	*gusto*	*justo*	–

Unfortunately you will find both *g* and *j* in the *ge/je* and *gi/ji* combination. Remember that words ending in *-aje*, often corresponding to English ones in '-age', always use a *j*, in spite of the final *e*, for example: *garaje*.

Because *u* is used as a buffer between *g* and *e/i*, for the *gw* sound plus *e/i* you have to resort to the 'diaeresis' (¨) to separate the *u* sound: *vergüenza*.

H (*ache*) is always silent: *hombre*, *prohibido*. Remember that you must use it before the 'radical change' diphthongs *ie* and *ue* at the beginning of a word: that is why the verb *oler* (to smell) is spelt *huelo*, *hueles*, *huele*, *huelen* in the parts where the vowel change occurs. **H** is often used at the beginning of a word where there was once an *f*. Remember this and a number of words become more easily guessable: *humo* (smoke), *hacer* (do, make [French *faire*]), even *hogar* (hearth, home – related to *fuego*!).

K (*ka*) is only used in foreign words and in the numerous variations on *kilo*, and is pronounced as in English: *kilómetro*.

L (*ele*) is pronounced roughly as in English, but with the tongue starting behind the top teeth: *la*, *le*, *Lima*, *lo*, *luz*.

LL (*elle*) was treated as a separate letter until 1994. It is pronounced rather more strongly than the '-lli-' combination in 'million'. In some parts of Spain and much of Latin America, it is pronounced like a very strong 'y', or even the English 'j': *llamar*, *llevar*, *llover*.

M (*eme*) as in English: *madre*, *mamá*.

N (*ene*) as in English: *no*, *nunca*. It can occur doubled, usually in words beginning with *n-* with the prefix *in-* added: *innegable*, *innovación*, and also *perenne*; note that you get *inm-*, however, in combination with *m*: *inmóvil*, *inmediatamente* (no double *mm*).

Ñ (*eñe*) as 'ni' in 'onion': **se_ñ_or**, **a_ñ_o**. This letter is still regarded as a separate letter of the alphabet and comes after **N** in the dictionary.

P (*pé*) as in English, but blowing out less air: **_p_apá**, **_p_e_p_ino**, **_p_o_p_a**.

Q (*cu*) (always written *qu*): see notes and table under **C**. But place names transliterated from Arabic have **Q** without *u*: **Qatar**.

R (*ere*) is trilled, even at the end of words: **to_r_o**, **cla_r_o**, **cha_rl_ar**.

• **rr** (*dos eres*), one of the few double consonants, is strongly trilled. Compare: **pe_r_o/pe_rr_o**, **to_r_o/to_rr_e**, **ca_r_o/ca_rr_o**, **ce_r_o/ce_rr_o**.

S (*ese*): much as in English, though sometimes through clenched teeth. Before *m*, like English 'z': **mi_s_mo**, **abi_s_mo**.

T (*té*): said with your tongue against your top teeth. In fact, say 'top teeth' like this and notice the difference! *TH* is not used, and words spelt with 'th' in English or French are reduced to just *t*: **_t_é**, **_t_eoría**, **disco_t_eca**.

V: see **B**

W (*uve doble*) only occurs in foreign words, mainly names (e.g. Washington, Wagner), and is now normally pronounced as in the language of origin. Words derived from names beginning with *w* have usually had this changed to *v*, and pronounced accordingly: **_v_atio** (watt). **WC** (toilet) is usually pronounced **vecé**, and the rather old-fashioned term **wáter** is now more often written and pronounced **váter**.

X (*equis*): before a consonant, like 's': **e_x_tento**, **e_x_posición**; between vowels, like 'ks': **e_x_amen**, **é_x_ito**, **e_x_igir.**

Y (*i griega*): as a consonant, it is similar to but stronger than the English 'y': **_y_acer**, **_y_endo**, **A_y_amonte**; see also its use as a vowel under **I**.

Z: see notes and table under **C**.

➡ **Exercise 2**

48.2 Stress and accents

In any word of more than one syllable in Spanish, one syllable is stressed, i.e. it is emphasised more than the others. There is nothing new in this – we do it in English: h_a_mster, c_o_ckroach, prolifer_a_tion.

You can even change the meaning of a word by changing the stress.

For example: When the dustmen go on strike, they ref_u_se to collect the r_e_fuse!

The same can happen in Spanish.

h_a_blo	I speak
*habl_ó_*	he/she spoke

The accent on **habló** is the clue to the stress system in Spanish. There are three stress rules:

1) Words ending in a vowel or **-n** or **-s** are stressed on the next to last syllable, without the need for an accent:

c*a*so, c*a*sas, c*a*sa, c*a*san; f*e*o, f*e*os, f*e*a, f*e*as; v*i*no, v*i*nos; qui*e*ro, qui*e*res, qui*e*re, qui*e*ren

You can now see why **-n** and **-s** are included in this rule. When you give nouns, adjectives and verbs plural endings, you do not usually have to worry about accents.

2) Words ending in a consonant except **n** or **s** are stressed on the last syllable and do not need an accent.

co*ñac*, ciu*dad*, re*loj*, princi*pal*, ha*blar*, co*mer*, vi*vir* (and all verb infinitives), *estoy*, *arroz*

Words which do not behave according to rules 1 and 2 above bear an acute accent (') on the stressed syllable.

48.2.1 Accented words

They fall mainly into the following groups:

a) words with a stressed final vowel:
café, *israelí*, *champú*, *ojalá*
including a number of preterite and future endings:
hablé, *habló*, *comí*, *comió*; *comeré*, *comerá*

b) words ending in **-n** or **-s** and stressed on the last syllable:
future endings: *comerás*, *comeréis*, *comerán*
present tense (*vosotros*) endings: *habláis*, *coméis*, *vivís*
many words ending **-ión**, **-ón**, **-és**: *estación*, *mandón*, *inglés*
(which lose the accent in the plural or feminine because then they observe rule 1:
estaciones, *mandones*, *mandonas*, *ingleses*, *inglesas*)

c) words ending in a consonant other than **-n** or **-s** and stressed on the next to last syllable:
alcázar, *almíbar*, *Almodóvar*, *Cádiz*

d) words stressed on any other syllable (usually the second from last):
buenísimo, *teléfono*, *polígono*, *kilómetro*, *Córdoba*
Watch out for imperatives, infinitives and gerunds with pronouns at the end:
dígame, *decírtelo*, *escribiéndole*
and words ending in unstressed **-en** in the plural: *imagen* ⟶ *imágenes*, etc.

e) words in which the accent is used to separate and stress a 'weak' vowel (see above, section 48.1.2):
panadería, *comían*, *continúa*

f)   words where the accent is used to distinguish:

- between two words which are otherwise spelt in the same way:

de	of	*dé*	give (imperative)
mas	but	*más*	more
se	(reflexive pronoun)	*sé*	I know; be! (imperative)
mi	my	*mí*	me
tu	your	*tú*	you
te	you	*té*	tea
solo	alone	*sólo*	only
si	if	*sí*	yes; oneself

- between demonstrative adjectives and pronouns (see Chapter 7):

este libro y ése   this book and that one
esa mesa y aquélla   that table and the one over there

You can tell the pronoun form because it is never immediately followed by a noun, and the accent always comes on the first **e** (even if there is only one!): *éste*, *ésos*, *aquéllas*.

Remember, though, that the neuter forms *esto*, *eso*, *aquello* have no accent because there is no corresponding adjective.

- interrogative words *¿dónde? ¿cuándo?* etc. (see Chapter 45).

Note: the only other accents you will find in Spanish are:

- the tilde (~) on the *ñ*:

señor, *mañana*

- the 'diaeresis' (¨) used in the combination *güe* and *güi* to indicate that the *u* is pronounced:

vergüenza, *argüir*

- There is no 'grave' (`) or 'circumflex' (^) accent in Spanish!

48.3 Punctuation

Punctuation is largely as in English, with the following exceptions.

48.3.1 Inverted question and exclamation marks

These are used as a warning that a question or exclamation is coming, as, unless there is a noun subject, you can't invert the verb and subject in Spanish:

¿Adónde vas? Pues ¡que sea pronto!
Where are you going? Well, make it quick!

Direct speech

To indicate direct speech (see Chapter 46) Spanish uses the long dash, or **raya** (–):

Buenos días – dijo. –¿Qué tal estás?

You will occasionally see **comillas** (« »), although these are more commonly used for quotations within a text and titles.

 Exercise 3

 ¡PONTE A PUNTO!

1 Cuestión de sílabas

Haz dos listas de las siguientes palabras. En la lista A, pondrás las palabras en que dos vocales forman diptongos de una sílaba, y en la lista B, las palabras en que los dos vocales forman dos sílabas.

cae	caos	cuarto	euro	feo	furia	hoy	huele
Jaime	lees	leí	ley	mío	roa	Ruiz	sea	seis
siete	soez	traes	traigo	viuda			

2 Manolo no sabe deletrear

Manolo se forma para reportero, pero su ortografía no es nada buena. He aquí dos párrafos que ha escrito sobre la playa de Isla Canela en el suroeste de España. ¿Sabes corregir sus 50 errores? ¡Vuelve a escribir este trozo de su reportaje con la ortografía correcta! (Nota: los nombres de los sitios están escritos correctamente.)

Conosida tradithionalmente commo la Puerta de España, al lindar con Portugal, es un lujar de repherencia parra el tourismo. A la atractiba offerta vacational se le mesclan activizades tradizionales que an conservado sus cuidadanos, dentro de un marquo imcomparable.

Isla Canela es la primmera de las plajas existentes en Huelva, nada más passar de Portugal. Es un lujar donde el dessarrollo del turizmo ha experrimentado un mayor camvio en los óltimos anos. En la playa se obcervan numerosos chiringitos y algún bar de kopas. En sus orilias, los pezcadores varan las emvarcaciones, algunas de ellas poseyen vasijas de baro, yamadas cajirones, que sirben para la pezca del pulpo. Ay un accesso cómmodo y rápido por careterra; tanbién, existe un cervicio de transbordadores que cruca el río Guadiana y lega asta la localidá portuguessa de Vila Real de Santo Antonio.

Cambio 16 no. 1503, 25.9.00, supplement p.5

3 ¡Acentos!

Arregla las palabras siguientes en columnas, añadiendo acentos cuando faltan.

Columna A: las que deben llevar acento;
Columna B: las que no tienen acento;
Columna C: las que llevan acento o no según su sentido.

administrativo	revolver	hospital	cesped	traigame	naciones
firmo vino	te lapiz	anden	vengo	racion	construyo
cambio trae	guardia	champu	vereis	monton	imagen
alemanes saco	pijama	como	Valladolid	telefono	frances
arabe verdad	marroqui	continuo			

Ejemplo:

A	**B**	**C**	
		i) con acento	ii) sin acento
nación	*debajo*	*habló*	*hablo*

4 ¿Sabes descifrar textos?

Acabas de recibir estos tres textos de tu novio/a español(a). ¡Descífralos y escríbelos con la ortografía normal! La clave en la próxima página podría ayudarte.

```
Q tl sts xico/a? Ns vemos sta trde o no? Q t prece kedr n l bar Malaga
a ls 8?

T veo n la prta dl cole a la slida d clse

Oye me prgntaba si kieres q m pase sta tarde. No es xq kera hacer na xo
x str jnts.
```

¡... Y EN MARCHA!

5 Lee un minuto, por favor

En grupos de tres o cuatro o en la clase entera, tomad un texto de la prensa o la literatura españolas. Un(a) estudiante empieza a leer en voz alta y los otros tienen que ser muy críticos de la precisión de su pronunciación, incluso el acento tónico, e interrumpir cuando creen que es incorrecta. Si el que interrumpe tiene razón, tiene que seguir con la lectura. Si no, el lector original sigue leyendo hasta cumplir un minuto.

6 Dictado comunal

Cada miembro de la clase escoge una frase de dos o tres renglones en un libro o artículo que estudiáis juntos y la dicta a los otros, que tienen que escribirlo. ¡A ver quién escribe más correctamente!

7 ¡Mándame un texto!

Con la ayuda de esta clave, mandaos textos unos a otros.

a2 – adiós; bn – bien; bss – besos; cmr – comer; d – de; dl – del; exo – hecho; kdms – quedamos; ktl – qué tal; mña – mañana; muxo – mucho; na – nada; str – estar; sts – estás; t – te; tk – te quiero; tkm – te quiero mucho; tmb – también; tmpc – tampoco; tngo – tengo; wenas – buenas; x – por; xd – por dios; xfa – por favor; xo – pero; xq – porque

49 An introduction to Spanish vocabulary

 MECANISMOS

49.1 The origins of Spanish

Modern Castilian Spanish (*castellano*) is derived from Vulgar Latin, the Latin spoken by ordinary Romans. The halfway stage, Romance, also gave rise to other languages and dialects of the Iberian Peninsula. The Castilians won political and military dominance over much of Spain, so it was their 'dialect' which eventually became the national language of Spain. Thus, Spanish comes from the same source as Italian, French, Portuguese and so on, and almost all other Iberian Peninsula languages, such as *catalán*, *valenciano* and *gallego*.

Much vocabulary in English also comes from Latin, either via Norman French, from other Romance languages, or direct from Latin in more recent times (largely in the fields of science or culture). Hence, Spanish and English have a lot of vocabulary in common, and many words new to you in Spanish will be recognisable via English or any other Romance language you happen to know.

Spanish has also imported words from many other languages over the centuries, among them Arabic (e.g. *algodón* – cotton), French (e.g. *boutique*), English (e.g. *márketing*) and Latin-American Indian languages (e.g. *tomate* – tomato). Many of the more recent importations are from English, mostly in the fields of sport, pop music, business, science and computing. Some imported words keep more or less their original spelling, but with pronunciation adapted to Spanish: this is usually the case with words adopted in written form (e.g. *iceberg*). Words imported through spoken language on the other hand tend to do the opposite, and have spelling adapted to keep the pronunciation similar to the original (e.g. *fútbol*). It is interesting to compare two words with similar meanings – *jersey* and *suéter*: the former was probably adopted from written English and is now usually pronounced in a Spanish way as something like 'hersei'; the latter was obviously adopted in spoken form, and a form of spelling was evolved which produces the right sound when said aloud. It is worth noting that verbs based on imported words tend to be in the *-ar* verb family, (e.g. *dopar*, *esnifar*, *xerocopiar*).

49.2 Survival skills in Spanish: making sensible guesses

a) Bearing in mind the origins of Spanish, new words should not always send you rushing for a dictionary. Often, you will be able to work out the likely meaning for yourself from your own resources, and from experience, especially if you already know the core of the new word, or recognise it through English or another language. (But beware of '*falsos amigos*', which look the same but are not!) Clearly, it is easier to make sensible guesses at written words – you are in control, and can look at them again and again – than at spoken words – you may not hear the spoken words more than once, and in any case it is often difficult in a piece of speech to tell where one word ends and another begins, as Spanish is such a flowing language. Practice helps, especially if you are able to spend time listening to recorded material and following a written transcript at the same time. Sometimes the sound or appearance of a word will help, sometimes it will hinder. This is the case with two examples of imported words: *jersey* is easy to read but difficult if heard – unless you can 'visualise' its spelling (a useful technique), whilst **suéter** (= sweater) is easy to hear and understand, but difficult to grasp in written form unless you try saying it aloud or imagining its sound (again, a useful technique).

b) In both written and spoken Spanish, it often helps to 'undress' a new word to get at its core, which may then be recognisable. First, some basic principles:

- Generally speaking, Spanish likes singular nouns to end in a vowel.
- Many nouns have both masculine and feminine forms.
- Adjectives match nouns they describe in gender and number.
- Plurals of nouns, pronouns, adjectives and articles which have plural forms all end in **-s**.
- Verbs have different forms for each person referred to.
- Words are often built up from core words, adding prefixes and/or suffixes.
- Spanish, like English, makes great use of affixes to alter the meaning of words or to make new words: prefixes are put at the beginning of a word and suffixes at the end; removing them helps you identify the core of the word, which you may then recognise.
- Like English, Spanish has many compound words made up of two base words; whilst in English these are mostly made up of two nouns, in Spanish many are made from a verb and a noun; English words consisting of two nouns are rendered in Spanish as two nouns linked by **de**.

The next section will help you develop the necessary 'feel' for Spanish to make the most of these techniques.

49.3 Guessing made easier

49.3.1 Spelling quirks of Castilian Spanish

For various reasons, several letters or combinations of letters changed in written form in the transition from Latin to modern Castilian Spanish. If you are aware of these, you can quite easily work out the meanings of many words which are similar in English but not otherwise easily recognisable. NB: often the changed Castilian form and a form closer to Latin, without the change, exist side by side, though sometimes with slightly different meanings.

a) 'vowel stretching' of **e** and **o**

Many Latin words which contain these two letters in a stressed situation have undergone a spelling change in the transition into Spanish; you should be familiar with this in radical/stem-changing verbs. Effectively, the stresssed **e** or **i** has 'stretched' as follows:

---

e ⟶ **ie**, and **o** ⟶ **ue**; and in addition, sometimes **e** ⟶ **i, o** ⟶ **u** and **u** ⟶ **ue**

e ⟶ **ie**; **bien** = well; c.f. Latin/Italian *bene*, English beneficial

o ⟶ **ue**: **bueno** = good; c.f. French **bon**, English bonus

e ⟶ **i**: **pido** = I ask for, from **pedir**; c.f. petition

o ⟶ **u**: **durmió** = he slept, from **dormir** (to sleep); c.f. dormitory

u ⟶ **ue**: **agüero** = omen, c.f. augur

NB: Some of these can work the other way round:

e.g. **precio** = price; **descuento** = discount

---

b) *esc-, esp-, est-*

You may notice that some native speakers of Spanish have problems pronouncing English words beginning '*sc-*', '*sp-*', '*st-*'; they tend to begin them with an *e* sound instead – with *esc-, esp-, est-*; it just happens that many such words in English, French, etc. tend to begin in Spanish with *esc-, esp-, est-*; so, to help your 'guess' at new words with these beginnings, simply take off the *e-*. You'll be surprised at how many new words you will now be able to 'guess'.

> *e + sc*: *escuela* = **sc**hool
> *e + sp*: *español* = **Sp**anish
> *e + st*: *estudiante* = **st**udent

c) *i/y*

Spanish replaces 'y' with an *i*, and *-ía* or *-ia* at the end of a word.

> *sistema* = system; *ritmo* = rhythm; *síntoma* = symptom
> *biología* = biology; *farmacia* = pharmacy; *Italia* = Italy

d) double consonants (see Chapter 48, section 48.1.3)

Spanish has very few double consonants, and such combinations in, for example, English are usually simplified in Spanish. However, *cc, ll, rr* are all very common. Up to 1994, *ll* was treated as a separate letter, along with *ch*, and you may well find this in textbooks and dictionaries published before that date. *nn* occurs in a few words, usually ones beginning with the prefix *in-*.

> *abadía, aceptar, efecto, balón, mamut, opresor, profesor*

- *innecesario* – unnecessary (**in-** negating/opposite)
- *innovar* – to innovate (**in-** meaning 'into')
- *cc* = 'ct'; *acción, diccionario, elección*

Note the following further examples of how Spanish simplifies complex combinations of consonants:

> *psicología, melancólico, caótico, ciencia, conciencia*

e) *f/ph* (see Chapter 48, section 48.1.3)

Spanish does not have 'ph' spellings, and uses *f* instead.

> *atmósfera, farmacia, filosofía, geografía, profeta, semáforo*

f) *f/h* (see Chapter 48, section 48.1.3)

Castilian Spanish often uses *h* instead of *f*, and two words with similar meanings but different spellings often coexist.

h ⟵ ⟶ **f**: *hogar* = hearth + *fuego* = fire; c.f. focus (means fireplace in Latin)
hijo = son + filial; c.f. French *fils*

g) *g/h*

Spanish sometimes begins words with **h** instead of **g**.

h ⟵ **g**: *hermano* = brother c.f. **g**ermane (related to)

NB: in Latin American pronunciation, **g** with **e** and **i**, and **j**, sound like the English 'h' sound.

h) *g/w* (see Chapter 48, section 48.1.3)

Spanish has problems with 'w' sounds, especially at the beginning of words; it tends to use **g** (**g** or **gu**) instead.

w ⟶ **g**: (*el País de Gales* = Wales; c.f. *Galicia*)
guerra = war; c.f. *guerrilla/guerrillero*

NB: also **wh**isky is often pronounced or written *güiski*

i) *j/x* (see Chapter 48, section 48.1.3)

Spanish usually uses **j** where English uses '**x**'.

j ⟵ **x**: *Méjico* = Mexico; *fijo* = fixed

j) *ll*

Castilian Spanish often uses *ll* instead of *cl*, *fl* and *pl* at the beginning of words.

cl ⟶ *ll*: *llamar* = to call; c.f. **cl**aim (call)
fl ⟶ *ll*: *llama* = **fl**ame (also the South American animal)
pl ⟶ *ll*: *llano* = flat, **pl**ain

k) *t/th* (see Chapter 48, section 48.1.3)

Spanish does not have 'th' spellings, using **t** instead.

teología, *terapia*, *teatro*, *ateo*, *simpatía*

49.3.2 Cognates and derivatives

Many Spanish words can be identified in a straightforward way and, for various reasons, either as a result of obvious similarity to known words in Spanish or other languages (coming from the same origin – cognates), or through being derived from known words, with bits added at the beginning or end of the word. In the case of the latter, you can often predict the existence of a word by knowing how similar words are built up from a base word; equally, you can work out the meaning of an unfamiliar word by 'undressing' it to get back to the base word at its core. Here are some of the commonest.

49.3.3 Cognates

a) English words absorbed into Spanish without change of meaning.

álbum, *récord*, *líder*, *fútbol*, *mánager*

NB: many have spellings which have been 'adapted' into Spanish.

b) Spanish words with equivalents in English or which English has borrowed from Spanish:

paella, *matador*, *fiesta*, *aficionado*

c) Words identical in form to their English equivalent and with comparable pronunciation.

casual, *panorama*

d) Words similar in form to their English equivalent and with comparable pronunciation.

documento, *militar*, *sistema*, *clima*, *movimiento*, *millón*

e) Verbs whose stem is identical or similar in form to their English equivalent.

admirar, *contener*, *consistir*, *aplaudir*

f) Words containing certain frequently occurring Spanish orthographic features which, once known, allow ready identification with English equivalents.

libertad, *turismo*, *indicación*, *potencia*

Note the equivalent English–Spanish suffixes:

* *-dad* = 'ty' e.g. *ciudad* – city; *capacidad* – capacity
* *-ción* = 'tion' e.g. *acción* – action; *elección* – election
* *-ía*, *-ia* = 'y' e.g. *energía* – energy; *farmacia* – pharmacy

g) Spanish words closer to Latin which exist alongside later Spanish forms with spelling changes. These pairs of words sometimes have slightly different meanings.

fuego – hueco; clave – llave; plano – llano

49.3.4 Derivatives: word building and undressing

a) Words whose meaning is determined by common prefixes or suffixes, but whose base element is already known or easily identifiable.

con-: contener

des-: deshacer, desnudo

dis-: disuadir

in-/im-: incorrecto, imposible

re-: revolver

sub-: submarino, subcontinente

-miento: pensar ⟶ *pensamiento*

-oso: arena ⟶ *arenoso*

-able: salud ⟶ *saludable*

-ería: zapatero ⟶ *zapatería*

b) Nouns denoting people and other concepts, which are characterised by endings such as *-ero/a, -or/a, -ista*.

-ero/era: zapatero, niñera

-ista: pianista, taxista

-or/ora: pescador, pintora

These are mostly based on another noun or a verb.

c) Adverbs formed by adding the ending *-mente* to known or easily identifiable adjectives.

totalmente, activamente

Note: it can be seen that in Spanish most adverbs end in *-mente*, just as in English most end in '-ly'.

d) Adjectives with ending *-able*, which compare with English equivalents ending in '-able' or '-ible', deriving from easily known or identifiable words.

imaginable, admirable

e) Adjectives with ending *-oso/-osa*, comparable with English equivalents ending in '-ous' or '-y', and which are easily identifiable.

religioso, furioso, vigoroso, vicioso; arenoso, rocoso, lluvioso, sabroso

f) Adjectives with ending *-és/esa, -(i)ense, -eno/a, -eño/a* comparing with English '-ese' or '-(i)an', usually indicating place of origin.

inglés, japonesa, canadiense, chileno, brasileña

g) Diminutives ending in *-ito, -illo, -ico* deriving from known words or other easily identifiable words (see Chapter 47).

señorito, panecillo, casita, perico

h) Augmentative and pejorative suffixes such as *-ón/ona, -azo, -ucho* (see Chapter 47).

hombrón, mujerona, manotazo, casucha

i) Compound nouns, consisting of combinations of known words.

abrelatas, *sacacorchos*, *cortacésped*

j) Words derived from adjectives.

tranquilizar, *ensuciar*, *limpieza*

k) Words mainly derived from verbs, with endings *-ante* or *-ente*.

cantante, *oyente*

l) Place names with identical or similar spelling to their English equivalents.

Italia, *América*, *Brasil*

m) Common acronyms and initials, often in a different order.

UNO = *ONU – Organización de las Naciones Unidas*
NATO = *OTAN – Organización del Tratado del Atlántico del Norte*

Note: USA = *EEUU – los Estados Unidos* (plural words have doubled-up letters when given as acronyms).

 ¡PONTE A PUNTO!

1 El detective

Busca la palabra española que equivale a estas palabras inglesas.

premier	certain	port	scale	special	station	geography
gymnasium	christian	procession	affect	photography	flame	
plain	theory	gothic				

2 Viceversa

Busca cualquier palabra inglesa que corresponda más o menos a estas palabras españolas, por tener el mismo origen.

precio	sierra	revuelto	escuela	especular	estudiar	geología
girar	concienzudo	batería	sección	fonético	llamar	
antropología	osteópata					

3 Derivaciones

Busca al menos una palabra derivada de las siguientes.

persuadir	tóxico	solución	cruel	imaginar	Italia	joven
arena	rascar	cigarro				

4 Orígenes

Busca la palabra que está a raíz de las siguientes.

rocoso	desviación	probabilidad	resolucíon	imposibilitar
reconocimiento	paulatinamente	desafortunadamente	madrileño	
inutilidad				

¡... Y EN MARCHA!

5 Juego eliminatorio

Haz cualquiera de los ejercicios de *¡Ponte a punto!* buscando o sugiriendo palabras, alternando con un(a) compañero/a; también los podrías hacer en grupo, como juego eliminatorio, y con un límite de tiempo para contestar. Luego podéis continuar, a base de vuestras propias listas de palabras.

6 ¡Los que no!

Seguid jugando tú y tus compañeros/as, tratando cada uno de sugerir palabras españolas que no tengan ninguna conexión con palabras inglesas, siguiendo el alfabeto según la primera letra de cada palabra.

Ejemplo:

Estudiante 1: ajo
Estudiante 2: burro
Estudiante 3: caso
Estudiantes 1 y 2: No vale, pues tenemos la palabra inglesa 'case'.

7 ¡Los que sí!

Luego podéis continuar, pero esta vez buscando palabras españolas que no tengan otras palabras derivadas.

Ejemplo:

Estudiante 1: a
Estudiante 2: bacalao
Estudiante 3: calor
Estudiante 1: No vale, pues está la palabra 'caluroso'
Estudiante 2: ... y 'caliente', 'calentar', 'caloría'

50 To put it another way

Throughout this book you have learnt about the various parts of speech and how they work in Spanish. (On the way, you may even have strengthened your knowledge of the grammar of your own language!) This chapter will give you some examples of how to vary your Spanish by using different parts of speech. We will also take a look at words which mean much the same thing, i.e. synonyms.

 MECANISMOS

50.1 Varying the parts of speech

50.1.1 Using nouns instead of verbs or verbs instead of nouns

You can often say the same thing in a different way by using a noun instead of a verb or vice versa.

Verb	*Santi **está** muy **motivado**.* Santi is very motivated.
Noun	***La motivación** de Santi es buena.* Santi's motivation is good.
	*Santi tiene buena **motivación**.* Santi has good motivation.
Verb	*Anita **trabaja** con precisión.* Anita works with accuracy.
Noun	***El trabajo** de Anita es preciso.* Anita's work is accurate.
Noun	*La contaminación de la playa es **causa** de gran preocupación entre los turistas.* The pollution of the beach is a cause for great concern amongst the tourists.
Verb	*La contaminación de la playa **causa** gran preocupación entre los turistas.* The pollution of the beach causes great concern amongst the tourists.
or	*Los turistas **se preocupan** mucho por la contaminación de la playa.* The tourists are very concerned about the pollution of the beach.
or	*Los turistas **se preocupan** mucho de que la playa se contamine.* The tourists are very concerned that the beach is being polluted.

Noun + adjective	**Las reformas recientes** del hotel han sido recibidas con aprobación por los clientes. The recent improvements to the hotel have been received with approval by the guests.
Noun + adjective	Los clientes han aprobado **las reformas recientes** del hotel. The guests have approved the recent improvements to the hotel.
Verb + adverb	Los clientes aprueban el hecho de que **se haya reformado recientemente** el hotel. The guests approve the fact that the hotel has been recently improved.

Sometimes there might be a slight difference in emphasis or nuance, and sometimes you might reject a particular way of expressing things as clumsy, too involved or long-winded (the last example might come into this category) but, basically, all the sentences in each group mean the same thing.

Note: because adjectives qualify nouns and adverbs qualify verbs, it is often necessary to change these as well, as in the examples above and the following:

* Noun + adjective:

  La subida en el precio de la gasolina ha sido **astronómica**.
  The rise in the price of petrol has been **astronomical**.

  El precio de la gasolina ha sufrido **una subida astronómica**.
  The price of petrol has undergone **an astronomical rise**.

  Por todo este trauma **el apoyo** de su amigo fue **incansable**.
  Throughout this trauma her friend's **support** was **untiring**.

  Por todo este trauma su amigo le prestó **un apoyo incansable**.
  Throughout this trauma her friend gave her **untiring support**.

* Verb + adverb or adverbial phrase:

  El precio de la gasolina **ha subido astronómicamente**.
  The price of petrol **has risen astronomically**.

  El precio de la gasolina **ha subido de una manera astronómica**.
  The price of petrol **has risen in an astronomical way**.

  Por todo este trauma su amigo **la apoyó incansablemente**.
  Throughout this trauma her friend **supported her untiringly**.

  Por todo este trauma su amigo **la apoyó de un modo incansable**.
  Throughout this trauma her friend **supported her in an untiring manner**.

Exercises 1, 2

50.1.2 Turning adjectives into verbs

A device which Spanish often uses is to create a verb which denotes the taking on or imparting of the quality described by the adjective:

Imposibilitar means *hacer imposible:*

*El viento **imposibilitó** la carrera.*
The wind **made** the race **impossible**.

Similarly:

posibilitar(se) = hacer(se) posible	to make/become possible
capacitar(se) = hacer(se) capaz	to render/become capable
incapacitar(se) = hacer(se) incapaz	to render/become incapable, incapacitate/become incapacitated
independizar(se) = hacer(se) independiente	to make/become independent
amarillear = volverse amarillo	to turn yellow
verdear = volverse verde	to turn green

Often the verb is of the *-ecer* type, with *-zc-* spelling change (see p. 83), sometimes with prefix *em-/en-*:

enloquecer(se) = volver(se) loco	to drive/become mad
enrojecer(se) = volver(se) rojo	to turn red, blush
humedecer(se) = hacer(se) húmedo	to moisten/become moist/damp
palidecer = volverse pálido	to turn pale

Note: you will see that the reflexive form is often (but not always) used in Spanish for the intransitive form in English.

*A esa edad los jóvenes **se independizan** de sus padres.*
At that age young people **become independent** from their parents.

*Luisa **palideció** al oír la noticia.*
Luisa **turned pale** when she heard the news.

Exercise 3

50.2 Using synonyms

A synonym is a word that means the same as another. An English example would be 'start', 'begin' and 'commence', which all mean about the same, although they may not always be completely interchangeable. Spanish is a rich language, in the sense that there is often a variety of words meaning approximately the same thing. For 'begin', etc. Spanish also has *empezar, comenzar, principiar, iniciar(se), ponerse a* and a number of other verbs.

*De repente **empezó/comenzó/se puso** a llover.*
Suddenly it **started/began** to rain.

*Rosario habla varias **lenguas**/varios **idiomas**.*
Rosario speaks several **languages**.

*Roberto **resbaló/se deslizó** y **se rompió/se quebró** el tobillo.*
Roberto **slipped** and **broke** his ankle.

*El espectáculo fue recibido con **aplausos/palmadas**.*
The show was received with **applause**.

*Merche **se ha marchado/se ha ido** a Madrid.*
Merche **has gone off** to Madrid.

➡ **Exercises 4, 5**

 ¡PONTE A PUNTO!

1 Palabras relacionadas

Con la ayuda del diccionario si te hace falta, rellena los espacios en blanco de cada columna con palabras relacionadas con la que se da. Cuidado: a veces no será posible rellenar todos los espacios, otras veces podría haber dos o más palabras.

sustantivo	verbo	adjetivo	adverbio o frase adverbial	otro
Ejemplo: peso/pesar	pesar	pesado	pesadamente	a pesar de
1		alegre		
2	entristecer(se)			
3		gordo		
4	oír			
5 belleza				
6		tonto		
7			de rodillas	
8 cabeza				
9	simpatizar			
10 vista				

2 Una empresa familiar

El sr. Pereda escribe la historia de su empresa y busca la mejor manera de expresarse. Tienes que ofrecerle por lo menos una, quizás más, maneras de expresar las frases en cursiva.

Ejemplo:

El establecimiento de la empresa tuvo lugar en 1921.

La empresa se estableció en 1921.

1 En ese año mi abuelo *hizo la compra de* dos empresas más pequeñas.
2 *La base del éxito de la nueva empresa fue* la lealtad de sus empleados.
3 *La desaparición de la empresa por poco ocurrió* durante la recesión mundial de los años veinte.
4 *Poco antes del estallido de la guerra civil española, la opinión de mi abuelo fue* que la vida en España iba a *tener sus dificultades*.
5 Entonces mi abuelo decidió *en el traslado de* la entera empresa a Argentina.
6 *Su estancia transatlántica tuvo una duración más larga de la que* esperaba, puesto que la Segunda Guerra Mundial *tuvo su principio* poco después.
7 *El hecho de que España estuviera aislada políticamente* del resto de Europa hasta los años sesenta *tuvo el resultado de* que *su vuelta a España no se verificara* hasta 1969.
8 Pero la empresa familiar *había sacado beneficio de los sucesos políticos: éramos los dueños de* una empresa establecida en dos países: Argentina y España.
9 *A su muerte en 1975, mi abuelo era rico y feliz*, y mi generación *se siente honrada pero a la vez obligada a* mantener *su creación*.

Ahora escribe la historia sin los números en un solo párrafo sin interrupción, escogiendo la frase que parezca mejor en cada caso: es decir, la original del sr. Pereda, o la tuya.

3 Dicho de otra manera

Vuelve a escribir las frases siguientes, utilizando un verbo en lugar de los adjetivos. Aviso: ¡a veces tendrás que buscar en el diccionario entre las palabras que empiezan con *em-* o *en-*!

Ejemplo:

El dinero que le dejó su tío <u>hizo posible</u> un viaje a Argentina.
El dinero que le dejó su tío <u>posibilitó</u> un viaje a Argentina.

1 Cuando estábamos en España en octubre, los árboles ya se volvían amarillos.
2 Los efectos del calor y del alcohol me volvían torpe.
3 La huelga de pilotos hizo imposible nuestro viaje a España.
4 Rosita se puso roja de vergüenza.
5 Recientemente Tomás se ha puesto más viejo.
6 La polución había vuelto negras las paredes.
7 A Maite le gustaría hacerse independiente de su hermana mayor.
8 Esteban se hizo responsable de los preparativos.
9 El apagón de la electricidad hizo inútiles todos los ordenadores.
10 ¡Esperamos que este ejercicio haga mejor tu conocimiento de algunos verbos españoles!

4 ¿Es igual o es lo mismo?

Busca una palabra sinónima de las que aparecen en cursiva.

1   ¡Qué vista tan *bella*!
2   ¡Qué niña tan *charlatana*!
3   Es un *chico* muy inteligente.
4   El programa *se iniciará* mañana.
5   *Se acabó* la fiesta.
6   ¡Me gusta ese *jersey*!
7   ¿Cuándo *te vas*?
8   Voy a *oír* la radio.
9   Estos vaqueros son *distintos*.
10 Voy a *mandar* este paquete a mi amigo en Perú.
11 Yo tengo razón: tú *no tienes razón*.
12 Voy a jugar en mi *computadora*.
13 ¿Dónde están *los demás*?
14 Estaban en *el borde* del lago.
15 Todos saben el secreto *salvo* María.
16 Franco *falleció* en 1975.
17 ¡Cuidado de que no te *resbales*!
18 ¿Qué *te parece*?
19 *Nos divertimos* estupendamente ayer.
20 Nos sentíamos algo *desilusionados* de la exposición.
21 Marco *quebrantó* su promesa a Conchi.
22 Quisiera *reparar* mi transistor.
23 La *vendimia* de uvas de 2005.
24 El ejército *derrotó* al enemigo.
25 El viejo edificio *se desplomó*.

5 Desarticulemos un artículo

Los siguientes párrafos se sacaron de un artículo aparecido en *El País*. Utilizando sinónimos o cambiando las partes de la oración, tienes que expresar de otra manera las palabras o frases que vienen en cursiva. Discute con tus compañeros/as de clase las varias maneras de expresar estas frases, y luego vuelve a escribir el artículo en un estilo aceptable.

Varios expertos *opinan* que *el turismo salvará el patrimonio*.
El auge del turismo cultural aparece como la principal esperanza *de salvación del* patrimonio histórico y artístico del país. *A esta conclusión ha llegado* un grupo de expertos que *ha participado* en los últimos días en el curso 'Patrimonio cultural y turismo', que *comenzó* el pasado lunes en El Escorial y que *termina* hoy. *La directora* del curso, Araceli Sánchez Garrido, *comentó* ayer que 'la preservación del patrimonio inmueble, *en especial* el *emplazado* en pequeñas ciudades y pueblos, depende *en buena medida* del *aumento del turismo.*'
   Según los especialistas, entre las ventajas *indiscutibles* del turismo cultural se encuentran *el impulso* de las inversiones *privadas*, la conservación de *recintos* arquitectónicos o el mantenimiento y rejuvenecimiento de *la población* en los centros históricos. *No obstante*, las afluencias de visitantes también *están en el origen de* fenómenos negativos como el *descontrol urbanístico* o la *adulteración de* fiestas y tradiciones populares. '*Hay que tener muy en claro* que la población de *zonas* de interés cultural no son *aborígenes* preparados para que les saquen una foto', señala Sánchez Garrido. Añade '*Se trata de alcanzar un equilibrio entre* la conservación del patrimonio, sus nuevos usos y el impacto del turismo. *El modelo podría ser un país como Francia.*'

El País

¡... Y EN MARCHA!

6 Palabras similares, sentidos distintos

a) Piensa en unos diez verbos españoles o que tengan un sinónimo perfecto o parcial, o que tengan dos o más sentidos distintos. Luego escribe frases que ilustran la diferencia.

Ejemplo:

andar/pasear

Me gusta pasear a orillas del río pero por el momento no puedo andar porque me he roto la pierna.

b) Ahora hazlo con unos diez sustantivos.

Ejemplo:

la experiencia

Fue una experiencia inolvidable.
En clase de química hicimos algunas experiencias.

c) Y unos diez adjetivos.

Ejemplo:

viejo

Ricardo es un viejo amigo; con sus noventa años, ya es un hombre muy viejo.

7 Juego de palabras

La clase se divide en dos equipos. Un(a) estudiante del equipo A tiene que decir una palabra española y un(a) contrincante del equipo B tiene que responder con otra palabra directamente relacionada con la primera palabra o con una que tenga un sentido similar. Si lo hace correctamente gana 2 puntos. Los dos equipos se alternan. Si el/la estudiante no sabe una palabra que esté estrechamente relacionada, puede decir una palabra sugerida por el sentido de la palabra de su rival, ganando así 1 punto.

Ejemplos:

Equipo A, estudiante 1: calor; Equipo B, estudiante 1: caliente (2 puntos); A2: calentas (2); B2: Caluroso (2); A3 ...

Equipo B, estudiante 1: queso; Equipo A, estudiante 1: quesero (2 puntos); B2: quesería (2); A2: lechería (1); B3 ...

8 Más desarticulación

Toma un párrafo de cualquier texto de una revista o periódico español, o de tu manual normal de español, y escríbelo de otra manera.

9 Historia con moraleja

En este extracto de una carta al redactor de *El País*, hay muchas posibilidades de variar las palabras y frases que se utilizan. Escribe un resumen del extracto en tus propias palabras.

Resulta que hace poquísimo tiempo los ictiólogos acaban de descubrir en las aguas poco profundas del Pacífico sur un pequeño tipo de pez, más bien normalito de forma y color, un pececito, en definitiva, que les había pasado inadvertido hasta ahora a los biólogos marinos, precisamente por su falta absoluta de características visualmente notables y que, por lo que aseguran, es presa fácil para especies mayores que él, que son la práctica totalidad del resto. Pero, al observar con detenimiento sus hábitos de comportamiento, los científicos se quedaron atónitos. Claro que era presa fácil, es que además se comportaba más como un suicida que como una víctima desprevenida, exhibiéndose descarado ante sus posibles captores como si no fuera con él la cosa. Así, tan tranquilo, a la vista de todos, cuando, de repente, ¡zas!, un destello de luz y una boca negra y enorme que literalmente lo engulle vivo y entero; ya está, se acabó … ¿Se suicidió? ¡Qué va! Resulta que el *inocente* pececillo de marras, una vez en el tubo digestivo del depredador de turno, comienza inmediatamente a comerse las entrañas de su casero, tardando de dos a tres minutos en salir por la cloaca de tan acogedor restaurante para, bien alimentado con su manjar favorito, volverse a poner de nuevo a la vista de cualquiera, abandonando a su suerte al infortunado captor, vivo y moribundo, a merced de la bellísima, abundante y siempre hambrienta naturaleza marina, circundante y multicolor.

Ricardo Moreno Moratinos, Sevilla

El País

KEY TO THE *¡PONTE A PUNTO!* EXERCISES

Chapter 2

1   la bronquitis, el diploma, el parabrisas, el cuidado, la igualdad, la civilización, el dilema, el ama de casa (*fem*.), la tesis, la goma, el Ecuador, el equipaje, el amor, el tragaperras, la cumbre, el programa, el Paraguay, la Argentina, el paraguas, el footing, el software, el coma (*coma*)/la coma (*comma*), el rugby, el/la guitarrista

2   dos – rinocerontes, hipopótamos, cocodrilos, gatos, ratones, ratas, gorriones, serpientes, pitones, jabalíes, reses, chimpancés; crisis, toses, inundaciones, regímenes, series de problemas, clubs/clubes de vela, ingleses, portuguesas, israelíes.

3   1) del 2) el 3) la 4) el 5) un 6) las 7) del 8) la 9) la 10) la 11) un 12) el 13) la 14) la 15) la 16) la 17) el 18) las 19) la 20) – 21) el 22) la 23) el 24) la 25) del 26) las 27) del 28) las 29) la 30) el 31) las 32) al 33) la 34) –

Chapter 3

1   Any combination that makes sense is possible. Check with your teacher that you have the agreements correct.

2   1) moreno 2) largo 3) redonda 4) marrón 5) grandes 6) vaqueros 7) azules 8) desgarrados 9) negras 10) de charol 11) alto 12) sucias 13) extranjero 14) pocas 15) pronunciadas 16) peligroso 17) seguros

3   1) un pueblo antiguo 2) varios pueblos 3) una región pobre 4) la renta media 5) ciertas ventajas, aire puro 6) el puro placer 7) medio kilómetro 8) su antigua maestra 9) una cosa cierta

Chapter 4

1   1) lentamente 2) rápidamente 3) estúpidamente 4) lógicamente 5) personalmente 6) regularmente 7) correctamente 8) bien

2   1) recientemente 2) fácilmente 3) atentamente 4) persuasivamente 5) categóricamente 6) diplomáticamente 7) airadamente 8) difícilmente 9) entusiasmadamente 10) profundamente

3   1) b 2) g 3) e 4) i 5) a 6) j 7) d 8) f 9) c 10) h

Chapter 5

1   1) Brasil es más grande que Chile.
    2) Llueve más en las selvas de Brasil que … en Chile.
    3) Menos personas hablan portugués que español/No tantas personas hablan portugués como español en Latinoamérica.
    4) Hay menos capitalistas en Cuba que en el resto de Latinoamérica/No hay tantos capitalistas en Cuba como …
    5) Acapulco está menos contaminada que la Ciudad de Méjico/no está tan contaminada como Méjico.
    6) El Río Grande es menos largo que el Río Orinoco/no es tan largo como el Río Orinoco.
    7) Hace menos frío/hace más calor en Caracas que en la Tierra del Fuego/No hace tanto frío en Caracas como …
    8) Hay más galeses en Gales que en Patagonia.
    9) Más norteamericanos que ingleses/Menos ingleses que norteamericanos/No tantos ingleses como norteamericanos visitan los países de Sudamérica.
    10) Los habitantes de las Islas Malvinas hablan más inglés que español/menos español que inglés.

2   Many versions are possible: consult your teacher.

3   1) de 2) de los que 3) de lo que 4) de los que 5) que 6) de 7) de lo que 8) de la que 9) de lo que

Chapter 6

1   1) La Rioja es la autonomía más pequeña de toda España.
2) El vino es el producto más importante de la Rioja.
3) Las drogas son el problema más preocupante de/para la juventud española.
4) Pedro Almodóvar es el director de cine más conocido de la actualidad española.
5) Torrelavega es la ciudad menos turística de Cantabria.
6) El AVE es el tren más rápido y moderno de la RENFE.
7) El turismo es el factor más imprescindible de/para la economía española.
8) El autobús es el modo de viajar menos cómodo de todos.
9) El Ebro es el río más largo de España.
10) Granada es la ciudad con más influencia árabe de toda Andalucía.

2   1) Está friísimo. 2) Son lindísimos. 3) Son riquísimas. 4) Son buenísimos.
5) Es simpatiquísima. 6) Son grandísimos. 7) Es sabrosísima. 8) Trabaja
muchísimo. 9) Estoy contentísima. 10) Te sirven rapidísimamente.

Chapter 7

1   1) este 2) esta 3) aquélla 4) Este 5) este 6) ése 7) aquél 8) estos 9) esta
10) aquélla 11) esto 12) Estas 13) aquéllas 14) ésta 15) aquélla 16) éstos

Chapter 8

1   1) No, no son sus zapatos. 2) Sí, es su CD. 3) No, no es su chaqueta. 4) Sí, son sus zapatillas rojas.
5) Sí, son sus monopatines. 6) No, no es su MP3. 7) Sí, es mi MP3. 8) Sí, son sus naipes. 9) No, no
son tus gafas. 10) Sí, es nuestro/vuestro vídeo. 11) No, no son nuestros/vuestros. 12) Sí, es tu DVD.

2   1) Es de Marcos. 2) Es de Ángel. 3) Es de Anita. 4) Sí, es suyo. 5) Sí, es mía. 6) Sí, es tuyo/suyo.
7) Sí, es nuestro. 8) Sí, es nuestra/vuestra/suya. 9) Son de Miriam González. 10) Son de Pablo
Picazo. 11) Sí, son mías. 12) Sí, son suyos. 13) Sí, son suyas. 14) Sí, son suyos. 15) Sí, son
nuestros. 16) Sí, son nuestras.

3   1) mi 2) la tuya 3) Mis 4) los tuyos 5) tu 6) la mía 7) mi 8) la tuya 9) mi 10) la tuya 11) vuestras 12) las
nuestras 13) Tu 14) la mía 15) la mía 16) la tuya 17) Vuestras 18) las nuestras 19) tu 20) la mía
21) vuestras/tus 22) las nuestras/mías 23) mías 24) tu

4   *All possible answers are given, both in the affirmative and in the negative.*
1) No, mi moto es más rápida que la tuya/Sí, tu moto es más rápida que la mía.
2) No, tu novio/a es más feo/a que el mío/la mía/Sí, mi novio/a es más feo/a que el tuyo/la tuya.
3) No, nuestra abuela es más vieja que la vuestra/Sí, vuestra abuela es más vieja que la nuestra.
4) No, tus tíos son más simpáticos que los míos/Sí, mis tíos son más simpáticos que los tuyos.
5) No, su perro es más feroz que el tuyo/Sí, tu perro es más feroz que el suyo.
6) No, tu amiga es más tonta que la mía/Sí, mi amiga es más tonta que la tuya.
7) No, mi móvil costó más dinero que el tuyo/Sí, tu móvil costó más dinero que el mío.
8) No, sus deberes son más difíciles que los nuestros/Sí, nuestros deberes son más difíciles que los
suyos.
9) No, vuestro profesor es mejor que el nuestro/Sí, nuestro profesor es mejor que el vuestro.
10) No, los mensajes que mandamos nosotros son más aburridos que los suyos/Sí, los mensajes
que mandan ellos son más aburridos que los nuestros.

Chapter 9

1a *Across columns:* veinticuatro, cuarenta y tres, sesenta y cinco, noventa y dos; cincuenta y uno, ciento uno, ciento doce, ciento cuarenta y ocho; ciento ochenta y siete, doscientos dos, trescientos cuarenta y dos, cuatrocientos cinco; cuatrocientos sesenta y seis, quinientos tres, quinientos trece, seiscientos setenta y tres; setecientos setenta y dos, ochocientos veintiuno, novecientos cincuenta y cuatro, mil uno; mil doscientos treinta y cuatro, dos mil trescientos setenta y ocho, ocho mil setecientos cuarenta y tres, doce mil ochocientos setenta y seis; cincuenta y nueve mil cuatrocientos ochenta y tres, ochenta y tres mil seiscientos ochenta y nueve, un millón uno, cuatro millones novecientos ochenta y seis mil quinientos veintitrés; cincuenta y seis millones cuatrocientos nueve mil cuatro, cuatrocientos cincuenta y dos millones seiscientos noventa y cuatro mil quinientos setenta

1b Isabel primera de Inglaterra, el papa Pablo sexto, el rey Alfonso décimo, el quinto aniversario, su octavo cumpleaños, su quince cumpleaños.

Chapter 10

2 Se vierte un litro de vino del jarro A al jarro C, que estará lleno con tres litros. Luego se vierte del jarro C al jarro B, donde cabrán dos litros, y te quedará un solo litro en el jarro C – ¡justamente lo que necesitabas!

Chapter 11

1 There are a variety of possible permutations: consult your teacher!

2 *Habrá nubes* a primeras horas en el norte de Galicia, *y lloverá débilmente* en toda Galicia. Por la tarde *hará sol*, *y hará más calor. Estará nublado/nuboso/Habrá nubes* en el norte de Castilla y León. *Estará despejado/No habrá nubes* en el resto del centro. En las costas este y sur *hará much(ísim)o calor*; en la región de Almería *hará unos 42 grados. Habrá nieblas* y *hará más fresco* en los Pirineos. *No nevará* en ningún sitio.

3 1g 2h 3e 4f 5c 6j 7i 8b 9a 10d

4 1) Tenía mucho frío. 2) Tuve/Había tenido éxito. 3) Tuve (mucha) suerte. 4) Tuve/Tenía mucho calor. 5) Tenía sueño. 6) Tenía mucha sed. 7) No tenía ganas de salir. 8) Tenía much(ísima) hambre. 9) Tenía prisa. 10) Tenía/Tuve razón.

Chapter 12

1a 1) Oye, **él** tiene un coche nuevo. 2) **Ellos** no tienen hijos. 3) **Nosotros** somos amigos, ¿no? 4) ¿Qué te parece **él**? 5) **Ella** es un poco tonta, ¿verdad?

 b 6) La profesora **los** pidió. 7) Pobre Susana: ¡ayer nuestro gato **lo** mató! 8) ¿Dónde **las** encontraste? 9) Vamos a ver, ¿**lo** compraste o no? 10) ¿Sabes a qué hora nos **la** traerá?

 c 11) Por favor, ¿puedes pasar**les** / **les** puedes pasar el pan? 12) ¡No deberías decir**le** / no **le** deberías decir tonterías! 13) Vamos a mandar**le** / **Le** vamos a mandar un crismas. 14) Sabes contar**les** /**Les** sabes contar chistes, ¡a que sí! 15) ¿Por qué no **le** dijiste nada?

 d 16) Vaya, ¡no le digas nada a **ella**! 17) ¿Sabes por qué no vamos a visitarles a **ellos**? 18) María y Juan vinieron con **nosotros**. 19) Siéntate al lado de **mí**; quiero hablar contigo. 20) Vamos a viajar en el coche de **él**.

 e 1) No, mis hijos pueden bañar**se** / **se** pueden bañar. 2) No, el perro puede pasear**se** / **se** puede pasear. 3) Sí, vamos a sentar**nos** / **nos** vamos a sentar aquí. 4) Sí, quiero duchar**me** / **me** quiero duchar. 5) Sí, vamos a acostar**nos** / **nos** vamos a acostar.

2 1) Tú, yo 2) nosotros, tú 3) ellos/ellas/ustedes 4) me 5) los 6) os/les 7) Les 8) ofrecerte 9) le 10) se 11) te 12) bañarnos 13) mí 14) ustedes 15) mí/nosotros

3 él, a ella, ella, a él, a ellos, a ella, ella, ellos, ellos, de ella, él, ellos

4 1) la 2) nos 3) me 4) decirles 5) la 6) ellos 7) La 8) ellos 9) Los 10) nos 11) se 12) me 13) me 14) ella

Chapter 13

1 *Sample answers:*
    1) Porque me encanta ver las películas.
    2) Sí, me apetece tomar una Coca-Cola.
    3) Sí, quiero ver un programa que ponen esta tarde.
    4) Porque me gusta escuchar música.
    5) Pues, sí, necesito ponerme un vestido/traje nuevo para la fiesta.
    6) ¡Claro! Tengo que aprobar el examen de español.
    7) Porque quiero hacerme médico.
    8) Sí, pues prefiero comer manzanas y nada más.
    9) Porque espero ver a mis amigos allí.
    10) Pues, porque me interesa ver la obra que ponen esta tarde.
    11) Porque deseo ayudarla: ¡es muy vieja ya!
    12) Porque ya sé conducir.
    13) No, no puedo ir porque no me dejan mis padres.
    14) No, ¡ya sabes que no me interesa escuchar los CDs que tienes tú!
    15) No, pienso jugar al dominó con mi hermano.
    16) Es que no sé hacerlos.
    17) No, ¡no me gusta estar contigo!
    18) Porque voy a comprarme un reloj de oro.
    19) No, no me apetece ser profesor(a).
2 1) Limpiar las mesas 2) Preparar las legumbres 3) Poner las mesas 4) Freír la carne 5) Hacer la sangría 6) Ponerme el uniforme 7) Servir las comidas 8) Lavar los platos 9) Barrer el suelo del restaurante 10) Escribir los menús para mañana
3 *Sample answers:*
    1) Claro, esta tarde voy a prestarte el DVD.
    2) Ya te dije que te voy a llevar al club.
    3) Sí, te voy a ayudar con los deberes.
    4) Claro que te voy a contar lo que pasó.
    5) Sí, sí, te voy a dejar mi moto.
4 *Sample answers:*
    1) Porque me encanta comer.
    2) Porque tengo que hacer un examen mañana.
    3) Porque prefiero llevar colores fuertes.
    4) Porque no puedo olvidarlos.
    5) Porque no me apetece cambiar de psiquiatra.

Chapter 14

1 1) estamos, estamos 2) mira, prepara 3) busca 4) sacamos, queremos 5) tenemos 6) vamos
    7) se encuentran 8) dicen, llueve 9) hace, podemos, hay 10) necesitamos
2 1) llama 2) contiene 3) son 4) hay 5) cultivan 6) crían 7) conoce 8) es 9) atrae 10) pueden 11) puede
    12) hace 13) vienen 14) ven 15) debe

Chapter 15

1 a) tienen, piensan, prefieren, vuelven, empiezan, se sientan, quieren, se esfuerzan, se acuestan, duermen, cuenta, cierran, encuentran, entienden, pueden
    b) tenemos, nos cuidamos, pensamos, comemos, bebemos, preferimos, nos volvemos, hacemos, empezamos, nuestras (horas de ocio), nos sentamos, queremos, nos esforzamos, nos acostamos, dormimos, nos (cuenta), deberíamos, nuestra (salud), cerramos, encontramos, nuestro (modo de ser), entendemos, nos (dice), darnos (cuenta), podemos, nuestro (estilo de vida)
2 1) piensa 2) tienen 3) Queréis 4) sientas 5) huele 6) cierra 7) puede 8) bebe 9) duermen 10) prefiere

Chapter 16

1   Esta mañana, *me desperté* en mi dormitorio, *me bañé* en el cuarto de baño, luego *me afeité* delante del espejo. Antes de tomar el desayuno *me vestí* en el dormitorio, luego *me senté* en la cocina para desayunar. Como hacía buen tiempo, decidí *pasearme* en el parque, pues *me puse* el abrigo antes de salir. Allí, con mi móvil, *me puse* en contacto con mi novia, y *nos encontramos* media hora después delante del estanque. A las once *nos sentamos* en la terraza de un café y *nos tomamos* un chocolate y unos churros. *Nos levantamos* a mediodía, y después de *pasearnos* un rato *me despedí* de mi novia, y *me dirigí* a mi casa. Por la tarde, *me quedé* en casa, y *me divertí* viendo la tele. Bastante cansado, *me duché* a las diez, y *me acosté* en mi dormitorio a las once. De repente, *me di* cuenta de que había sido un día de trabajo ... ¡y de que *me volvía* loco!

2   1) se lava 2) ducharnos, bañarnos 3) se pasean 4) afeitarse 5) mirarse
6) mantenerse 7) se divierten 8) se encuentra 9) se hace/se hizo 10) se vuelve/se volvió, se va/se fue

3   volví, Llegué, me dirigí, me di, necesitaba, me dije, (me) quedaba, empecé, me sentía, tenía, quería, podía, oí, me decidí, podía, tuve, me sentía, Volví, subí, Me senté, empecé, tenía, podía, me dormí.

Chapter 17

1   Part 1:
1) Lo arreglaré mañana. 2) Las lavaré mañana. 3) Los haré mañana. 4) Los fregaré mañana. 5) Lo barreré mañana. 6) La limpiaré mañana. 7) Lo leeré mañana. 8) La visitaré mañana/Iré a visitarla mañana. 9) La pondré en el garaje mañana. 10) Volveré a la biblioteca mañana. 11) Los compraré mañana. 12) Lo buscaré mañana. 13) Le escribiré mañana. 14) Les/Los llamaré mañana.
Part 2:
1) Voy a arreglarlo en seguida. 2) Voy a lavarlas en seguida. 3) Voy a hacerlos en seguida. 4) Voy a fregarlos en seguida. 5) Voy a barrerlo en seguida. 6) Voy a limpiarla en seguida. 7) Voy a leerlo en seguida. 8) Voy a visitarla en seguida. 9) Voy a ponerla en el garaje en seguida. 10) Voy a volver a la biblioteca en seguida. 11) Voy a comprarlos en seguida. 12) Voy a buscarlo en seguida. 13) Voy a escribirle en seguida. 14) Voy a llamarles/llamarlos en seguida.

2   *Suggested versions:*
Novio: La víspera de la boda, saldré por la tarde con unos amigos. Tomaremos unas copitas, luego iremos a cenar a un restaurante. Después, bueno, no lo recordaré bien, ¡ni querré recordarlo!
El día de la boda me levantaré a las ocho y desayunaré con el padrino de boda que llegará a las ocho y pico. Los dos saldremos a dar un paseo al lado del río y a las diez volveremos a mi casa a vestirnos para la boda.
Llegaremos a la iglesia a las doce menos cuarto; muchos parientes y amigos ya estarán allí, y otros llegarán después de nosotros. El cura entrará a las doce en punto, y, por fin, llegará Juanita con su padre. ¡Qué hermosa estará! Con ella llegarán también las damas de honor, mis sobrinas Mariana y Sara. Ellas también estarán muy guapas. La ceremonia durará un poco menos de una hora, y después se harán las fotos delante de la iglesia.
A las dos iremos todos al hotel donde almorzaremos, bailaremos y nos divertiremos. Por fin, Juanita y yo nos despediremos de todos y nos pondremos en camino para nuestra luna de miel. ¡Y ya no escribo más!
Novia: La víspera de la boda, saldré por la tarde con unas amigas: tomaremos unas copitas, luego iremos a cenar a un restaurante. Después, bueno, no lo recordaré bien, ¡ni querré recordarlo!
El día de la boda, me levantaré a las ocho y desayunaré con las damas de honor, las sobrinas de mi novio, Mariana y Sara. Pasaremos una hora y media preparándonos para la boda. Llegaremos a la iglesia a las doce y pico; todos los parientes y amigos ya estarán allí y también Andrés que estará esperándome en el altar. ¡Qué guapo estará! El cura empezará la ceremonia que durará un poco menos de una hora, y después harán las fotos delante de la iglesia. A las dos iremos todos al hotel donde almorzaremos, bailaremos y nos divertiremos. Por fin, Andrés y yo nos despediremos de todos y nos pondremos en camino para nuestra luna de miel. ¡Y ya no escribo más!

Chapter 18

1   1) Lo limpiaría mi robot. 2) Lo lavaría mi robot. 3) Los fregaría mi robot. 4) Lo barrería mi robot.
5) La prepararía mi robot. 6) La pondría mi robot. 7) La llevaría mi robot. 8) Los secaría mi robot.
9) Lo buscaría mi robot. 10) Lo cortaría mi robot.

2

¡Hola!

Te escribo para contarte cómo será el día de la boda de mi tío y lo que tendré yo que hacer como dama de honor de su novia. Juanita me escribió recientemente para explicármelo todo.

Juanita me dijo que la víspera de la boda, tendría yo que llegar a su casa a las ocho; mi prima, Sara, ya estaría allí. Prepararíamos varias cosas para la boda, luego saldríamos a cenar con unas amigas suyas. Dijo que el día de la boda, nos levantaríamos a las ocho, y después del desayuno iríamos a la peluquería. A las diez y cuarto volveríamos a su casa a vestirnos para la boda. ¡Todas estaríamos guapísimas!

Escribió Juanita que iríamos con su padre a la iglesia y que llegaríamos a las doce y pico: ¡siendo la novia, tendría que llegar un poquito tarde! Los parientes y amigos ya estarían allí, pues seríamos los últimos en llegar.

Al entrar, Sara y yo iríamos detrás de ella. Me dijo que el cura me diría lo que tuviera que hacer durante la ceremonia; y que la ceremonia duraría un poco menos de una hora, y después se harían las fotos delante de la iglesia.

Dijo que a las dos iríamos todos al hotel, donde almorzaríamos, bailaríamos y nos divertiríamos. Me contó Juanita que, por fin, ella y Andrés se despedirían de todos nosotros y se pondrían en camino para su luna de miel.

¡Y ya no me contó más! ¡Hasta pronto!

Un beso,
Mariana

3   (*suggested answers*) 1) Compraría un coche muy elegante. 2) Buscaría un chalet cerca de la playa. 3) Le regalaría un collar de oro muy precioso a mi madre. 4) Le ayudaría a mi hermano a comprar un negocio. 5) Vendría a visitar a mi amigo en España. 6) Le daría mucho dinero a unas obras de caridad. 7) Me casaría con mi novio/a / con un(a) chico/a muy guapo/a. 8) Tendría(mos) muchos hijos. 9) No trabajaría más excepto para divertirme. 10) Iría de vacaciones a Chile.

Chapter 19

1   era, llevaba, Vivía, tenía, iba, almorzaba, estaba, encontraba, gustaban, traía, daba, compraban, veía, quería

2   se prohibía, había, podía, quería, existían, empezaban, se decía, leía, negaban, insistía, se daba, estaba ocurriendo, restringía, podía(n)

3   pasaba, jugaban, trepaba, roía, dormía, quemaba, estaba, trataba, se escapaba, se desbordaba, corrían, saltaban, comían, cortaba, caían, pensaban, hacían, cuidábamos, ibas, soñaba, era.

Chapter 20

1 Son las nueve y está saliendo de casa. **Está cruzando** la calle y ahora **está esperando** el autobús. **Está llegando** el autobús. Está **subiendo** y **pagando** el billete. **Está bajando** delante del ayuntamiento, y **está tomando** la calle de Toledo. Ahora **está subiendo** la avenida de Burgos, y **está entrando** en el edificio de la empresa donde trabaja. **Está cogiendo** el ascensor al cuarto piso. Ahora **está saliendo** y **se está dirigiendo** a su despacho. **Está saludando** a su secretaria, y **se está sentando** detrás de su escritorio. **Está comenzando** a abrir el correo y (**está comenzando**) a redactar sus respuestas a las cartas. Ahora **está entrando** su secretaria con una taza de café, y **se está preparando** para tomar unos apuntes. Ahora **está llamando** por teléfono a su jefe. **Está entrando** un colega: le **está mostrando** unos dibujos. Es mediodía: los dos **están saliendo** y **están entrando** en el bar que se encuentra enfrente de la oficina. **Están tomando** un aperitivo. Ahora **se están dirigiendo** al restaurante Salamanca. **Se están sentando** cerca de la ventana. **Están pidiendo** algo de comer y una botella de vino tinto. **Están charlando** con el camarero. **Están tomando** café y ahora **están volviendo** al trabajo.

2 *Sample answers:*
   1) Ayer a las diez de la mañana vi a Concha en el parque y estaba dando de comer a los patos.
   2) A las diez y media la vi en la biblioteca y estaba leyendo una revista.
   3) A las once la vi en el café Chinchón y estaba tomando un coñac.
   4) A mediodía la vi salir de la panadería y estaba llevando un pastel.
   5) A la una la vi entrar en el Restaurante Zeluán y estaba comiendo un bistec.
   6) A las dos la vi en la playa y estaba tomando el sol.
   7) A las cuatro la vi en la Calle Mayor y estaba mirando escaparates.
   8) A las siete la vi entrar en la Discoteca Marisol y estaba bailando con un chico alto y rubio.
   9) A las nueve la vi en Bodegas Muñoz-Rivas y estaba charlando con el chico alto y rubio.
   10) A medianoche la vi volver a casa y estaba besando al chico.

Chapter 21

1 resultó, se celebró, sucedieron, descubrió, se organizaron, emprendieron, recorrieron, recibió, asistieron, acudieron, visitaron, llamó

2 se prepararon, volvieron, compraron, pagaron, se enfadaron, empezaron, continuaron

Chapter 22

1 1) cogía 2) cogió 3) dejé 4) dejaba 5) hacía 6) hizo 7) comíamos 8) comimos 9) estaba
   10) estuvo

2 1) éramos, comíamos 2) veía, trabajaba 3) cayó, leía 4) fue/iba, se cayó 5) cruzaron, conquistaron
   6) sabías, dejaste 7) estaba, era 8) tenía, compré 9) erais, estudiabais 10) iba, se cayó

3 *Sample answers:*
   1) Mientras veía la televisión, entró mi tío.
   2) Hacía los deberes cuando salió mi hermano.
   3) Cuando escuchaba un disco, alguien llamó por teléfono.
   4) Mientras lavaba los platos, rompí un vaso.
   5) Cuando iba por la calle, vio un accidente.
   6) Mientras cogía manzanas, se cayó del árbol.
   7) Jugaba al fútbol cuando se hizo daño en el pie.
   8) Mientras subíamos la colina, vimos un pájaro muy raro.
   9) Tomé el sol en la playa y cogí una insolación.
   10) Mientras estaban en el jardín, oyeron el primer cuclillo.

4 fui, Hacía, nos pusimos, Había, llegamos, encontramos, decidió, Dio, se cayó, tuvieron, decía, sabía, se ahogó, Se quedó, volvió, pasó, estaba, gustaba, criticaba, se quedaba/quedó

Chapter 23

1   Sí, claro que … 1) … la he preparado. 2) … los he encontrado. 3) … lo he reservado. 4) … los he conseguido. 5) … lo he visto. 6) … (se) la he dejado. 7) … la he hecho. 8) … lo he comprobado. 9) … las he cerrado.

2   ha visto, se han creado, han fomentado, se ha devuelto, ha ganado, se han alternado, han vuelto, ha pedido, (ha) conseguido, ha causado, ha traído, se ha seleccionado, ha celebrado, han construido, han proyectado, ha logrado, ha hecho, ha cumplido, ha completado, ha elegido, se ha casado, ha tenido, ha dicho

Chapter 24

1   1f, 2d, 3e, 4a, 5g, 6b, 7h, 8c

2   había sido, habían tenido, había ido, habría/hubiera gustado, habría/hubiera tenido, habría/hubiera sido, había aumentado, había hecho, había podido, han construido, ha sido, ha pasado

3   1) ¿Habrá llegado ya? 2) ¿Habrá venido/llegado el avión a tiempo? 3) ¿Habrá puesto sus calcetines en la maleta? 4) ¿Se habrá mareado en el avión? 5) ¿Habrá sido desviado el avión si hay niebla? 6) ¿Habrá estado allí mi hermana para esperarle? 7) ¿Se habrá acordado de darle el regalo? 8) ¿Habrá llevado bastante dinero? 9) ¿Habría/Hubiera sido mejor llevar cheques de viajero? 10) ¿Qué (le) habrá dicho a su tía?

Chapter 25

1   NB the answers given are those preferable in the context but not necessarily the only ones possible: 1) Carmen debió/A Carmen le hizo falta 2) Tenía que/Le hacía falta 3) no debía/no tenía que 4) tienes que/debes/(te) hace falta 5) tengo que/me hace falta/hay que 6) no debo 7) tengo que/debo 8) tuvo que/debió 9) no tenías que 10) tendremos que/deberemos

2   1c, 2a, 3e, 4b, 5d

3   1e, 2a, 3d, 4c, 5b

4   1) Debe de haberse ido ya. 2) Tenemos que marcharnos antes de las diez. 3) Tendrás que darte prisa para coger aquel tren. 4) Habrá sido un gran problema para usted. 5) Los españoles ya no tienen que hacer la mili. 6) El equipo de Inglaterra ha debido tener un día malo. 7) Debe de estar lloviendo. Veo a gente que lleva paraguas. 8) Deberás llevarte el impermeable. 9) Hay que aprender a respetar la ley. 10) ¡Ha debido ser un ejercicio bastante difícil!

5   1) Podía haber estudiado más. 2) No debía haber trabajado tanto en el supermercado. 3) Podía haber trabajado sólamente los sábados. 4) Podía haberse levantado más temprano. 5) No debía haber pasado tanto tiempo con aquella chica. 6) Debería darse cuenta de que necesita aprobar sus exámenes. 7) Podría volver a hacer los exámenes el año que viene, claro. 8) Podría aprobar en español si intentara. 9) Trató de estudiar francés pero no podía hacerlo. 10) Yo debía haber tenido más simpatía, pero traté y no podía/pude.

Chapter 26

1   1) nosotros 2) les 3) le 4) a ti 5) gustan 6) gustaría 7) os 8) a usted 9) a mis padres 10) vivir

2   1) me gustaban 2) me gustaría 3) me encantan 4) me interesa 5) me faltan 6) me queda 7) Me sobran 8) me interesan 9) me apetecería 10) me dolería

3   1) A Miguel no le gusta la Coca-Cola. 2) A Pedro no le gustó la película. 3) A Sandra le encanta jugar al tenis. 4) A Andrés no le interesa trabajar aquí. 5) A nuestros hijos les apetece ir a España este año. 6) A mi padre no le entusiasma el jardín. 7) A Bárbara le emocionó ese libro. 8) No quedan ejemplares. 9) A la abuela le sobra dinero. 10) A ese coche le faltaban dos ruedas. 11) A María le duelen/dolían las piernas. 12) A papá le hacía falta un nuevo traje.

Chapter 27

1   1) decidió pasar 2) empezó a/por informarse 3) prefirió ir 4) se dedicaron a finalizar 5) nos preparamos para ponernos a 6) pudimos coger 7) tratamos de encontrar 8) logramos viajar 9) comenzamos a broncearnos 10) nos dispusimos a volver

2   1) me preparaba para 2) tuve que 3) me esforcé a 4) dejé de 5) necesitaba 6) decidí 7) quería 8) (Había) decidido 9) (había) optado por 10) me dispuse a 11) me dedicaba/dediqué a 12) me resigné a 13) logré 14) invitaron a 15) persuadieron a 16) aconsejaban 17) deseaba 18) resolví 19) disuadieron de 20) me comprometí a

3   1) Al llegar a casa, preparé la cena. 2) Veré el partido hasta ver el primer gol. 3) Compré este regalo para dárselo a mi novia. 4) Volví a casa inmediatamente por haber perdido la cartera. 5) Llegué al cole sin ver a mi amigo. 6) Vamos a pararnos a tomar algo de beber antes de ir a casa. 7) Después de ir al cine, iremos al restaurante.

Chapter 28

1

Infinitivo	Participio pasado	Gerundio	Infinitivo	Participio pasado	Gerundio
decir	dicho	diciendo	descubrir	descubierto	descubriendo
hacer	hecho	haciendo	regresar	regresado	regresando
saber	sabido	sabiendo	componer	compuesto	componiendo
salir	salido	saliendo	quemar	quemado	quemando
reparar	reparado	reparando	oír	oído	oyendo
ver	visto	viendo	querer	querido	queriendo
escribir	escrito	escribiendo	volver	vuelto	volviendo
conocer	conocido	conociendo	pensar	pensado	pensando
mantener	mantenido	manteniendo	dormir	dormido	durmiendo
romper	roto	rompiendo	ir	ido	yendo

2   1) Viajando a España … 2) Jugando al fútbol … 3) Comiendo pescado … 4) Besando a su amiguita … 5) Mirando la carrera … 6) Corriendo, don Eduardo … 7) Viendo la corrida … 8) Paseando por el parque … 9) Subiendo una cuesta … 10) Durmiendo, doña Gimena …

3   El verano pasado, como nos sentíamos aventureros, mi hermana y yo decidimos pasar las vacaciones visitando el País de Gales a pie. El primer día, después de andar unos veinte kilómetros, teníamos las piernas cansadas y nos apetecía pasar una semana durmiendo, por lo tanto nos pusimos a buscar un albergue para jóvenes. ¡Por desgracia, no teníamos el mapa de los albergues pues yo lo había dejado olvidado en casa, en la mesa de la cocina! Después de andar durante otra hora más, encontramos un albergue al lado de un río. Cuando entramos, una joven estaba reservando una habitación, así que mientras esperábamos, nos pusimos a mirar pasar el río fluyendo. Después de reservar dos habitaciones con agua corriente, fuimos a la cocina a preparar nuestra cena. Luego nos sentamos a ver la televisión antes de acostarnos a las diez, agotados después de andar el primer día pero convencidos de que íbamos a divertirnos durante el resto de nuestras vacaciones, explorando esta región del País de Gales.

4   1) rota 2) visto 3) sentados 4) corriente 5) helado 6) andante 7) fritos 8) pendientes 9) vuelta 10) pendientes

5

Infinitivo	Adjetivo	Sustantivo
cubrir	cubierto	cubierta
abrir	abierto	apertura/abertura
freír	frito	frito/fritura
satisfacer	satisfecho	satisfacción
ver	visto	vista
cerrar	cerrado	cerradura
volver	vuelto	vuelta
parecer	parecido	parecido
permitir	permitido	permisión/permiso
caer	caído	caída
poner	puesto	puesta/puesto
variar	variado	variedad/variación

6

1	carne	f	picada
2	leche	d	desnatado
3	tomate	g	frito
4	patatas	j	fritas
5	huevos	k	escalfados
6	pollo	a	asado
7	pan	b	tostado
8	manzanas	n	asadas
9	filete	l	empanado
10	bistec	o	estofado
11	huevo	i	pasado por agua
12	agua	h	hervida
13	queso	c	fundido
14	nata	m	batida
15	bacalao	e	salado

Chapter 29

1 a) *Tú:* toma, lava, pela, córtalas, casca, bate, pon, caliéntalo, añade, fríelas, echa, mézclalas, añade, mezcla, pon, añade, fríe, sirve
b) *Usted:* tome, lave, pele, córtelas, casque, bata, ponga, caliéntelo, añada, fríalas, eche, mézclelas, añada, mezcle, ponga, añada, fría, sirva
c) *Vosotros:* tomad, lavad, pelad, cortadlas, cascad, batid, poned, calentadlo, añadid, freídlas, echad, mezcladlas, añadid, mezclad, poned, añadid, freíd, servid
2 1) Conserve 2) Mantenga 3) No lave 4) Sirva 5) No deje

3   Ejemplos: ¡hay otras posibilidades!
1) ¡Sí, lávalas, luego pélalas! 2) ¡No, no las batas, córtalas en trozos! 3) ¡Sí, bátelos! 4) ¡No, no la pongas en la sartén, pon media taza de aceite! 5) ¡No, no los peles, rómpelos! 6) ¡No, no los cortes, bátelos! 7) ¡Sí, mézclalas con los huevos batidos! 8) ¡No, no la ases, fríela! 9) ¡Sírvela fría o caliente!
1) ¡Sí, lavadlas, luego peladlas! 2) ¡No, no las batáis, cortadlas en trozos! 3) ¡Sí, batidlos/batirlos! 4) ¡No, no la pongáis en la sartén, poned media taza de aceite! 5) ¡ No, no los peléis, rompedlos! 6) ¡No, no los cortéis, batidlos/batirlos! 7) ¡Sí, mezcladlas con los huevos batidos! 8) ¡No, no la aséis, freídla/freírla! 9) ¡Servidla/Servirla fría o caliente!

Chapter 30

1   1) está 2) es 3) Está 4) es 5) Es 6) está 7) es 8) es 9) Fue 10) es 11) es 12) fue 13) fueron 14) está 15) es 16) está 17) está 18) está 19) está
2   1) es 2) Está 3) es 4) están 5) son 6) Fueron/Han sido 7) estaba 8) fue 9) ha sido/está 10) es

Chapter 31

1   fue cortada, fue despejada, fueron traídos, fueron alojados, fueron preparadas, fue prevista, son sorprendidas, será/sea hecho, será mejorado, serán transmitidos
2   1) Plasencia fue fundada por el rey … 2) Fue ubicada por este rey … 3) Fue amurallada por las autoridades. 4) El mercado fue iniciado por el rey … 5) El ayuntamiento fue restaurado por el concejo … 6) Nombres fueron puestos a las varias puertas de la ciudad. 7) La catedral vieja fue comenzada … 8) Una de las torres fue derribada … 9) Una Ciudad Deportiva ha sido construida.
3   Ayer cayó mucha nieve y la carretera Burgos–San Sebastián **se cortó** en dos sitios. La carretera **la despejaron dos grandes quitanieves** que **se trajeron** desde Burgos. Mientras tanto **a los chóferes de** los coches y camiones atascados **se los alojó/los alojaron** en el colegio de un pueblo vecino. **Las comidas de emergencia las prepararon el personal de cantina y unos padres de los colegiales**. Aunque ésta es una circunstancia que **previeron las autoridades**, casi siempre **las sorprenden las dificultades** que trae. Los usuarios de dicha carretera esperan que algo **se hará/haga** antes del próximo invierno. El MOPU (Ministerio de Obras Públicas) ha asegurado que el trayecto de la carretera **se mejorará** y que si va a haber problemas de nieve, unos avisos **se transmitirán** por medio de la emisora de radio local.
4   1) se toman 2) se distribuye 3) se gasta 4) se ingresa 5) se ingresa 6) me ponen 7) Me prohíben 8) usan 9) Dicen 10) me consideran
5   *A possible version, but not the only one, might be:*
La semana pasada la pasamos en un hotel en el noreste de España, donde se nos trató muy bien. Por las noches se nos daba/proporcionaba una cena de tres platos y una botella de vino. Si queríamos, se servía el desayuno en nuestra habitación. Se decía en el folleto del touroperador que el hotel tenía dos estrellas, pero se nos enteró/nos enteraron al llegar que esto se había cambiado a tres estrellas este año. El martes se nos llevó/nos llevaron a los Picos de Europa, y el hotel nos proporcionó/dio una comida merienda. Al llegar al pueblo de Fuente Dé, se nos dijo que nos llevarían hasta lo alto de la montaña en el teleférico y que luego bajaríamos y el autocar nos recogería a las seis. Se consideró que la mayoría pasamos un día agradable.

Chapter 33

1   1) disfruten 2) jueguen 3) se metan 4) vengan 5) fumen 6) beban 7) ofrezca(n) 8) contribuya 9) sean 10) quiera
2   quiera, siga, escoja/haya escogido, cambie, desempeñe, decida/haya decidido, marche, haya firmado, tomen/hayan tomado

3 1) ¡No me gusta que Jaime escriba en las paredes!
   2) ¡Prefiero que ambos niños jueguen fuera!
   3) ¡Dile a Pablo que se lave las manos!
   4) ¡Dile a Pablo que baje la tele!
   5) ¡No quiero que pinten el/al gato!
   6) ¡Diles que no pongan zapatos sucios en la mesa!
   7) ¡Pide a Pablo que no salte sobre la cama!
   8) ¡Es terrible/horroroso que se acuesten tan tarde!
   9) ¡Más vale/Es mejor que todos os vayáis a casa mañana!

Chapter 34

1 Es posible/dudoso que (*or similar phrase*) …
   1) … haga 2) … nieve 3) … haga 4) … sople 5) … se formen 6) … sean 7) … no bajen 8) … caigan
2a 1) quiera 2) tenga 3) gusten 4) case 5) me quede 6) decida 7) atraiga 8) venga
2b 1) quisiera/quisiese 2) tuviera/tuviese 3) gustaran/gustasen 4) casara/casase
   5) me quedara/quedase 6) decidiera/decidiese 7) atrajera/atrajese 8) viniera/viniese
3 Ya sabemos que España **está** de moda tanto en Europa como en el mundo entero. Es probable
   que esta popularidad **siga**. No cabe duda de que se **puede** ver toda clase de producto español en
   las tiendas europeas. Es dudoso que **haya** una buena discoteca en Londres o París donde no se
   oiga algún conjunto español. Para los españoles mayores, es difícil creer que la actitud de los
   extranjeros hacia su país **haya** cambiado tanto. A fin de cuentas, algunos de ellos no creían que la
   democracia se **estableciera/estableciese**. Lo que es cierto es que España ya **puede** contarse
   como uno de los países principales en la diplomacia europea. ¿Quién hubiera creído hace treinta
   años que Madrid se **hiciera/hiciese** centro diplomático europeo o que España
   participara/participase plenamente en la UE? ¿Puede que lo **esté/estemos** soñando?

Chapter 35

1 1) En cuanto/Así que 2) Cuando 3) … para que 4) Cuando/En cuanto/Así que 5) Antes de que
   6) Cuando 7) con tal que/a condición de que 8) Cuando 9) Cuando/Con tal que (*Note: not* Si …!)
   10) a condición de que 11) En cuanto/Así que/Cuando 12) con tal que/a condición de que
2 ¿De quién es Gibraltar? En la época de Franco, los gibraltareños decían que no querían ser
   españoles, hasta que España **fuera/fuese** democrática. Los ingleses decían que no dejarían la
   soberanía sin que los habitantes del Peñón lo **quisieran/quisiesen**. Antes de que **muriera/muriese**
   Franco, la situación no iba a resolverse. Desde la muerte de Franco, en efecto la situación ha ido
   cambiando, pero para que los gibraltareños **cambien** de parecer, todavía hace falta tiempo. Con tal
   que lo que pase **sea** según sus deseos, un día el problema se resolverá, pero quizás no mientras
   tengan sus recuerdos de la España de la dictadura. Tampoco habrá solución hasta que España y el
   Reino Unido **hablen** en serio y **hagan** un verdadero acuerdo. En cuanto **ocurra** esto, entonces
   todos los partidos podrán estar contentos.
3 1) en cuanto el proceso se complete/esté completo 2) cuando el producto esté listo 3) en cuanto
   sepamos las dimensiones 4) mientras continúe/siga esta situación 5) hasta que nos den la luz verde
   6) una vez que recibamos un pedido definitivo 7) con tal que sepamos lo que quieren 8) a menos
   que nos manden/envíen un fax 9) aunque el pedido sea pequeño 10) a condición de que se firme
   pronto el contrato
4 1) aprendas 2) sabes 3) te acostumbres 4) entiendes 5) estés 6) aprobar

Chapter 36

1 Si buscas un deporte que te **mantenga** en buena forma y que al mismo tiempo **mezcle** la destreza
   física con el arte, ¿por qué no **pruebas** el tae-kwondo? No es una actividad que **requiera** gran
   fuerza, pero es un deporte que se **hace** muy popular entre los españoles. Esto no es porque **sea** un
   deporte con orígenes europeos, puesto que **tiene** sus raíces en el Oriente. Unos dicen que los
   españoles **necesitan** un deporte que **canalice** la violencia. El tae-kwondo no es un deporte que se
   pueda practicar donde y como se **quiera**. Hay que haber un local que **ofrezca** sitio suficiente y un
   sitio donde los practicantes se **cambien** y se **pongan** el uniforme, que **es** de rigor.

2 El cielo es:
   a) ... una casa que sea totalmente automática
   b) ... un criado que me prepare las comidas
   c) ... un(a) compañero/a que me traiga la felicidad
   d) ... dos niños hermosos que me mantengan ocupado/a
   e) ... un trabajo que me dé satisfacción
   f) ... un sueldo que lo pague todo
   g) ... no tener problemas financieros que me preocupen
   h) ... un jardín precioso donde descansemos
   i) ... y el sentido común que me devuelva a la realidad.
   El cielo sería:
   aa) ... una casa que fuera/fuese totalmente automática
   bb) ... un criado que me preparara/preparase las comidas
   cc) ... un(a) compañero/a que me trajera/trajese la felicidad
   dd) ... dos niños hermosos que me mantuvieran/mantuviesen ocupado/a
   ee) ... un trabajo que me diera/diese satisfacción
   ff) ... un sueldo que lo pagara/pagase todo
   gg) ... no tener problemas financieros que me preocuparan/preocupasen
   hh) ... un jardín precioso donde descansáramos/descansásemos
   ii) ... y el sentido común que me devolviera/devolviese a la realidad.

3 Las vacaciones del año pasado fueron un desastre. Buscamos unas vacaciones que **fueran/fuesen** interesantes y que no **costaran/costasen** un dineral. Llamamos por teléfono a cierta agencia que **anunciaba** vacaciones de montar a caballo. Como no hay ningún sitio por aquí donde se **pueda** aprender a montar a caballo, pedimos una escuela donde se nos **enseñara/enseñase**. Llegó julio y fuimos en coche a la granja en Gales que **elegimos/habíamos elegido**. Al llegar ¡no había nadie que nos **recibiera/recibiese**! ¡La granja estaba desierta! Tuvimos que buscar quien nos **indicara/indicase** algún pueblo de donde **pudiéramos/pudiésemos** llamar a la agencia. Como ya eran las nueve de la noche no conseguimos hablar con nadie que nos **ayudara/ayudase**. Por fin pasó un granjero en un tractor, a quien preguntamos si conocía un hotel donde nos **alojáramos/alojásemos**. Él dijo que no, en esa región, no hay quien se **dedique** siquiera a alquilar habitaciones. Tuvimos que dormir en el coche y a la mañana siguiente volvimos a casa. Como, claro, apenas había palabras que **expresaran/expresasen** nuestro descontento, mis padres escribieron una carta muy fuerte a la agencia. Ahora buscamos alguna medida que les **obligue** a devolvernos nuestro dinero. No es que **seamos** tacaños, pero vamos, ¡qué desastre!

Chapter 37

1 1) ¡Que pongas ... 2) ¡Que pases ... 3) ¡Que termines ... 4) ¡Que no ocupes 5) ¡Que quitéis 6) ¡Y que lavéis ... 7) ¡Que vayáis ... 8) ¡Y que sea ... 9) ¡Que tu padre baje ... 10) ¡Que esos condenados perros se larguen ...

2 2) ojalá pases, pusieras/pusieses 3) ojalá termines, terminaras/terminases 4) ojalá no ocupes, no ocuparas/ocupases 5) ojalá quitéis, quitarais/quitaseis 6) ojalá lavéis, lavarais/lavaseis 7) ojalá vayáis, fuerais/fueseis 8) ojalá sea, fuera/fuese 9) ojalá baje, bajara/bajase 10) ojalá se larguen, se largaran/se largasen

3 1) Por mucho/más que grite ese diputado ... 2) Por tonto que fuese el gobierno ... 3) Por más/mucho que amemos al Presidente ... 4) Por muchos escaños que ganen los comunistas ... 5) Por contentos que estemos con el resultado ... 6) Por listos que sean los políticos ... 7) Por seguro que fuese el gobierno de ganar ... 8) Por rápidamente que se declare el resultado ...

4 1) Quizás/Tal vez la derecha gane las elecciones. 2) ¡Ojalá no las ganen los comunistas! 3) Quienquiera que diga eso tiene que ser muy optimista. 4) Comoquiera que hable el presidente, siempre tiene éxito. 5) Pase lo que pase, pasado mañana tendremos un nuevo gobierno. 6) Cualquiera que sea el gobierno, me es igual. 7) Quizás/Tal vez/Ojalá el próximo sea mejor.

Chapter 38

1 Si no hay … Si hace … Mi marido dice que si pasamos … Me pregunto qué pasaría si cogiéramos/cogiésemos … Si mi marido sigue bebiendo … Si llueve … Si nos hubiésemos/hubiéramos puesto … Si tuviésemos/tuviéramos … Si llego … Si encontrara/encontrase … Si aquella muñeca no hubiera/hubiese sido … Si supiese/supiera … Si el avión lleva retraso … Si hubiera/hubiese quedado …

2 En 1969, el General Franco dijo que si los ingleses no **entraran/entrasen** en negociaciones sobre la soberanía del Peñón, cerraría la verja. Si los gibraltareños **hubiesen/hubieran querido** unirse a España, los británicos hubieran empezado a negociar, pero entonces aquéllos querían quedarse bajo la soberanía británica. Es de conjeturarse lo que habría pasado si los habitantes de la Roca **hubiesen/hubieran votado** por unirse a la dictadura. Ahora que España es una democracia y miembro de la UE, si los gibraltareños **quieren** unirse a España, quizás habrá menos problemas. Pero si los ingleses **fueran/fuesen** verdaderamente sinceros hacia España al asunto de la soberanía, no habría tantas procrastinaciones. Pero, ¿si los gibraltareños no **tienen/tuvieran/tuviesen** ganas de hacerse españoles? ¿Qué se debería hacer entonces? O ¡¿si Gran Bretaña **se hiciera/hiciese** dictadura?!

3 1) estuviera/estuviese 2) llevaran/llevasen 3) tuviera/tuviese 4) agotara/agotase 5) atracaran/atracasen 6) robara/robase 7) encontráramos/encontrásemos 8) fuera/fuese 9) llegáramos/llegásemos, perdiéramos/perdiésemos 10) saliera/saliese

Chapter 39

1 1) nadie 2) nada 3) nunca 4) ninguno 5) Nunca/en mi vida   6) en ninguna parte 7) ni 8) ni 9) nada 10) alguno 11) tampoco 12) en su vida/nunca
2 1) Mateo *nunca/jamás* ayuda (*no* ayuda *nunca/jamás*) a su madre.
2) A Mateo no le gusta invitar *a nadie* a casa.
3) Mateo *no* invita *ni* a sus compañeros *ni* a sus compañeras.
4) Mateo *no* invita *tampoco* a su novia.
5) A Mateo no le interesa *nada* (*ninguna cosa*).
6) Mateo no juega *a nada*.
7) Y no viaja *a ninguna parte/ningún sitio* con el equipo.
8) Mateo *ya no* tiene éxito con sus estudios.
3 1) Nadie ha llegado. 2) Ni Pedro ni Ana lo sabe. 3) Tampoco lo sé yo. 5) Nadie me conoce. 7) Nada ocurre. 8) En mi vida no he hecho tal cosa. 9) Esto nunca ocurre.
(*Note:* 4, 6, 10, 11 – you wouldn't normally change the word order.)

Chapter 40

1 1) En 2) de 3) En 4) en/sobre 5) Delante de/Enfrente de 6) sobre/encima de 7) Sobre/En 8) dentro del/en 9) Encima de/Sobre 10) En 11) con 12) En/Sobre 13) En 14) Frente a/A causa de/A razón de 15) encima del/sobre 16) Alrededor de 17) a pesar de/pese a 18) Con/Para 19) ¿De 20) a razón de/debido a 21) en 22) hasta 23) Con/A causa del 24) en contra de 25) con 26) al lado

Chapter 41

1 The personal *a* is used only in the following phrases: 2) conocimos al director; 3) preguntó a nuestra profe; 5) fuimos a ver a la encargada; 7) la fábrica emplea a cincuenta personas; 9) preguntamos a un hombre; 10) que paseaba a su perro/a; 11) no quería ayudar a nadie; 12) encontramos a alguien; 13) vimos a un taxista; 15) llevar a un grupo; 16) llamó por radio a sus colegas; 17) encontramos a muchas personas.

Chapter 42

1   1) por 2) por 3) por 4) por 5) Para 6) por 7) por 8) por 9) por 10) Para 11) para 12) Para 13) para 14) para 15) Por

2   1) Por 2) para 3) por 4) Para 5) Para 6) Para 7) Por 8) para 9) por 10) por 11) para 12) para

Chapter 43

1   1) Llevo diez años sabiendo nadar. 2) Llevo once años viajando al extranjero. 3) Llevamos siete meses viviendo en esta ciudad. 4) Llevo año y medio saliendo con mi novio/a. 5) Llevo nueve meses haciendo mis *A levels*. 6) Llevo mucho tiempo hablando español. 7) Llevamos un año en esta clase. 8) Llevamos varios años admirando a nuestro/a profesor(a) de español.

2   1) ¿Desde cuándo/Cuánto tiempo hace que vives en Torrenueva?/¿Cuánto tiempo llevas viviendo en Torrenueva? 2) ¿Desde cuándo/Cuánto tiempo hace que aprendes el inglés?/Cuánto tiempo llevas aprendiendo el inglés? 3) ¿Cuánto tiempo estuviste en el avión desde Alicante? 4) ¿Hacía mucho tiempo que esperabas/Esperabas desde hace mucho tiempo/Llevabas mucho tiempo esperando en el aeropuerto cuando llegamos? 5) Aprendo el español desde hace tres meses/Hace tres meses que aprendo el español/Llevo tres meses aprendiendo el español. 6) Lo aprendo desde enero. 7) Vivimos aquí desde que mi papá cambió su trabajo. 8) Hacía cinco años que trabajaba/Trabajaba desde hacía cinco años/Llevaba cinco años trabajando para su empresa/compañía cuando mudamos de casa. 9) Antes vivimos cinco años en América/Antes vivimos en América por/durante cinco años. 10) Vinimos aquí hace cuatro años.

Chapter 44

1   1) que 2) cuyo 3) el que 4) que 5) que/quien/el cual 6) que/quienes/los cuales 7) quien/el cual 8) que/quien 9) cuya 10) el cual 11) que/el cual 12) que 13) con quienes/los cuales 14) que 15) que 16) donde/en que 17) las que/las cuales 18) las que 19) que

2   1) que 2) de la que/la cual 3) que 4) que 5) cuyo 6) del que/del cual 7) que 8) que 9) lo que 10) cuyo 11) que 12) los que/los cuales 13) de quien/del que/del cual 14) cuya

Chapter 45

1   *In some cases, other answers are possible:*
    1) ¿Quién… ? 2) ¿Cuánta gente … ? 3) ¿Por qué … ? 4) ¿Cómo … ? 5) ¿Cómo … ? 6) ¿Cuál … ? 7) ¿Qué … ? 8) ¿Cómo … ? 9) ¿Dónde … ? 10) ¿Adónde … ? 11) ¿Cuándo … ? 12) ¡Cómo … ! 13) ¡Qué! 14) ¡Qué … ! 15) ¡Cuánta … ! 16) ¡Cuántos … ! 17) ¡Cómo … ! 18) ¡Qué … !

2   1) dónde 2) Qué 3) Por qué 4) cuándo 5) Cuánta 6) cuántos 7) Cuántos 8) Cuántas 9) Cómo 10) cuánta 11) Qué 12) qué 13) Qué 14) De quién 15) Quién 16) Cómo

Chapter 46

1   1) Paco dijo que hacía buen tiempo. 2) Manuela contestó que estaba lloviendo. 3) El cartero confesó que había perdido muchas cartas. 4) Le dijimos que teníamos un problema. 5) La señora Ruiz me preguntó cómo se escribía mi nombre. 6) Nos dijo Malení que iban a Alicante. 7) Me preguntó Alicia por qué era yo tan estúpido. 8) Le respondió Alejandro que no sabía nada. 9) Preguntó Juana qué le parecía esta blusa. 10) Contestó Pablo que le gustaba. 11) Dijo que iría cuando terminara/terminase su trabajo. 12) Explicó que estaría dos días en Madrid antes de que llegara/llegase su hermana.

2   *Suggested version (variations are possible):*
    Julio dijo que él y Marisa iban a ir a la fiesta esta tarde. Le preguntó qué le parecía. Marisa contestó que le parecía bien, y le preguntó a qué hora iban a salir. Julio contestó que sobre las ocho. Pero dijo que primero irían a cenar a la cafetería. Marisa se preguntó qué se pusiera; quería saber si Julio prefería su vestido rojo o el azul. Julio contestó que prefería el azul. Añadió que él iba a ponerse unos tejanos y una camiseta verde. Marisa le preguntó si tenían que llevar una botella a la fiesta. Julio explicó que Manuel había dicho que no hacía falta. Luego preguntó dónde iban a verse/encontrarse. Marisa sugirió que delante de su casa. Por fin se despidieron.

Chapter 47

1 1) un sillazo 2) peludo 3) una niñita 4) Miguelito 5) una mujercilla 6) un cuartucho 7) un librote
8) un limonazo 9) ojudo 10) una callejuela/calleja

Chapter 48

1 A: 1-syllable diphthong: cuarto, euro, furia, hoy, huele, Jaime, ley, Ruiz, seis, siete, traigo, viuda.
B: 2 syllables: cae, caos, feo, lees, leí, mío, roa, sea, soez, traes.

2 Conocida tradicionalmente como la Puerta de España, al lindar con Portugal, es un lugar de
referencia para el turismo. A la atractiva oferta vacacional se le mezclan actividades tradicionales
que han conservado sus ciudadanos, dentro de un marco incomparable.
Isla Canela es la primera de las playas existentes en Huelva, nada más pasar de Portugal. Es un
lugar donde el desarrollo del turismo ha experimentado un mayor cambio en los últimos años. En la
playa se observan numerosos chiringuitos y algún bar de copas. En sus orillas, los pescadores
varan las embarcaciones, algunas de ellas poseen vasijas de barro, llamadas cajirones, que sirven
para la pesca del pulpo. Hay un acceso cómodo y rápido por carretera; también, existe un servicio
de transbordadores que cruza el río Guadiana y llega hasta la localidad portuguesa de Vila Real de
Santo Antonio.

3

A	B
árabe	administrativo
césped	alemanes
champú	guardia
francés	hospital
lápiz	imagen
marroquí	naciones
montón	pijama
ración	Valladolid
teléfono	verdad
tráigame	vino (*wine; he/she came*)
veréis	

C (i) con acento	C (ii) sin acento
andén (*platform*)	anden (*they walk*) (*subj*)
cambió (*he/she changed*)	cambio (*exchange; I change*)
cómo (*how*)	como (*like/as; I eat*)
continúo (*I continue*)	continuo (*continuous*)
continuó (*he/she continued*)	
construyó (*he/she built*)	construyo (*I build*)
firmó (*he/she signed*)	firmo (*I sign*)
revólver (*revolver*)	revolver (*to stir up*)
sacó (*he/she took out*)	saco (*sack; I take out*)
té (*tea*)	te (*you as obj pron*)
vengó (*he/she avenged*)	vengo (*I come; I avenge*)

4   ¿Qué tal estás chico/a? ¿Nos vemos esta tarde o no? ¿Qué te parece quedar en el bar Málaga a las ocho?

Te veo en la puerta del cole a la salida de clase.

Oye me preguntaba si quieres que me pase esta tarde. No es porque quiera hacer nada, pero por estar juntos.

Chapter 49

1   primero; cierto; puerto; escala; especial; estación; geografía; gimnasio; cristiano; procesión; afectar; fotografía; llama; llano; teoría; gótico
2   price; serrate(d); revolved; school; speculate; study; geology; gyrate; conscientious; battery; section; phonetic; claim; anthropology; osteopath
3   Ejemplos: disuadir/persuasión/persuasivo; toxicómano/intoxificar/intoxicación; solucionar/disolución; crueldad/cruelmente; imaginable/imaginación; italiano; juventud/juvenil; arenoso; rascacielos; cigarrillo
4   (En algunos casos hay otras posibilidades): roca; desviar; probable; resolver; posible; conocer; paulatino; fortuna; Madrid; útil

Chapter 50

1   Here is a selection of related words: the list is not exhaustive and you may well have found more.

sustantivo	verbo	adjetivo	adverbio o frase adverbial	otro
1. alegría	alegrar(se)	alegre	alegremente/ con alegría	
2. tristeza	entristecer(se)	triste	tristemente/ con tristeza	
3. gordura/ el gordo	engordar	gordo/engordador		
4. oída/oído/ oyente	oír	(oído – past part)	de oídas	
5. belleza	embellecer	bello	bellamente	
6. tontería	tontear	tonto	tontamente	
7. rodilla	arrodillarse	arrodillado	de rodillas	
8. cabeza	encabezar	cabezudo	cabezudamente/ de cabeza	a la cabeza de
9. simpatía	simpatizar	simpático	simpáticamente/ con simpatía	
10. vista/ vistazo	ver	visto/vistoso	en vista por lo visto vistosamente	en vista de con vistas a

2   Best versions are: 1) compró 2) El éxito de la nueva empresa se basó en 3) La empresa casi/por poco desapareció 4) Poco antes de que se estallara/ase la guerra civil española; mi abuelo opinó; ser/resultar difícil 5) trasladar/que tendría que trasladar 6) Se quedó al otro lado del Atlántico más tiempo del que; empezó/comenzó/principió/estalló 7) El aislamiento político de España; resultó en que no volviera/ese a España 8) había beneficiado; lo que ocurrió/sucedió políticamente; poseíamos 9) mi abuelo murió en 1975, rico y contento; siente honor pero a la vez obligación de; lo que creó.

3   1) amarilleaban 2) entorpecían 3) imposibilitó 4) se enrojeció 5) (se) ha envejecido 6) había
    ennegrecido 7) independizarse 8) se responsabilizó 9) inutilizó 10) mejore
4   *The words in brackets are possible but may have a slightly different shade of meaning or may not
    cover the whole range of meaning of the original.*
    1) hermosa (preciosa) 2) habladora 3) muchacho/(niño)/(chaval) 4) empezará/comenzará/(se
    inaugurará) 5) se terminó/se llevó a cabo 6) suéter 7) te marchas 8) escuchar 9) diferentes
    10) enviar 11) te equivocas 12) ordenador 13) los otros 14) la orilla 15) excepto/con la excepción
    de/menos 16) murió 17) te deslices 18) piensas/opinas 19) lo pasamos 20) decepcionados
    21) rompió 22) arreglar 23) cosecha 24) venció 25) se derrumbó/se cayó
5   *These are only suggestions: other ways are often possible.*
    piensan/tienen la opinión de que; el turismo será la salvación del patrimonio; la popularidad/el
    aumento/el boom; de que se salve; esto (lo) concluyó; ha tomado parte; empezó; concluye/(se)
    acaba; jefa/gerente/organizadora; observó/declaró/dijo; especialmente; situado/ubicado;
    mayormente/en gran parte/en alto grado; del crecimiento del turismo/de la expansión del turismo/de
    que se aumente/crezca el turismo
    innegables/indudables; el ímpetu/el empuje/la atracción; particulares; lugares; los habitantes/los que
    viven; sin embargo; son la causa de/causan/ocasionan/dan lugar a; la falta de control en la
    planificación/urbanización; el hecho de que se adulteren/estropeen/arruinen; es necesario/hay
    que/hace falta comprender muy bien; barrios/regiones/áreas; indígenas; es necesario que/es
    cuestión de que se equilibren; un país como Francia podría servir de modelo

Verb table

Regular verbs

Infinitive	Present indicative	Present subjunctive	Imperative	Future	Conditional
-ar verbs	paso	pase		pasaré	pasaría
pasar	pasas	pases	pasa (tú)	pasarás	pasarías
to pass,	pasa	pase	pase Vd	pasará	pasaría
spend (time),	pasamos	pasemos		pasaremos	pasaríamos
happen	pasáis	paséis	pasad (vosotros)	pasaréis	pasaríais
	pasan	pasen	pasen Vds	pasarán	pasarían
-er verbs	bebo	beba		beberé	bebería
beber	bebes	bebas	bebe (tú)	beberás	beberías
to drink	bebe	beba	beba Vd	beberá	bebería
	beb**emos***	bebamos		beberemos	beberíamos
	beb**éis***	bebáis	beb**ed*** (vosotros)	beberéis	beberíais
	beben	beban	beban Vds	beberán	beberían
-ir verbs	subo	suba		subiré	subiría
subir	subes	subas	sube (tú)	subirás	subirías
to go up,	sube	suba	suba Vd	subirá	subiría
come up	sub**imos***	subamos		subiremos	subiríamos
	sub**ís***	subáis	sub**id*** (vosotros)	subiréis	subiríais
	suben	suban	suban Vds	subirán	subirían

*These are the only three places where regular **-er** and **-ir** verbs have different endings.

The main irregular verbs

Infinitive	Present indicative	Present subjunctive	Imperative	Future	Conditional
caber	**quepo**	**quepa**		cabré	cabría
to fit, be	cabes	**quepas**	cabe	etc.	etc.
contained	cabe	**quepa**	**quepa** Vd		
	cabemos	**quepamos**			
	cabéis	**quepáis**	cabed		
	caben	**quepan**	**quepan** Vds		
caer	**caigo**	**caiga**		caeré	caería
to fall	caes	**caigas**	cae	etc.	etc.
	cae	**caiga**	**caiga** Vd		
	caemos	**caigamos**			
	caéis	**caigáis**	caed		
	caen	**caigan**	**caigan** Vds		

Imperfect indicative	Preterite	Imperfect subjunctive		Gerund	Past participle
pasaba	pasé	pasara	pasase	pasando	pasado
pasabas	pasaste	pasaras	pasases		
pasaba	pasó	pasara	pasase		
pasábamos	pasamos	pasáramos	pasásemos		
pasabais	pasasteis	pasarais	pasaseis		
pasaban	pasaron	pasaran	pasasen		
bebía	bebí	bebiera	bebiese	bebiendo	bebido
bebías	bebiste	bebieras	bebieses		
bebía	bebió	bebiera	bebiese		
bebíamos	bebimos	bebiéramos	bebiésemos		
bebíais	bebisteis	bebierais	bebieseis		
bebían	bebieron	bebieran	bebiesen		
subía	subí	subiera	subiese	subiendo	subido
subías	subiste	subieras	subieses		
subía	subió	subiera	subiese		
subíamos	subimos	subiéramos	subiésemos		
subíais	subisteis	subierais	subieseis		
subían	subieron	subieran	subiesen		

Imperfect indicative	Preterite	Imperfect subjunctive		Gerund	Past participle
cabía	cupe	cupiera	cupiese	cabiendo	cabido
cabías	cupiste	cupieras	cupieses		
cabía	cupo	cupiera	cupiese		
cabíamos	cupimos	cupiéramos	cupiésemos		
cabíais	cupisteis	cupierais	cupieseis		
cabían	cupieron	cupieran	cupiesen		
caía	caí	cayera	cayese	cayendo	caído
caías	caíste	cayeras	cayeses		
caía	cayó	cayera	cayese		
caíamos	caímos	cayéramos	cayésemos		
caíais	caísteis	cayerais	cayeseis		
caían	cayeron	cayeran	cayesen		

Infinitive	Present indicative	Present subjunctive	Imperative	Future	Conditional
conducir *to drive, lead* and all verbs ending in **-ducir**	**conduzco** conduces conduce conducimos conducís conducen	**conduzca** **conduzcas** **conduzca** **conduzcamos** **conduzcáis** **conduzcan**	conduce **conduzca** Vd conducid **conduzcan** Vds	conduciré *etc.*	conduciría *etc.*
dar *to give*	**doy** das da damos dais dan	**dé** des **dé** demos deis den	da **dé** Vd dad den Vds	daré *etc.*	daría *etc.*
decir *to say, tell*	**digo** dices **dice** decimos decís **dicen**	**diga** **digas** **diga** **digamos** **digáis** **digan**	di **diga** Vd decid **digan** Vds	diré *etc.*	diría *etc.*
estar *to be*	**estoy** **estás** **está** estamos estáis **están**	**esté** **estés** **esté** estemos estéis **estén**	**está** **esté** Vd estad **estén** Vds	estaré *etc.*	estaría *etc.*
haber *to have* (as auxiliary verb only) **hay** = there is/are	**he** **has** **ha (hay)** **hemos** habéis **han**	**haya** **hayas** **haya** **hayamos** **hayáis** **hayan**	– –	**habré** *etc.*	**habría** *etc.*
hacer *to do, make*	**hago** haces hace hacemos hacéis hacen	**haga** **hagas** **haga** **hagamos** **hagáis** **hagan**	haz **haga** Vd haced **hagan** Vds	**haré** *etc.*	**haría** *etc.*
ir *to go*	**voy** **vas** **va** **vamos** **vais** **van**	**vaya** **vayas** **vaya** **vayamos** **vayáis** **vayan**	ve **vaya** Vd id **vayan** Vds	iré *etc.*	iría *etc.*
oír *to hear*	**oigo** **oyes** **oye** oímos oís **oyen**	**oiga** **oigas** **oiga** **oigamos** **oigáis** **oigan**	**oye** **oiga** Vd oíd **oigan** Vds	oiré *etc.*	oiría *etc.*

Imperfect indicative	Preterite	Imperfect subjunctive		Gerund	Past participle
conducía	conduje	condujera	condujese	conduciendo	conducido
conducías	condujiste	condujeras	condujeses		
conducía	condujo	condujera	condujese		
conducíamos	condujimos	condujéramos	condujésemos		
conducíais	condujisteis	condujerais	condujeseis		
conducían	condujeron	condujeran	condujesen		
daba	di	diera	diese	dando	dado
dabas	diste	dieras	dieses		
daba	dio	diera	diese		
dábamos	dimos	diéramos	diésemos		
dabais	disteis	dierais	dieseis		
daban	dieron	dieran	diesen		
decía	dije	dijera	dijese	diciendo	dicho
decías	dijiste	dijeras	dijeses		
decía	dijo	dijera	dijese		
decíamos	dijimos	dijéramos	dijésemos		
decíais	dijisteis	dijerais	dijeseis		
decían	dijeron	dijeran	dijesen		
estaba	estuve	estuviera	estuviese	estando	estado
estabas	estuviste	estuvieras	estuvieses		
estaba	estuvo	estuviera	estuviese		
estábamos	estuvimos	estuviéramos	estuviésemos		
estabais	estuvisteis	estuvierais	estuvieseis		
estaban	estuvieron	estuvieran	estuviesen		
había	hube	hubiera	hubiese	habiendo	habido
habías	hubiste	hubieras	hubieses		
había	hubo	hubiera	hubiese		
habíamos	hubimos	hubiéramos	hubiésemos		
habíais	hubisteis	hubierais	hubieseis		
habían	hubieron	hubieran	hubiesen		
hacía	hice	hiciera	hiciese	haciendo	hecho
hacías	hiciste	hicieras	hicieses		
hacía	hizo	hiciera	hiciese		
hacíamos	hicimos	hiciéramos	hiciésemos		
hacíais	hicisteis	hicierais	hicieseis		
hacían	hicieron	hicieran	hiciesen		
iba	fui	fuera	fuese	yendo	ido
ibas	fuiste	fueras	fueses		
iba	fue	fuera	fuese		
íbamos	fuimos	fuéramos	fuésemos		
ibais	fuisteis	fuerais	fueseis		
iban	fueron	fueran	fuesen		
oía	oí	oyera	oyese	oyendo	oído
oías	oíste	oyeras	oyeses		
oía	oyó	oyera	oyese		
oíamos	oímos	oyéramos	oyésemos		
oíais	oísteis	oyerais	oyeseis		
oían	oyeron	oyeran	oyesen		

Infinitive	Present indicative	Present subjunctive	Imperative	Future	Conditional
poder *to be able, can*	**puedo** **puedes** **puede** podemos podéis **pueden**	**pueda** **puedas** **pueda** podamos podáis **puedan**	– –	**podré** *etc.*	**podría** *etc.*
poner *to put*	**pongo** pones pone ponemos ponéis ponen	**ponga** **pongas** **ponga** **pongamos** **pongáis** **pongan**	**pon** **ponga** Vd poned **pongan** Vds	**pondré** *etc.*	**pondría** *etc.*
querer *to want, love*	**quiero** **quieres** **quiere** queremos queréis **quieren**	**quiera** **quieras** **quiera** queramos queráis **quieran**	**quiere** **quiera** Vd quered **quieran** Vds	**querré** *etc.*	**querría** *etc.*
saber *to know*	**sé** sabes sabe sabemos sabéis saben	**sepa** **sepas** **sepa** **sepamos** **sepáis** **sepan**	sabe **sepa** Vd sabed **sepan** Vds	**sabré** *etc.*	**sabría** *etc.*
salir *to go out, come out*	**salgo** sales sale salimos salís salen	**salga** **salgas** **salga** **salgamos** **salgáis** **salgan**	**sal** **salga** Vd salid **salgan** Vds	**saldré** *etc.*	**saldría** *etc.*
ser *to be*	**soy** **eres** **es** **somos** **sois** **son**	**sea** **seas** **sea** **seamos** **seáis** **sean**	**sé** **sea** Vd sed **sean** Vds	seré *etc.*	sería *etc.*
tener *to have*	**tengo** **tienes** **tiene** tenemos tenéis **tienen**	**tenga** **tengas** **tenga** **tengamos** **tengáis** **tengan**	**ten** **tenga** Vd tened **tengan** Vds	**tendré** *etc.*	**tendría** *etc.*
traer *to bring*	**traigo** traes trae traemos traéis traen	**traiga** **traigas** **traiga** **traigamos** **traigáis** **traigan**	trae **traiga** Vd traed **traigan** Vds	traeré *etc.*	traería *etc.*

Imperfect indicative	Preterite	Imperfect subjunctive		Gerund	Past participle
podía	pude	pudiera	pudiese	pudiendo	podido
podías	pudiste	pudieras	pudieses		
podía	pudo	pudiera	pudiese		
podíamos	pudimos	pudiéramos	pudiésemos		
podíais	pudisteis	pudierais	pudieseis		
podían	pudieron	pudieran	pudiesen		
ponía	puse	pusiera	pusiese	poniendo	**puesto**
ponías	pusiste	pusieras	pusieses		
ponía	puso	pusiera	pusiese		
poníamos	pusimos	pusiéramos	pusiésemos		
poníais	pusisteis	pusierais	pusieseis		
ponían	pusieron	pusieran	pusiesen		
quería	quise	quisiera	quisiese	queriendo	querido
querías	quisiste	quisieras	quisieses		
quería	quiso	quisiera	quisiese		
queríamos	quisimos	quisiéramos	quisiésemos		
queríais	quisisteis	quisierais	quisieseis		
querían	quisieron	quisieran	quisiesen		
sabía	supe	supiera	supiese	sabiendo	sabido
sabías	supiste	supieras	supieses		
sabía	supo	supiera	supiese		
sabíamos	supimos	supiéramos	supiésemos		
sabíais	supisteis	supierais	supieseis		
sabían	supieron	supieran	supiesen		
salía	salí	saliera	saliese	saliendo	salido
salías	saliste	salieras	salieses		
salía	salió	saliera	saliese		
salíamos	salimos	saliéramos	saliésemos		
salíais	salisteis	salierais	salieseis		
salían	salieron	salieran	saliesen		
era	fui	fuera	fuese	siendo	sido
eras	fuiste	fueras	fueses		
era	fue	fuera	fuese		
éramos	fuimos	fuéramos	fuésemos		
erais	fuisteis	fuerais	fueseis		
eran	fueron	fueran	fuesen		
tenía	tuve	tuviera	tuviese	teniendo	tenido
tenías	tuviste	tuvieras	tuvieses		
tenía	tuvo	tuviera	tuviese		
teníamos	tuvimos	tuviéramos	tuviésemos		
teníais	tuvisteis	tuvierais	tuvieseis		
tenían	tuvieron	tuvieran	tuviesen		
traía	traje	trajera	trajese	**trayendo**	traído
traías	trajiste	trajeras	trajeses		
traía	trajo	trajera	trajese		
traíamos	trajimos	trajéramos	trajésemos		
traíais	trajisteis	trajerais	trajeseis		
traían	trajeron	trajeran	trajesen		

Infinitive	Present indicative	Present subjunctive	Imperative	Future	Conditional
venir *to come*	vengo vienes viene venimos venís vienen	venga vengas venga vengamos vengáis vengan	 ven venga Vd venid vengan Vds	vendré *etc.*	vendría *etc.*

Note also:

- **andar** has a *'Pretérito grave'* (**anduve**, etc.) and therefore the imperfect subjunctive is **anduviera/anduvies**
- **ver** has **veo, ves**, etc. in present indicative, **vea**, etc. in present subjunctive and **veía**, etc. in imperfect ind
- **abrir, cubrir, descubrir, freír, romper, volver** and verbs ending in **-solver** have irregular past participles – Chapter 23.
- For the tenses of radical-changing verbs, see the box in Chapter 15, section 15.1 on page 86, and for 'sp change' verbs see notes on the tense you need in the relevant chapter.

Imperfect indicative	Preterite	Imperfect subjunctive		Gerund	Past participle
venía	vine	viniera	viniese	viniendo	venido
venías	viniste	vinieras	vinieses		
venía	vino	viniera	viniese		
veníamos	vinimos	viniéramos	viniésemos		
veníais	vinisteis	vinierais	vinieseis		
venían	vinieron	vinieran	viniesen		

Index

Section numbers are given first, followed by page numbers in brackets.